For Reference

Not to be taken from this room

Twentieth-Century Short Story Explication

Supplement I to Third Edition

With Checklists of Books and Journals Used

Compiled by
WARREN S. WALKER
Horn Professor of English
Texas Tech University

THE SHOE STRING PRESS, INC.
1980

First edition published 1961
Supplement I to first edition published 1963
Supplement II to first edition published 1965
Second edition published 1967
Supplement I to second edition published 1970
Supplement II to second edition published 1973
Third edition published 1977
Supplement I to third edition published 1980

Third Edition, Supplement I
© The Shoe String Press, Inc., 1980
Hamden, Connecticut   06514

Library of Congress Cataloging in Publication Data

Walker, Warren S
    Twentieth-century short story explication.

    Includes index.
    1. Short story—Indexes.   I. Title.
Z5917.S5W33   1977, Supl [PN3373]   016.8093'1   80-16175
ISBN 0-208-01813-1

CONTENTS

PREFACE

Twentieth-Century Short Story Explication is a bibliography of interpretations which have appeared since 1900 of short stories published after 1800. In the Third Edition (1977) were materials on the works of more than 850 short story authors, and this Supplement lists explications of the fiction of 186 additional authors. The Third Edition carried the coverage through 31 December 1975; the present volume is devoted primarily to studies done during the calendar years 1976, 1977, and 1978. Also included, however, are items previously overlooked, as well as recent reprintings of explications in the Third Edition. Reprinted entries are preceded by asterisks.

The term *short story* here has the same meaning it carries in the Wilson Company's *Short Story Index:* " . . . a brief narrative of not more than 150 average-sized pages." By *explication* I suggest simply interpretation or explanation of the meaning of a story, including observations on theme, symbol, and sometimes structure. This excludes from the bibliography what are primarily studies of sources, biographical data, and background materials. Occasionally there are explicatory passages cited in other works otherwise devoted to one of these external considerations. Page numbers refer strictly to explicatory passages, not to the longer studies in which they may appear.

Although the entries refer predominantly to materials written in English, the reader will also find citations to key studies in several other major languages of Western Europe. Attention is called to many important books published abroad as well as to articles in such readily available foreign-language journals as *Hispamerica, Monatshefte, French Review,* and *Slavic & East European Journal.*

The recent profusion of interpretive material required that, beginning with the Third Edition, we adopt a system of coding and consequently a format different from that used in the first two editions. Each book is cited by author or editor and a short title; the full title and publication data are provided in a Checklist of Books Used. For an article in a journal or an essay in a critical collection, the full publication information is provided the first time the study is cited. In subsequent entries only the critic's or scholar's name and a short title are used as long as these entries appear under the name of the same short story writer; if an article or essay explicates stories by two or more writers, a complete initial entry is made for each writer. Now, for the first time, we have also included a Checklist of Journals Used. This should be especially helpful to students who may not be familiar with the titles of professional journals, much less the abbreviations for such titles.

Again I am indebted to the editors of such literary journals as *PMLA, Modern Fiction Studies, Journal of Modern Literature,* and *Abstracts of English Studies.* I wish to extend personal thanks to Gloria Lyerla, Interlibrary Loan Librarian at Texas Tech University, and to the reference librarians at Mahon Library, Lubbock, Texas. As always, my greatest debt is to my wife, Barbara K. Walker, for her untiring assistance.

Warren S. Walker
Texas Tech University

ROBERT ABERNATHY

"Hostage of Tomorrow"
   Carter, Paul A. *The Creation* . . ., 132–133.

THOMAS ABRAMS

"And When I Die Be Sure to Let Me Know"
   Reader, Willie. "'And When I Die Be Sure to Let Me Know,'" in Dietrich,
   R. F., and Roger H. Sundell. *Instructor's Manual* . . ., 3rd ed., 143–145.

CHINUA ACHEBE

"Akeuke"
   Killam, G. D. . . . *Chinua Achebe*, 105–106.

"Civil Peace"
   Killam, G. D. . . . *Chinua Achebe*, 108–109.

"Dead Man's Path"
   Killam, G. D. . . . *Chinua Achebe*, 103–104.

"Girls at War"
   Elias, Mohamed. "Time in Achebe's 'Girls at War': Presence of Nigerian Past,"
      Commonwealth Q, 2, vi (1978), 17–23.
   Killam, G. D. . . .*Chinua Achebe*, 109–112.
   Sarvan, Ponnuthurai. "The Mirror and the Image: Achebe's 'Girls at War,'"
      Stud Short Fiction, 14 (1977), 277–279.

"The Madman"
   Killam, G. D. . . . *Chinua Achebe*, 99–100.

"Marriage Is a Private Affair"
   Killam, G. D. . . . *Chinua Achebe*, 104–105.

"The Sacrificial Egg"
   Killam, G. D. . . . *Chinua Achebe*, 102–103.

"Uncle Ben's Choice"
   Killam, G. D. . . . *Chinua Achebe*, 100–102.

"Vengeful Creditor"
   Killam, G. D. . . . *Chinua Achebe*, 107–108.

"The Voter"
   Killam, G. D. . . . *Chinua Achebe*, 106–107.

1

JAMES AGEE

"Bound for the Promised Land"
Moreau, Geneviève. *The Restless Journey* . . ., 72–73.

"Boys Will Be Brutes"
Moreau, Geneviève. *The Restless Journey* . . ., 87–88.

"Death in the Desert"
Moreau, Geneviève. *The Restless Journey* . . ., 91–92.

"Dedication Day"
Moreau, Geneviève. *The Restless Journey* . . ., 211–214.

"The House"
Moreau, Geneviève. *The Restless Journey* . . ., 150–153.

"The Morning Watch"
Kramer, Victor A. " 'Religion at Its Deepest Intensity': The Stasis of Agee's
'The Morning Watch,' " *Renascence,* 27 (1975), 221–230.

"A Mother's Tale"
Moreau, Geneviève. *The Restless Journey* . . ., 246–248.

"They That Sow in Sorrow Shall Reap"
Moreau, Geneviève. *The Restless Journey* . . ., 92–94.

"A Walk Before Mass"
Moreau, Geneviève. *The Restless Journey* . . ., 85–86.

"Wall"
Moreau, Geneviève. *The Restless Journey* . . ., 75–76.

SHMUEL YOSEF AGNON [SHMUEL YOSEF CZACZKES]

"Agunot"
Fisch, Harold. *S. Y. Agnon,* 16–18.

"Edo and Enam"
Fisch, Harold. *S. Y. Agnon,* 38–39.

"The House"
Fisch, Harold. *S. Y. Agnon,* 72–76.

"The Last Bus"
Fisch, Harold. *S. Y. Agnon,* 70–72.

"The Letter"
Fisch, Harold. *S. Y. Agnon,* 69–70.

"A Whole Loaf"
Fisch, Harold. *S. Y. Agnon,* 78–83.

LARS AHLIN

"Coming Home to Be Nice"
Lundell, Torborg. *Lars Ahlin*, 141.

"No Eyes Await Me"
Lundell, Torborg. *Lars Ahlin*, 141–142.

"Squeezed"
Lundell, Torborg. *Lars Ahlin*, 142–143.

"The Wonderful Nightgown"
Lundell, Torborg. *Lars Ahlin*, 142.

CONRAD AIKEN

"Impulse"
Winehouse, Bernard. "'Impulse': Calculated Artistry in Conrad Aiken," *Stud Short Fiction*, 15 (1978), 107–110.

AKUTAGAWA RYŪNOSUKE

"The Fires"
Ueda, Makoto. *Modern Japanese Writers . . .*, 132–134.

"Ways of the Philippes"
Ueda, Makoto. *Modern Japanese Writers . . .*, 132–134.

IGNACIO ALDECOA

"Amadís"
Díaz, Janet W. "Amadís Existentialized: A Posthumous Tale by Ignacio Aldecoa," in Landeira, Ricardo, and Carlos Mellizo, Eds. *Ignacio Aldecoa . . .*, 103–113.

"En el kilómetro 400"
Abbott, James H. "Ignacio Aldecoa and the Journey to Paradise (The Short Stories)," in Landeira, Ricardo, and Carlos Mellizo, Eds. *Ignacio Aldecoa . . .*, 60.

"Santa Olaja de Acero"
Abbott, James H. "Ignacio Aldecoa . . .," 59–60.
Estaban Soler, H. "Estructura y Sentido de 'Santa Olaja de Acero,'" in Landeira, Ricardo, and Carlos Mellizo, Eds. *Ignacio Aldecoa . . .*, 69–94.

"Solar del Paraiso"
Abbott, James H. "Ignacio Aldecoa . . .," 62–63.

BRIAN W. ALDISS

"Dumb Show"
  Mathews, Richard. *Aldiss Unbound* . . ., 6.

"The Failed Man" [same as "Ahead"]
  Mathews, Richard. *Aldiss Unbound* . . ., 6–7.

FERNANDO ALEGRÍA

"A qué lado de la cortina?"
  Carlos, Alberto J. "Tres cuentos de Fernando Alegría," in Giacoman, Helmy
    F., Ed. *Homenaje a Fernando Alegría* . . ., 229–232.

"El lazo"
  Carlos, Alberto J. "Tres cuentos . . .," 232–235.

"El poeta que se volvió gusano"
  Carlos, Alberto J. "Tres cuentos . . .," 235–237.

SHOLOM ALEICHEM [SHOLOM RABINOWITZ]

"The Enchanted Tailor"
  Butwin, Joseph. *Sholom Aleichem*, 80–84.

"The Fiddler"
  Butwin, Joseph. *Sholom Aleichem*, 44–46.

"Gymnasia"
  Gittleman, Sol. *From Shtetl to Suburbia* . . ., 90–91.

"Home for Passover"
  Butwin, Joseph. *Sholom Aleichem*, 72–74.

"The Little Pot"
  Butwin, Joseph. *Sholom Aleichem*, 106–110.

"On Account of a Hat"
  Butwin, Joseph. *Sholom Aleichem*, 74–77.

"The Penknife"
  Butwin, Joseph. *Sholom Aleichem*, 42–44.
  Gittleman, Sol. *From Shtetl to Suburbia* . . ., 55–56.

"The Purim Feast"
  Gittleman, Sol. *From Shtetl to Suburbia* . . ., 87–89.

NELSON ALGREN

"A Bottle of Milk for Mother"
  Cox, Martha H., and Wayne Chatterton. *Nelson Algren*, 46–47.

"The Captain Has Bad Dreams"
Cox, Martha H., and Wayne Chatterton. *Nelson Algren,* 47–49.

"The Captain Is Impaled"
Cox, Martha H., and Wayne Chatterton. *Nelson Algren,* 47–49.

"Depend on Aunt Elly"
Cox, Martha H., and Wayne Chatterton. *Nelson Algren,* 53.

"The Face on the Barroom Floor"
Cox, Martha H., and Wayne Chatterton. *Nelson Algren,* 55–56.

"How the Devil Came Down Division Street"
Cox, Martha H., and Wayne Chatterton. *Nelson Algren,* 44–45.

"So Help Me"
Cox, Martha H., and Wayne Chatterton. *Nelson Algren,* 39–41.

CARL JONAS LOVE ALMQVIST

"The Palace"
Romberg, Berthil. *Carl . . . Almqvist,* 106–109.

"Skällnora Mill"
Romberg, Berthil. *Carl . . . Almqvist,* 115–116.

"The Urn"
Romberg, Berthil. *Carl . . . Almqvist,* 103–104.

JORGE AMANDO

"The Two Deaths of Quincas Wateryell"
Silverman, Malcolm. "Duality in Jorge Amando's 'The Two Deaths of Quincas Wateryell,'" *Stud Short Fiction,* 15 (1978), 196–199.

SHERWOOD ANDERSON

"Adventure"
Glicksberg, Charles I. *The Sexual Revolution . . .,* 51–52.
Taylor, Welford D. *Sherwood Anderson,* 24–27.

"The Book of the Grotesque"
Alsen, Eberhard. "The Futile Pursuit of Truth in Twain's 'What Is Man?' and Anderson's 'The Book of the Grotesque,'" *Mark Twain J,* 17, iii (1975), 12–14.
Francoeur, Marie and Louis. "Deux contes nordaméricains considérés comme actes de langage narratifs," *Études Littéraires,* 8 (1975), 57–80.
Mavrocordato, Alexandre. "Le Prisonnier de Winesburg: Reflexions sur le 'Livre des Grotesque,'" *Études Anglaises,* 29 (1976), 424–428.
Taylor, Welford D. *Sherwood Anderson,* 19–21.

"Brother Death"
Taylor, Welford D. *Sherwood Anderson*, 70–73.

"Death"
Fertig, Martin. "'A Great Deal of Wonder in Me': Inspiration and Transformation in *Winesburg, Ohio*," *Markham R*, 6 (1977), 68–69.

"Death in the Woods"
Cassill, R. V. *Instructor's Handbook* . . ., 4–5.
Martin, Robert A. "Primitivism in Stories by Willa Cather and Sherwood Anderson," *Midamerica*, 3 (1976), 42–44.

"The Egg"
Cassill, R. V. *Instructor's Handbook* . . ., 1–3.
Groene, Horst. "The American Idea of Success in Sherwood Anderson's 'The Egg,'" *Neusprachliche Mitteilungen aus Wissenschaft und Praxis*, 28 (1975), 162–166.
Taylor, Welford D. *Sherwood Anderson*, 49–52.

"Godliness"
Glicksberg, Charles I. *The Sexual Revolution* . . ., 51.
O'Neill, John. "Anderson Writ Large: 'Godliness' in *Winesburg, Ohio*," *Twentieth Century Lit*, 23 (1977), 67–83.
Taylor, Welford D. *Sherwood Anderson*, 22–24.

"I Want to Know Why"
*Abcarian, Richard, and Marvin Klotz. *Instructor's Manual* . . ., 2nd ed., 1.
Naugle, Helen H. "The Name 'Bildad,'" *Mod Fiction Stud*, 22 (1977), 591–594.

"I'm a Fool"
*Perrine, Laurence. *Instructor's Manual* . . . "*Story* . . .," 7–8; *Instructor's Manual* . . . "*Literature* . . .," 7–8.
Taylor, Welford D. *Sherwood Anderson*, 61–62.

"Loneliness"
Fertig, Martin. "'A Great Deal . . .,'" 67–68.

"The Man Who Became a Woman"
Taylor, Welford D. *Sherwood Anderson*, 65–67.

"The New Englander"
Taylor, Welford D. *Sherwood Anderson*, 52–55.

"Paper Pills"
Taylor, Welford D. *Sherwood Anderson*, 25–27.

"The Strength of God"
Glicksberg, Charles I. *The Sexual Revolution* . . ., 53–54.

"Tandy"
Taylor, Welford D. *Sherwood Anderson*, 31–32.

"Unlighted Lamps"
Taylor, Welford D. *Sherwood Anderson*, 55–57.

"Unused"
Taylor, Welford D. *Sherwood Anderson*, 57–61.

ANONYMOUS

"The Captain of Banditti: A True Story"
Pitcher, E. W. "Changes in Short Fiction in Britain 1785–1810: Philosophic
Tales, Gothic Tales, and Fragments and Visions," *Stud Short Fiction*, 13
(1976), 344.

JUAN JOSÉ ARREOLA

"The Switchman"
McMurray, George R. "Albert Camus' Concept of the Absurd and Juan José
Arreola's 'The Switchman,' " *Latin Am Lit R*, 11 (1977), 30–35.

ISAAC ASIMOV

"The Dying Night"
Pierce, Hazel. " 'Elementary, My Dear . . .': Asimov's Science Fiction Mysteries," in Olander, Joseph D., and Martin H. Greenberg, Eds. *Isaac Asimov*,
53–55.

"Escape"
Fiedler, Jean, and Jim Mele. "Asimov's Robots," in Riley, Dick, Ed. *Critical
Encounters . . .*, 5–6.

"The Evitable Conflict"
Fiedler, Jean, and Jim Mele. "Asimov's Robots," 6–8.

"Franchise"
Rhodes, Carolyn. "Tyranny by Computer: Automated Data Processing and
Oppressive Government in Science Fiction," in Clareson, Thomas D., Ed.
Many Futures . . ., 82–83.

"Nightfall"
Moore, Maxine. "The Use of Technical Metaphors in Asimov's Fiction," in
Olander, Joseph D., and Martin H. Greenberg, Eds. *Isaac Asimov*, 66–70.

"Risk"
Fiedler, Jean, and Jim Mele. "Asimov's Robots," 9–10.

"Robbie"
Fiedler, Jean, and Jim Mele. "Asimov's Robots," 2–3.

"Runaround"
Fiedler, Jean, and Jim Mele. "Asimov's Robots," 3–4.

"Satisfaction Guaranteed"
  Fiedler, Jean, and Jim Mele. "Asimov's Robots," 8–9.

PERCY ATKINSON

"Votes for Men"
  Moskowitz, Sam. *Strange Horizons* . . ., 75–76.

ANTONIO AZORÍN

"El secreto oriental"
  Joiner, Lawrence D., and Joseph W. Zdenek. "Two Neglected Stories of
    Azorín," *Stud Short Fiction,* 15 (1978), 284–287.

"El topacio"
  Joiner, Lawrence D., and Joseph W. Zdenek. "Two Neglected Stories . . .,"
    287–288.

ISAAC BABEL

"Karl-Yankel"
  Cassill, R. V. *Instructor's Handbook* . . ., 6–7.

JAMES BALDWIN

"Come Out of the Wilderness"
  Pratt, Louis H. *James Baldwin,* 42–45.

"Going to Meet the Man"
  *Abcarian, Richard, and Marvin Klotz. *Instructor's Manual* . . ., 2nd ed., 1–3.
  Freese, Peter. "James Baldwin: 'Going to Meet the Man,'" in Bruck, Peter, Ed.
    The Black American Short Story . . ., 174–182.
  Millican, Arthenia B. "Fire as the Symbol of a Leadening Existence in 'Going to
    Meet the Man,'" in O'Daniel, Therman B., Ed. *James Baldwin* . . .,
    170–180.
  Pratt, Louis H. *James Baldwin,* 45–49.
  Vandyke, Patricia. "Choosing One's Side with Care: The Liberating Repartee,"
    Perspectives Contemp Lit, 1, i (1975), 111–116.

"The Man Child"
  Jones, Harry L. "Style, Form, and Content in the Short Fiction of James
    Baldwin," in O'Daniel, Therman B., Ed. *James Baldwin* . . ., 147–148.

"Previous Condition"
  *Bluefarb, Sam. "James Baldwin's 'Previous Condition': A Problem of Iden-
    tification," in O'Daniel, Therman B., Ed. *James Baldwin* . . ., 151–155.
  Jones, Harry L. "Style, Form, and Content . . .," 148–149.
  Pratt, Louis H. *James Baldwin,* 34–39.

"Sonny's Blues"
Cassill, R. V. *Instructor's Handbook* . . ., 7–9.
Kane, Thomas S., and Leonard J. Peters. *Some Suggestions* . . ., 34–35.
Murray, Donald C. "James Baldwin's 'Sonny's Blues': Complicated and Simple," *Stud Short Fiction*, 14 (1977), 353–357.
Ostendorf, Bernhard. "James Baldwin, 'Sonny's Blues,' " in Freese, Peter, Ed. . . . *Interpretationen*, 194–204.
Pratt, Louis H. *James Baldwin*, 32–34.
*Reilly, John M. " 'Sonny's Blues': James Baldwin's Image of Black Community," in O'Daniel, Therman B., Ed. *James Baldwin* . . ., 163–169.

"This Morning, This Evening, So Soon"
*Hagopian, John V. "James Baldwin: The Black and the Red-White-and-Blue," in O'Daniel, Therman B., Ed. *James Baldwin* . . ., 156–162.
Kimmey, John L. *Instructor's Manual* . . ., 20–22.
Pratt, Louis H. *James Baldwin*, 39–42.

BETTY T. BALKE

"Apostle to Alpha"
Moskowitz, Sam. *Strange Horizons* . . ., 20–21.

J. G. BALLARD

"The Drowned Giant"
Wright, A. J. "Allegory of the Ruin: J.G. Ballard's 'The Drowned Giant,' " *Notes Contemp Lit*, 6, iv (1976), 14–15.

HONORÉ DE BALZAC

"Adieu"
Brooks, Peter. *The Melodramatic Imagination* . . ., 149–150.

"Christ in Flanders"
Champagne, Roland A. "The Architectural Pattern of a Literary Artifact: A Lacanian Reading of Honoré Balzac's 'Jésus-Christ en Flandre,' " *Stud Short Fiction*, 15 (1978), 49–54.

"Gambara"
Luce, Louise F. "Alchemy and the Artist in Balzac's 'Gambara,' " *Centerpoint*, 3, i (1978), 67–74.

"Gobseck"
Clark, R. J. B. " 'Gobseck': Structure, images et signification d'une nouvelle de Balzac," *Symposium*, 31 (1977), 290–301.

"Louis Lambert"
Brooks, Peter. *The Melodramatic Imagination* . . ., 116–117.
Knapp, Bettina L. "Louis Lambert: The Legend of the Thinking Man," *Nineteenth-Century French Stud*, 6 (1977), 21–35.

"A Passion in the Desert"
   Cassill, R. V. *Instructor's Handbook* . . ., 10–11.
   Hoffmann, Léon-François. "Eros camouflé: En marge d'*Une Passion dans le désert*, de Balzac," *Hebrew Univ Stud Lit*, 5 (1977), 19–36.

IMAMU AMIRI BARAKA [formerly LeROI JONES]

"The Alternative"
   Coleman, Larry G. "LeRoi Jones' *Tales:* Sketches of the Artist as a Young Man Moving Toward a Blacker Art," *Black Lines*, 1, ii (1970), 20–21; rpt. Benston, Kimberly W., Ed. *Imamu Amiri Baraka* . . ., 87–89.
   Sollors, Werner. . . . "*Populist Modernism*," 146–149.
   Wakefield, John. "Amiri Baraka (LeRoi Jones): 'The Alternative,'" in Bruck, Peter, Ed. *The Black American Short Story* . . ., 191–201.

"A Chase (Alighieri's Dream)"
   Coleman, Larry G. "LeRoi Jones' *Tales* . . .," 19–20; rpt. Benston, Kimberly W., Ed. *Imamu Amiri Baraka* . . ., 86–87.

"Death of Horatio Alger"
   Coleman, Larry G. "LeRoi Jones' *Tales* . . .," 21–23; rpt. Benston, Kimberly W., Ed. *Imamu Amiri Baraka* . . ., 89–91.

"Going Down Slow"
   Sollors, Werner. . . . "*Populist Modernism*," 153–156.

"Heroes Are Gang Leaders"
   Sollors, Werner. . . . "*Populist Modernism*," 156–158.

"Round Trip"
   Sollors, Werner. . . . "*Populist Modernism*," 17–18.

"Salute"
   Sollors, Werner. . . . "*Populist Modernism*," 158–160.

"The Screamer"
   Sollors, Werner. "Amiri Baraka (LeRoi Jones), 'The Screamer,'" in Freese, Peter, Ed. . . . *Interpretationen*, 270–279.
   –––––. . . . "*Populist Modernism*," 160–167.

"Suppose Sorrow Was a Time Machine"
   Sollors, Werner. . . . "*Populist Modernism*," 49–51.

"Uncle Tom's Cabin: Alternate Ending"
   Sollors, Werner. . . . "*Populist Modernism*," 149–152.

"Words"
   Coleman, Larry G. "LeRoi Jones' *Tales* . . .," 23–24; rpt. Benston, Kimberly W., Ed. *Imamu Amiri Baraka* . . ., 92–94.

JULES AMÉDÉE BARBEY D'AUREVILLY

''A un dîner d'athées''
Chartier, Armand B. *Barbey D'Aurevilly,* 119–123.

''Le bonheur dans le crime''
Chartier, Armand B. *Barbey D'Aurevilly,* 111–115.

''Le dessous de cartes d'une partie de whist''
Chartier, Armand B. *Barbey D'Aurevilly,* 115–119.

''Le plus bel amour de Don Juan''
Chartier, Armand B. *Barbey D'Aurevilly,* 108–111.

''Le rideau cramoisi''
Chartier, Armand B. *Barbey D'Aurevilly,* 104–108.

''La vengeance d'une femme''
Chartier, Armand B. *Barbey D'Aurevilly,* 123–127.

DJUNA BARNES

''Aller et Retour''
Ferguson, Suzanne C. ''Djuna Barnes's Short Stories: An Estrangement of the
Heart,'' *Southern R,* 5 (1969), 33–34.
Kannenstine, Louis F. *The Art of Djuna Barnes . . .,* 64–68.
Scott, James B. *Djuna Barnes,* 29–31.

''A Boy Asks a Question of a Lady''
Scott, James B. *Djuna Barnes,* 28–29.

''Cassation'' [originally titled ''A Little Girl Tells a Story to a Lady'']
Kannenstine, Louis F. *The Art of Djuna Barnes . . .,* 68–71.
Scott, James B. *Djuna Barnes,* 32–33.

''The Doctors'' [originally titled ''Katrina Silverstaff'']
Ferguson, Suzanne C. ''. . . Estrangement of the Heart,'' 37–40.
Kannenstine, Louis F. *The Art of Djuna Barnes . . .,* 76–79.
Scott, James B. *Djuna Barnes,* 45–47.

''Dusie''
Ferguson, Suzanne C. ''. . . Estrangement of the Heart,'' 30.

''The Grande Malade'' [originally titled ''The Little Girl Continues'']
Scott, James B. *Djuna Barnes,* 33–35.

''Indian Summer''
Scott, James B. *Djuna Barnes,* 41–43.

''Mother''
Kannenstine, Louis F. *The Art of Djuna Barnes . . .,* 63–64.

"The Nigger"
Kannenstine, Louis F. *The Art of Djuna Barnes* . . ., 62–63.
Scott, James B. *Djuna Barnes,* 39–41.

"A Night Among the Horses"
Ferguson, Suzanne C. ". . . Estrangement of the Heart," 28–29.
Kannenstine, Louis F. *The Art of Djuna Barnes* . . ., 72–74.

"No-Man's Mare"
Scott, James B. *Djuna Barnes,* 38–39.

"The Passion"
Kannenstine, Louis F. *The Art of Djuna Barnes* . . ., 82–84.

"The Perfect Murder"
Kannenstine, Louis F. *The Art of Djuna Barnes* . . ., 60–61.

"The Rabbit"
Ferguson, Suzanne C. ". . . Estrangement of the Heart," 31–32.
Kannenstine, Louis F. *The Art of Djuna Barnes* . . ., 75–76.
Scott, James B. *Djuna Barnes,* 35–37.

"Spillway" [originally titled "Beyond the End"]
Ferguson, Suzanne C. ". . . Estrangement of the Heart," 34–37.
Kannenstine, Louis F. *The Art of Djuna Barnes* . . ., 79–81.
Scott, James B. *Djuna Barnes,* 47–49.

JOHN BARTH

"Ambrose His Mark"
Morrell, David. *John Barth* . . ., 89–90.

"Anonymiad"
Morrell, David. *John Barth* . . ., 95–96.
Trachtenberg, Stanley. "Berger and Barth: The Comedy of Decomposition," in
Cohen, Sarah B., Ed. *Comic Relief* . . ., 68–69.

"Autobiography: A Self-Recorded Fiction"
Morrell, David. *John Barth* . . ., 81–82.

"Bellerophoniad"
Cantrill, Dante. "'It's a Chimera': An Introduction to John Barth's Latest
Fiction," *Rendezvous,* 10, ii (1975), 24–28.
Morrell, David. *John Barth* . . ., 148–156.

"Dunyazadiad"
Cantrill, Dante. "'It's a Chimera' . . .," 19–21.
Morrell, David. *John Barth* . . ., 156–161.

"Echo"
Morrell, David. *John Barth* . . ., 83–84.

"Life-Story"
  Cassill, R. V. *Instructor's Handbook* . . ., 11–12.
  Trachtenberg, Stanley. "Berger and Barth . . .," 66–67.
  Westervelt, Linda A. "Teller, Tale, Told: Relationships in John Barth's Latest
  Fiction," *J Narrative Technique*, 8 (1978), 46–47.

"Lost in the Funhouse"
  Allen, Mary. *The Necessary Blankness* . . ., 36–37.
  Howard, Daniel F., and William Plummer. *Instructor's Manual* . . ., 3rd ed., 76.
  Kimmey, John L. *Instructor's Manual* . . ., 37–40.
  Morrell, David. *John Barth* . . ., 87–88.
  Schulz, Dieter. "John Barth, 'Lost in the Funhouse,'" in Freese, Peter, Ed. . . .
  Interpretationen, 289–300.
  Trachtenberg, Stanley. "Berger and Barth . . .," 64–66.
  Westervelt, Linda A. "Teller, Tale, Told . . .," 43–45.

"Menelaiad"
  Morrell, David. *John Barth* . . ., 94–95.
  Trachtenberg, Stanley. "Berger and Barth . . .," 67–68.
  Westervelt, Linda A. "Teller, Tale, Told . . .," 45–46.

"Night-Sea Journey"
  Deer, Irving. "'Night-Sea Journey,'" in Dietrich, R. F., and Roger H. Sundell.
  Instructor's Manual . . ., 3rd ed., 78–81.
  Howard, Daniel F., and William Plummer. *Instructor's Manual* . . ., 3rd ed., 77.

"Perseid"
  Cantrill, Dante. "'It's a Chimera' . . .," 21–24.
  Morrell, David. *John Barth* . . ., 139–148.

DONALD BARTHELME

"At the Tolstoy Museum"
  Goetsch, Paul. "Donald Barthelme, 'At the Tolstoy Museum,'" in Freese,
  Peter, Ed. . . . *Interpretationen*, 323–332.

"City Life"
  Kimmey, John L. *Instructor's Manual* . . ., 35–37.

"Daumier"
  Ditsky, John M. "'With Ingenuity and Hard Work Distracted': The Narrative
  Style of Donald Barthelme," *Style*, 9 (1975), 394–398.

"The Glass Mountain"
  Cassill, R. V. *Instructor's Handbook* . . ., 12–13.
  Detweiler, Robert. "Games and Play in Modern American Fiction," *Contemp
  Lit*, 17 (1976), 50.

"The Policemen's Ball"
  Howard, Daniel F., and William Plummer. *Instructor's Manual* . . ., 3rd ed.,
  79–80.

"Robert Kennedy Saved from Drowning"
  Giles, James R. "The 'Marivaudian Being' Drowns His Children: Dehumaniza-
    tion in Donald Barthelme's 'Robert Kennedy Saved from Drowning' and
    Joyce Carol Oates' *Wonderland*," *Southern Hum R*, 9 (1975), 63–75.

"The Sandman"
  Abcarian, Richard, and Marvin Klotz. *Instructor's Manual . . .*, 2nd ed., 3.

CHARLES BAUDELAIRE

"La Fanfarlo"
  Carter, A. B. *Charles Baudelaire*, 44–46.
  Heck, Francis S. "Baudelaire's 'La Fanfarlo': An Example of Romantic Irony,"
    French R, 49 (1976), 328–339.

PARDO BAZÁN

"Accidente"
  Feeny, Thomas. "The Child as Redeemer and Victim in Pardo Bazán's Short
    Fiction," *Revista de Estudios Hispánicos*, 11 (1977), 428–429.

"Jesusa"
  Feeny, Thomas. "The Child as Redeemer . . .," 429–430.

"La niña mártir"
  Feeny, Thomas. "The Child as Redeemer . . .," 429–430.

SAMUEL BECKETT

"Assumption"
  Bair, Deirdre. *Samuel Beckett*, 79–80.
  Pilling, John. *Samuel Beckett*, 122–123.

"The Calmative"
  Barge, Laura. "Life and Death in Beckett's Four Stories," *So Atlantic Q*, 76
    (1977), 332–347.

"Dante and the Lobster"
  Bernhart, Walter. " 'Human Nature's Intricacies' und 'Rigorous Truth': Joyce's
    'Clay,' Beckett's 'Dante and the Lobster,' und die Individuation (II),"
    Arbeiten aus Anglistik und Amerikanistik, 2 (1977), 67–82.
  Rosen, Steven J. *Samuel Beckett . . .*, 32–33.

"The End"
  Barge, Laura. "Life and Death . . .," 332–347.
  Finney, Brian. " 'Assumption' to 'Lessness': Beckett's Short Fiction," in
    Worth, Katharine, Ed. *Beckett the Shape Changer*, 71–72.
  Pilling, John. *Samuel Beckett*, 137–138.

"Enough"
  Finney, Brian. . . . *Beckett's Later Fiction*, 27–29.
  ———. ". . . Beckett's Short Fiction," 78–81.

"The Expelled"
  Barge, Laura. "Life and Death . . .," 332–347.
  Finney, Brian. ". . . Beckett's Short Fiction," 70–71.

"First Love"
  Barge, Laura. "Life and Death . . .," 332–347.
  Finney, Brian. " . . . Beckett's Short Fiction," 67–71.

"How It Is"
  Sage, Victor. "Innovation and Continuity in 'How It Is,'" in Worth, Katharine,
    Ed. *Beckett the Shape Changer*, 88–91, 95–102.
  Schwartz, Paul J. "Life and Death in the Mud: A Study of Beckett's 'Comment
    c'est,'" *Int'l Fiction R*, 2 (1975), 43–48.

"Imagination Dead Imagine"
  Finney, Brian. "A Reading of Beckett's 'Imagination Dead Imagine,'" *Twen-
    tieth Century Lit*, 17, ii (1971), 65–71.
  ———. . . . *Beckett's Later Fiction*, 26–27.

"Lessness"
  Finney, Brian. . . . *Beckett's Later Fiction*, 21.

"The Lost Ones"
  Brienza, Susan D. " 'The Lost Ones': The Reader as Searcher," *J Mod Lit*, 6
    (1977), 148–168.

"Ping"
  Bergman, Elisabeth. "Style and Structure in Beckett's 'Ping': 'That Something
    Itself,'" *J Mod Lit*, 6 (1977), 130–147.
  Finney, Brian. . . . *Beckett's Later Fiction*, 20–21.
  Lodge, David. "Samuel Beckett: Some Ping Understood," *Encounter*, 30
    (February, 1968), 85–89; rpt. in his *The Novel at the Crossroads*, 136–145;
    Hazell, Stephen, Ed. *The English Novel . . .*, 172–183.

"A Wet Night"
  Mercier, Vivian. *Beckett/Beckett*, 208–209.

SAUL BELLOW

"A Father-to-Be"
  *Dietrich, R. F. " 'A Father-to-Be,'" in Dietrich, R. F., and Roger H. Sundell.
    Instructor's Manual . . ., 3rd ed., 135–142.

"The Gonzaga Manuscript"
  Galloway, David. "Saul Bellow, 'The Gonzaga Manuscript,'" in Freese, Peter,
    Ed. . . . *Interpretationen*, 163–174.

"Leaving the Yellow House"
  Cassill, R. V. *Instructor's Handbook* . . ., 14–16.
  O'Connor, Shaun. "Bellow: Logic's Limits," *Massachusetts R,* 10 (1969), 185.

"Looking for Mr. Green"
  Kindilien, Glenn A. "The Meaning of the Name 'Green' in Saul Bellow's
    'Looking for Mr. Green,'" *Stud Short Fiction,* 15 (1978), 104–107.

"Mosby's Memoirs"
  O'Connor, Shaun. " . . . Logic's Limits," 185–186.

"Seize the Day"
  Alhadeff, Barbara. "The Divided Self: A Laingian Interpretation of 'Seize the
    Day,'" *Stud Am Jewish Lit,* 3, i (1977), 16–20.
  Handy, William J. "Saul Bellow and the Naturalistic Hero," *Texas Stud Lit &*
    Lang, 5 (1964), 539–545; rpt. in his *Modern Fiction* . . ., 119–130.
  *Howe, Irving, Ed. *Classics of Modern Fiction* . . ., 2nd ed., 511–520.
  Nelson, Gerald B. *Ten Versions of America,* 129–145.
  Raper, J.R. "Running Contrary Ways: Saul Bellow's 'Seize the Day,'"
    Southern Hum R, 10 (1976), 157–168.
  Sicherman, Carol M. "Bellow's 'Seize the Day': Reverberations and Hollow
    Sounds," *Stud Twentieth Century,* 15 (Spring, 1975), 1–31.

"A Sermon by Dr. Pep"
  Nakajima, Kenji. "A Study of S. Bellow's 'A Sermon by Dr. Pep,' " *Kyushu*
    Am Lit, 17 (1976), 12–19.

ANDREI BELY

"The Baptized Chinese"
  Mochulsky, Konstantin. *Andrei Bely* . . ., 189–193.

VÜS'AT O. BENER

"The Homecoming"
  Hickman, William. "Notes on Language and Style in 'The Homecoming,'"
    Edebiyat: J Middle Eastern Lit, 2 (1977), 219–226.

STEPHEN VINCENT BENÉT

"By the Waters of Babylon"
  Carter, Paul A. *The Creation* . . ., 232–233.

ANTONIO BENÍTEZ ROJO

"El escudo de hojas secas"
  Menton, Seymour. . . . *Cuban Revolution,* 192–194.

"Estatuas sepultadas"
  Menton, Seymour. . . . *Cuban Revolution*, 185–186.

"Primer balcon"
  Menton, Seymour. . . . *Cuban Revolution*, 184–185.

"La tierra y el cielo"
  Menton, Seymour. . . . *Cuban Revolution*, 191–192.

HJALMAR BERGMAN

"Sardanapal"
  Linder, Erik H. *Hjalmar Bergman*, 152–154.

ALFRED BESTER

"The Push of a Finger"
  Carter, Paul A. *The Creation* . . ., 101–105.

DORIS BETTS

"Beasts of the Southern Wild"
  Evans, Elizabeth. "Negro Characters in the Fiction of Doris Betts," *Critique*,
    17, ii (1975), 73–75.

"The Sympathetic Visitor"
  Evans, Elizabeth. "Negro Characters . . .," 59–60.

"The Ugliest Pilgrim"
  Evans, Elizabeth. "Negro Characters . . .," 72–73.

AMBROSE BIERCE

"The Boarded Window"
  Kennedy, X. J. *Instructor's Manual* . . ., 6–7.

"A Horseman in the Sky"
  Kimmey, John L. *Instructor's Manual* . . ., 2–3.

"An Occurrence at Owl Creek Bridge"
  *Abcarian, Richard, and Marvin Klotz. *Instructor's Manual* . . ., 2nd ed., 3–5.
  Brashers, Howard C. *Creative Writing* . . ., 194–195.
  Cassill, R. V. *Instructor's Handbook* . . ., 16–18.
  Logan, F. J. "The Wry Seriousness of 'Owl Creek Bridge,'" *Am Lit Realism*, 10
    (1977), 101–113.

RUDOLPH BLOCK

"End of the Task"
Fine, David M. *The City . . .*, 65–66.

HEINRICH BÖLL

"Murke's Collected Silences"
Kimmey, John L. *Instructor's Manual . . .*, 25–27.

SHERWOOD BONNER [KATHERINE S. B. McDOWELL]

"The Case of Eliza Bleylock"
Frank, William L. *Sherwood Bonner*, 89–90.

"Coming Home to Roost"
Frank, William L. *Sherwood Bonner*, 98–100.

"The Gentlemen of Sarsar"
Frank, William L. *Sherwood Bonner*, 80–81.

"Hieronymus Pop and the Baby"
Frank, William L. *Sherwood Bonner*, 83–84.

"In Aunt Mely's Cabin"
Frank, William L. *Sherwood Bonner*, 87–89.

"Lame Jerry"
Frank, William L. *Sherwood Bonner*, 91.

"On the Nine Mile"
Frank, William L. *Sherwood Bonner*, 82–83.

"The Revolution in the Life of Mr. Balingall"
Frank, William L. *Sherwood Bonner*, 110–111.

"Sister Weeden's Prayer"
Frank, William L. *Sherwood Bonner*, 84–85.

"The Valcours"
Frank, William L. *Sherwood Bonner*, 116–118.

"The Volcanic Interlude"
Frank, William L. *Sherwood Bonner*, 112–114.

ARNA W. BONTEMPS

"A Summer Tragedy"
Kuperman, David. "Dying: The Shape of Victory in 'A Summer Tragedy,'"
MELUS, 5, i (1978), 66–68.

JOHAN BORGEN

"Chance"
Birn, Randi. "Dream and Reality in Johan Borgen's Short Stories," *Scandinavian Stud*, 46 (1974), 62–65; rpt. in his *Johan Borgen*, 53–55.

"Honeysuckle Vine"
Birn, Randi. "Dream and Reality . . .," 61–62; rpt. in his *Johan Borgen*, 51–52.

"Legend"
Birn, Randi. "Dream and Reality . . .," 70–71; rpt. in his *Johan Borgen*, 62–63.

"Morning on Montparnasse"
Birn, Randi. *Johan Borgen*, 129–130.

"Night and Day 1"
Birn, Randi. "Dream and Reality . . .," 62–63; rpt. in his *Johan Borgen*, 51–53.

"Ocean in Winter"
Birn, Randi. "Dream and Reality . . .," 69–70; rpt. in his *Johan Borgen*, 61–62.

"She Willed It"
Birn, Randi. "Dream and Reality . . .," 66–67; rpt. in his *Johan Borgen*, 56–57.

"Star Song"
Birn, Randi. "Dream and Reality . . .," 67–68; rpt. in his *Johan Borgen*, 61–63.

"Trustworthy and Dutiful"
Birn, Randi. *Johan Borgen*, 131–132.

JORGE LUIS BORGES

"Abenjacán the Borjarí"
Sturrock, John. *Paper Tiger* . . ., 176–177.

"The Aleph"
Lévy, Salomón. "El 'Aleph,' simbolo cabalistico y sus implicaciones en la obra de Jorge Luis Borges," *Hispanic R*, 44 (1976), 143–161.
Lind, Georg R. "Die Dante-Parodie in J.L. Borges' 'El Aleph,' " in Rheinfelder, Hans, Pierre Christophorov, and Eberhard Müller-Bochat, Eds. *Literatur und Spiritualität* . . ., 145–151.
McBride, Mary. "Jorge Luis Borges, Existentialist: 'The Aleph' and the Relativity of Human Perception," *Stud Short Fiction*, 14 (1977), 401–403; rpt. Dietrich, R.F., and Roger H. Sundell. *Instructor's Manual* . . ., 3rd ed., 128–132.
Sturrock, John. *Paper Tiger* . . ., 106–107.

"Averroes' Search"
  King, James R. "'Averroes' Search': The 'Moment' as Labyrinth in the Fiction
    of Jorge Luis Borges," *Research Stud*, 45 (1977), 138–142.
  Sturrock, John. *Paper Tiger* . . ., 85–87.

"The Babylonian Lottery"
  Kane, Thomas S., and Leonard J. Peters. *Some Suggestions* . . ., 46–48.

"Biography of Tadeo Isidoro"
  Gyurko, Lanin A. "Borges and the Theme of the Double," *Ibero-Amerikan-
    isches Archiv*, 2, iii (1976), 197–198.

"Brodie's Report"
  Sturrock, John. *Paper Tiger* . . ., 81–83.

"The Circular Ruins"
  Gyurko, Lanin A. ". . . Theme of the Double," 211–213.
  Mikkelson, Holly. "Borges and the Negative of Time," *Romance Notes*, 17
    (1976), 97–98.

"The Dead Man"
  Lusky, Mary H. "Pére Menard: Autor," *Texas Q*, 18, i (1975), 113–115.

"Death and the Compass"
  Gyurko, Lanin A. ". . . Theme of the Double," 216–223.
  Sturrock, John. *Paper Tiger* . . ., 128–133.

"Deutsches Requiem"
  Sturrock, John. *Paper Tiger* . . ., 104–106.

"The Dreadful Redeemer Lazarus Morell"
  Sturrock, John. *Paper Tiger* . . ., 144–145.

"Emma Zunz"
  Chrzanowski, Joseph. "Psychological Motivation in Borges' 'Emma Zunz,'"
    Lit & Psych, 28 (1978), 100–104.
  Rabkin, Eric S. *The Fantastic* . . ., 219–220.
  Sturrock, John. *Paper Tiger* . . ., 68–70.

"The Encounter"
  Sturrock, John. *Paper Tiger* . . ., 170–171.

"The End"
  Sturrock, John. *Paper Tiger* . . ., 42–44.

"The Enigma of Edward Fitzgerald"
  Gyurko, Lanin A. ". . . Theme of the Double," 194–197.

"Examination of the Works of Herbert Quain"
  Sturrock, John. *Paper Tiger* . . ., 146–152.

"Funes the Memorious"
  Sturrock, John. *Paper Tiger* . . ., 109–112.

"The Garden of Forking Paths"
  Lusky, Mary H. "Pére Menard . . .," 105.
  Rabkin, Eric S. *The Fantastic* . . ., 170–174.
  Sturrock, John. *Paper Tiger* . . ., 189–192.

"Guayaquil"
  Sturrock, John. *Paper Tiger* . . ., 66–68.

"The House of Asterion"
  Fragoso, Milton. " 'The House of Asterion,' a God's Fall into Ignorance," in
    Finke, Wayne H., Ed. *Estudios de historia* . . ., 165–172.

"The Improbable Impostor Tom Castro"
  Sturrock, John. *Paper Tiger* . . ., 53–57.

"Juan Muraña"
  Sturrock, John. *Paper Tiger* . . ., 17–18.

"The Library of Babel"
  Sturrock, John. *Paper Tiger* . . ., 100–103.

"The Maker"
  Sturrock, John. *Paper Tiger* . . ., 194–195.

"The Other"
  Calaf de Aguera, Helen. "El doble en el tiempo en 'El otro' de Jorge L. Borges,"
    Explicación de Textos Literarios, 6, ii (1978), 167–173.
  Sturrock, John. *Paper Tiger* . . ., 14–15.

"The Other Death"
  Gyurko, Lanin A. ". . . Theme of the Double," 198–200.
  Sturrock, John. *Paper Tiger* . . ., 158–159.

"Pierre Menard, Author of *Quixote*"
  Cassill, R. V. *Instructor's Handbook* . . ., 19–20.
  Sturrock, John. *Paper Tiger* . . ., 163–165.

"The Secret Miracle"
  Gyurko, Lanin A. ". . . Theme of the Double," 214–216.
  Sturrock, John. *Paper Tiger* . . ., 39–41.

"The Sect of the Thirty"
  Sturrock, John. *Paper Tiger* . . ., 175–176.

"The Shape of the Sword"
  Sturrock, John. *Paper Tiger* . . ., 178–179.

"The Sorcerer Postponed"
  Sturrock, John. *Paper Tiger* . . ., 34–36.

"The South"
  Gyurko, Lanin A. ". . . Theme of the Double," 200–202.
  Sturrock, John. *Paper Tiger* . . ., 57–58, 209–212.

"The Story of Rosendo Juárez" [earlier versions entitled "Political Legend" and
  "Hombre de la esquina rosado"]
  Lusky, Mary H. "Pére Menard . . .," 110–112.

"Theme of the Traitor and the Hero"
  Sturrock, John. *Paper Tiger* . . ., 136–138.

"The Theologians"
  Gyurko, Lanin A. ". . . Theme of the Double," 207–211.
  Sturrock, John. *Paper Tiger* . . ., 160–162.

"Three Versions of Judas"
  Sturrock, John. *Paper Tiger* . . ., 174–175.

"Tlön, Uqbar, Orbis Tertius"
  Brivic, Sheldon. "Borges' 'Orbis Tertius,' " *Massachusetts R,* 16 (1975),
    387–399.
  Mikkelson, Holly. "Borges and the Negative . . .," 95–97.
  Pérez, Carlos A. "Tlön, el mundo en otro mundo," *Explicación de Textos
    Literarios,* 6, i (1977), 45–51.
  Sturrock, John. *Paper Tiger* . . ., 118–122.

"Utopia of a Man Who Is Tired"
  Sturrock, John. *Paper Tiger* . . ., 202–203.

"The Zahir"
  Sturrock, John. *Paper Tiger* . . ., 70–72.

ELIZABETH BOWEN

"Coming Home"
  Glendinning, Victoria. *Elizabeth Bowen* . . ., 42–43.

"The Demon Lover"
  Glendinning, Victoria. *Elizabeth Bowen* . . ., 144.

"The Happy Autumn Fields"
  Glendinning, Victoria. *Elizabeth Bowen* . . ., 143–144.

"Making Arrangements"
  Glendinning, Victoria. *Elizabeth Bowen* . . ., 54–55.

"Mysterious Kōr"
  Glendinning, Victoria. *Elizabeth Bowen* . . ., 144–145.

"Summer Night"
  Glendinning, Victoria. *Elizabeth Bowen* . . ., 111–112.

"A Walk in the Woods"
Glendinning, Victoria. *Elizabeth Bowen* . . ., 126–127.

"Woodby, John"
Glendinning, Victoria. *Elizabeth Bowen* . . ., 224–225.

KAY BOYLE

"Rest Cure"
Cassill, R. V. *Instructor's Handbook* . . ., 21–22.

RAY BRADBURY

"And So Died Riabouchinska"
Slusser, George E. . . . *Chronicle*, 41–42.

"The Anthem Sprinters"
Slusser, George E. . . . *Chronicle*, 48.

"The Beggar on O'Connell Bridge"
Slusser, George E. . . . *Chronicle*, 47–48.

"The Cistern"
Slusser, George E. . . . *Chronicle*, 36–37.

"The Concrete Mixer"
Johnson, Wayne L. "The Invasion Stories of Ray Bradbury," in Riley, Dick,
Ed. *Critical Encounters* . . ., 39–40.
Slusser, George E. . . . *Chronicle*, 29–30.

"The Crowd"
Slusser, George E. . . . *Chronicle*, 13–14.

"Dark They Were, and Golden Eyed"
Johnson, Wayne L. "The Invasion Stories . . .," 37–39.

"Death and the Maiden"
Slusser, George E. . . . *Chronicle*, 46.

"The Dwarf"
Slusser, George E. . . . *Chronicle*, 42–43.

"The Emissary"
Slusser, George E. . . . *Chronicle*, 20–21.

"The Exiles"
Cassill, R. V. *Instructor's Handbook* . . ., 22–24.

"Fever Dream"
Johnson, Wayne L. "The Invasion Stories . . .," 28–29.

"The Golden Apples of the Sun"
  Slusser, George E. . . . *Chronicle*, 32–33.

"The Great Wide World Over There"
  Slusser, George E. . . . *Chronicle*, 40.

"I Sing the Body Electric"
  Slusser, George E. . . . *Chronicle*, 50–52.

"Icarus Montgolfier"
  Slusser, George E. . . . *Chronicle*, 44–45.

"The Illustrated Man"
  Slusser, George E. . . . *Chronicle*, 39–40.

"Invisible Boy"
  Slusser, George E. . . . *Chronicle*, 25–26.

"Jack-in-the-Box"
  Slusser, George E. . . . *Chronicle*, 37–38.

"The Lake"
  Slusser, George E. . . . *Chronicle*, 23–24.

"The Machineries of Joy"
  Slusser, George E. . . . *Chronicle*, 46–47.

"The Man Upstairs"
  Slusser, George E. . . . *Chronicle*, 19–20.

"A Medicine for Melancholy"
  Slusser, George E. . . . *Chronicle*, 45–46.

"Night Call Collect"
  Stupple, A. James. "The Past, the Future, and Ray Bradbury," in Clareson,
  Thomas D., Ed. *Voices for the Future* . . . , 182–183.

"Night Meeting"
  Scholes, Robert, and Eric S. Rabkin. *Science Fiction* . . . , 178–179.

"No Particular Night or Morning"
  Favier, Jacques. "Space and Settor in Short Science Fiction," in Johnson, Ira
  and Christiane, Eds. *Les Américanistes* . . . , 186–187.

"Pillar of Fire"
  Slusser, George E. . . . *Chronicle*, 33.

"Powerhouse"
  Slusser, George E. . . . *Chronicle*, 38–39.

"The Rocket Man"
  Slusser, George E. . . . *Chronicle*, 32.

"The Scythe"
Slusser, George E. . . . *Chronicle*, 14–16.

"Skeleton"
Slusser, George E. . . . *Chronicle*, 17–19.

"There Was an Old Woman"
Slusser, George E. . . . *Chronicle*, 22–23.

"Uncle Einar"
Slusser, George E. . . . *Chronicle*, 37.

"The Watchful Poker Chip of H. Matisse"
Slusser, George E. . . . *Chronicle*, 44.

"Way in the Middle of the Air"
Moskowitz, Sam. *Strange Horizons* . . ., 50–51.

"The Wind"
Slusser, George E. . . . *Chronicle*, 12–13.

"The Wonderful Ice Cream Suit"
Slusser, George E. . . . *Chronicle*, 45.

"Zero Hour"
Johnson, Wayne L. "The Invasion Stories . . .," 25–28.

HOWARD C. BRASHERS

"Crack, Crash Orange Flame"
Brashers, Howard C. *Creative Writing* . . ., 235–239.

RICHARD BRAUTIGAN

"Homage to the San Francisco YMCA"
Hulseberg, Richard A. "'Homage to the San Francisco YMCA,'" in Dietrich, R. F., and Roger H. Sundell. *Instructor's Manual* . . ., 3rd ed., 1–4.

"The World War I Los Angeles Airplane"
Galloway, David. "Richard Brautigan, 'The World War I Los Angeles Airplane,'" in Freese, Peter, Ed. . . . *Interpretationen*, 333–339.

CLEMENS BRENTANO

"Brave Kasperl and Beautiful Annerl"
Leibowitz, Judith. *Narrative Purposes* . . ., 20–27.

MILES J. BREUER

"Paradise and Iron"
Carter, Paul A. *The Creation* . . ., 207–208.

CHARLOTTE BRONTË

"The Secret"
Holtz, William, Ed. *Two Tales by Charlotte Brontë* . . ., 39–41.

GEORG BÜCHNER

"Lenz"
Jansen, Peter K. "The Structural Function of the 'Kunstgespräch' in Büchner's 'Lenz,' " *Monatshefte*, 67 (1975), 145–156.
Swales, Martin. *The German "Novelle,"* 99–113.

WILLIAM BURROUGHS

"The Beginning Is Also the End"
Hoenisch, Michael. "William Burroughs, 'The Beginning Is Also the End,'" in Freese, Peter, Ed. . . . *Interpretationen,* 262–269.

ELLIS PARKER BUTLER

"Pigs Is Pigs"
Andrews, Clarence A. "The Comic Element in Iowa Literature," in Brack, O.M., Ed. *American Humor* . . ., 124–125.

FERNÁN CABALLERO

"The Daughter of the Sun"
Klibble, Lawrence H. *Fernán Caballero,* 144–145.

"The Flower of Ruins"
Klibble, Lawrence H. *Fernán Caballero,* 143–144.

"Silence in Life and Pardon in Death"
Klibble, Lawrence H. *Fernán Caballero,* 143.

"Time Is Longer Than Fortune"
Klibble, Lawrence H. *Fernán Caballero,* 145.

"The Two Friends"
Klibble, Lawrence H. *Fernán Caballero,* 144.

GEORGE WASHINGTON CABLE

"Belles Demoiselles Plantation"
Cleman, John. "College Girl Wildness: Nature in the Work of George W. Cable," *Markham R,* 5 (1976), 28–30.
Ringe, Donald A. "The Moral World of Cable's 'Belles Demoiselles Plantation,'" *Mississippi Q,* 29 (1976), 83–90.

"Jean-ah Poquelin"
Cleman, John. "College Girl Wildness . . .," 26–27.

"Madame Delphine"
Berzon, Judith R. *Neither White Nor Black . . .,* 105–106.

"The Solitary" [originally "Gregory's Island"]
Cleman, John. "College Girl Wildness . . .," 26.

"The Story of Bras-Coupé"
Cleman, John. "College Girl Wildness . . .," 28.

ABRAHAM CAHAN

"The Apostate of Chego-Chegg"
Chametzky, Jules. *From the Ghetto . . .,* 90–93.

"Circumstances"
Chametzky, Jules. *From the Ghetto . . .,* 78–80.
Fine, David M. *The City . . .,* 128–129.

"The Daughter of Avrom Leib"
Chametzky, Jules. *From the Ghetto . . .,* 97–99.

"Dumitru and Sigrid"
Chametzky, Jules. *From the Ghetto . . .,* 101–103.

"Fanny and Her Suitors" [same as "Fanny's Khasonim"]
Chametzky, Jules. *From the Ghetto . . .,* 109–114.

"A Ghetto Wedding"
Chametzky, Jules. *From the Ghetto . . .,* 80–81.

"The Imported Bridegroom"
Chametzky, Jules. *From the Ghetto . . .,* 81–87.
Fine, David M. *The City . . .,* 126–127.

"A Marriage by Proxy: A Story of the City"
Chametzky, Jules. *From the Ghetto . . .,* 100–101.

"A Providential Match" [same as "Mottke Arbel and His Romance"]
Chametzky, Jules. *From the Ghetto . . .,* 49–52.

"Rabbi Eliezer's Christmas"
   Chametzky, Jules. *From the Ghetto* . . ., 94–97.
   Fine, David M. *The City* . . ., 130–131.

"Rafael Naarizokh Becomes a Socialist"
   Chametzky, Jules. *From the Ghetto* . . ., 44–47.

"A Sweatshop Romance"
   Chametzky, Jules. *From the Ghetto* . . ., 52–53.

"Tzinchadzi of the Catskills"
   Chametzky, Jules. *From the Ghetto* . . ., 103–105.
   Fine, David M. *The City* . . ., 131–132.

ERSKINE CALDWELL

"Daughter"
   Cook, Sylvia J. *From Tobacco Road* . . ., 77–78.

"Kneel to the Rising Sun"
   Cook, Sylvia J. *From Tobacco Road* . . ., 79–80.

"Slow Death"
   Cook, Sylvia J. *From Tobacco Road* . . ., 78–79.

"Where the Girls Were Different"
   Cassill, R. V. *Instructor's Handbook* . . ., 24–25.

HORTENSE CALISHER

"The Scream on Fifty-Seventh Street"
   Hendricksen, Bruce. " 'The Scream on Fifty-Seventh Street,' " in Dietrich,
   R. F., and Roger H. Sundell. *Instructor's Manual* . . ., 3rd ed., 132–134.

JOHN W. CAMPBELL

"The Machine"
   Carter, Paul A. *The Creation* . . ., 214–216.

"Twilight"
   Carter, Paul A. *The Creation* . . ., 211–213.

ALBERT CAMUS

"Exile and the Kingdom"
   Curtis, Jerry L. "Alienation and the Foreigner in Camus' 'L'Exil et le
   royaume,' " *French Lit Series*, 2 (1975), 127–138.

"The Fall"

Barry, Catherine. "The Concepts of Community and Christology in Camus' 'The Fall,'" *Christianity & Lit,* 25, ii (1976), 37–42.

Goldschläger, Alain, and Jacques Lemaire. "Technique narrative parataxique et psychologie des personnages dans 'L'Étranger' et 'La Chute' d'Albert Camus," *Neophilologus,* 61 (1977), 188–192.

Jones, Rosemarie. "Modes of Discourse in 'La Chute,'" *Nottingham French Stud,* 15, ii (1976), 27–35.

Pratt, Bruce F.R. "Clamence, prophèt de Meursault," *La Revue des Lettres Modernes,* Nos. 479–483 (1976), 105–128.

Van-Huy, Pierre N. "Clamence ou le grand messager camusien," *Lang Q,* 14, iii–iv (1976), 5–9, 12; 15, i–ii (1976), 47–51.

Wasiolek, Edward. "Dostoevsky, Camus, and Faulkner: Transcendence and Mutilation," *Philosophy & Lit,* 1 (1977), 135–136.

"The Growing Stone"

Claire, Thomas. "Landscape and Religious Imagery in Camus' 'La Pierre que pousse,' " *Stud Short Fiction,* 13 (1976), 321–329.

Issacharoff, Michael. "Une Symbolique de l'espace: Lecture de 'La Pierre qui pousse' d'Albert Camus," *Cahiers de l'Association Internationale des Études Françaises,* 27 (1975), 255–272.

"The Guest"

Bovey, Shirley. "Albert Camus' 'The Guest,' " *Notes Contemp Lit,* 7, ii (1977), 9–10.

Gunter, G.O. "The Irony of Alienation in 'The Guest,'" *Notes Contemp Lit,* 8, ii (1978), 5–7.

*Perrine, Laurence. *Instructor's Manual . . . "Story . . .,"* 22–24; *Instructor's Manual . . . "Literature . . .,"* 22–24.

———. "Camus' 'The Guest': A Reply," *Notes Contemp Lit,* 8, iv (1978), 4.

Rooke, Constance. "Camus' 'The Guest': The Message on the Blackboard," *Stud Short Fiction,* 14 (1977), 78–81.

Womack, William R., and Francis S. Heck. "A Note on Camus' 'The Guest,'" *Int'l Fiction R,* 2 (1975), 163–165.

"Jonas, or The Artist at Work"

Bartfeld, Fernande. "Les Paradoxes du 'Jonas' de Camus," *Hebrew Univ Stud Lit,* 6 (1978), 129–142.

Curtis, Jerry L. "Structure and Space in Camus' 'Jonas,'" *Mod Fiction Stud,* 22 (1977), 571–576.

"The Renegade"

Joiner, Lawrence D. "Reverie and Silence in 'Le Renégat,'" *Romance Notes,* 16 (1975), 262–267.

———. "Camus' 'Le Renégat': Identity Denied," *Stud Short Fiction,* 13 (1976), 37–41.

"The Stranger"

Banks, G.V. *Camus: "L'Étranger,"* 1–64.

Brody, Jules. "Camus et la pensée tragique: 'L'Étranger,'" *Saggi,* 15 (1976), 511–554.

Fletcher, Dennis. "Camus between Yes and No: A Fresh Look at the Murder in 'L'Étranger,'" *Neophilologus*, 61 (1977), 523–533.

Gale, John E. "Meursault's Telegram," *Romance Notes*, 16 (1974), 29–32.

Goldschläger, Alain, and Jacques Lemaire. "Technique narrative paratax- ique . . .," 185–188.

Henry, Patrick. "Routine and Reflection in 'L'Étranger,' " *Essays in Arts & Sciences*, 4 (1975), 1–7.

Kellogg, Jean. *Dark Prophets* . . ., 92–96.

Leibowitz, Judith. *Narrative Purposes* . . ., 80–82.

Merad, Ghani. " 'L'Étranger' de Camus vu sous un angle psychosociologique," *Revue Romane*, 10 (1975), 51–91.

Otten, Terry. " 'Mamam' in Camus' 'The Stranger,'" *Coll Lit*, 2 (1975), 105–111.

Panter, James. "Remarks on a Phrase in Camus' 'L'Étranger,'" *Romance Notes*, 16 (1974), 25–28.

Pratt, Bruce. "Epicureanism in 'L'Étranger,'" *Essays French Lit*, 11 (1974), 74–82.

TRUMAN CAPOTE

"Master Misery"
Dörfell, Hanspeter. "Truman Capote, 'Master Misery,' " in Freese, Peter, Ed. . . . *Interpretationen*, 129–139.

"A Tree of Night"
Cassill, R. V. *Instructor's Handbook* . . ., 25–26.

PETER CAREY

"The Fat Man in History"
Bennett, Bruce. "Australian Experiments in Short Fiction," *World Lit Written Engl*, 15 (1976), 363–364.

WILLIAM CARLETON

"A Pilgrimage to Patrick's Purgatory"
Chesnutt, Margaret. . . . *William Carleton*, 30–36.

"Wildgoose Lodge" [originally titled "Confessions of a Reformed Ribbonman"]
Chesnutt, Margaret. . . . *William Carleton*, 126–129.

ALEJO CARPENTIER

"El año 59"
Menton, Seymour. . . . *Cuban Revolution*, 48–49.

"Los convidados de plata"
Menton, Seymour. . . . *Cuban Revolution*, 49–50.

"Lord, Praised Be Thou"
González Echevarría, Roberto. *Alejo Carpentier* . . ., 63–86.

"Manhunt"
González Echevarría, Roberto. *Alejo Carpentier* . . ., 189–212.

"Viaje a la Semilla"
Jiménez-Fajardo, Salvator. "The Redeeming Quest: Patterns of Unification in
Carpentier, Fuentes, and Cortázar," *Revista de Estudios Hispánicos,* 11
(1977), 90–102.

CALVERT CASEY

"En el Potosí"
Menton, Seymour. . . . *Cuban Revolution,* 176–177.

"In partenza"
Menton, Seymour. . . . *Cuban Revolution,* 241–242.

"Polacca brillante"
Menton, Seymour. . . . *Cuban Revolution,* 242–243.

"El regreso"
Menton, Seymour. . . . *Cuban Revolution,* 175–176.

R. V. CASSILL

"The Biggest Band"
Cassill, R. V. *Instructor's Handbook* . . ., 27.

ROSARIO CASTELLANOS

"La tregua"
Brodman, Barbara L. C. *The Mexican Cult* . . ., 65–67.

WILLA CATHER

"The Enchanted Bluff"
Bonham, Barbara. *Willa Cather,* 56–57.

"Neighbour Rosicky"
Martin, Robert A. "Primitivism in Stories by Willa Cather and Sherwood
Anderson," *Midamerica,* 3 (1976), 40–42.

"The Old Beauty"
Cassill, R. V. *Instructor's Handbook* . . ., 28–30.

"Paul's Case"
  *Perrine, Laurence. *Instructor's Manual* . . . *"Story* . . .," 18–19; *Instructor's Manual* . . . *"Literature* . . .," 18–19.

ADELBERT VON CHAMISSO

"Peter Schlemihl"
  Berger, Willy R. "Drei phantastische Erzählungen: Chamissos 'Peter Schlemihl,' E. T. A. Hoffmanns 'Abenteur der Silvester-Nacht,' und Gogols 'Die Nase,'" *Arcadia,* [n. v.], Special Issue (1978), 106–138.
  Butler, Colin A. "Hobson's Choice: A Note on 'Peter Schlemihl,' " *Monatshefte,* 69 (1979), 5–16.
  Massey, Irving. *The Gaping Pig* . . ., 138–154.
  Swales, Martin. "Mundane Magic: Some Observations on Chamisso's 'Peter Schlemihl,'" *Forum Mod Lang Stud,* 12 (1976), 250–262.
  ———. *The German "Novelle,"* 77–98.

EILEEN CHANG

"Blockade"
  Hsia, C. T. *A History* . . ., 413–414.

"Jasmine Tea"
  Hsia, C. T. *A History* . . ., 407–413.

CHANG T'IEN

"After Her Departure"
  Hsia, C. T. *A History* . . ., 228–231.

"The Bulwark"
  Hsia, C. T. *A History* . . ., 215–218.

"The Mid-Autumn Festival"
  Hsia, C. T. *A History* . . ., 220–221.

"On the Journey"
  Hsia, C. T. *A History* . . ., 218–220.

"Spring Breeze"
  Hsia, C. T. *A History* . . ., 223–227.

CHAO SHU-LI

"The Marriage of Hsiao Erh-hei"
  Hsia, C. T. *A History* . . ., 482–483.

FRANÇOIS RENÉ DE CHATEAUBRIAND

"Abencérage"
  Dubé, Pierre. "Les Aventures du dernier 'Abencérage': Étude spatio-temporelle," *Travaux de Linguistique et de Littérature* (Strasbourg), 15, ii (1977), 101–107.

"Atala"
  Amelinckx, Frans C. "Image et structure dans 'Atala,'" *Revue Romane*, 10 (1975), 367–372.
  Becker, Jon. "Archetype and Myth in Chateaubriand's 'Atala,'" *Symposium*, 31 (1977), 93–106.

"René"
  Hunt, Tony. "Chateaubriand's 'René' and Christian Apologetics," *Durham Univ J*, 36 (1975), 68–78.
  Massey, Irving. *The Uncreating Word . . .*, 48–50.

PADDY CHAYEFSKY

"A Few Kind Words from Newark"
  Clum, John M. *Paddy Chayefsky*, 25–26.

"The Giant Fan"
  Clum, John M. *Paddy Chayefsky*, 27–28.

JOHN CHEEVER

"The Angel of the Bridge"
  Burhans, C[linton] S. "John Cheever and the Grave of Social Coherence," *Twentieth Century Lit*, 14 (1969), 193.
  Coale, Samuel. *John Cheever*, 54–58.

"The Bella Lingua"
  Burhans, C[linton] S. "John Cheever . . .," 191.

"Clementina"
  Burhans, C[linton] S. "John Cheever . . .," 191–192.

"The Common Day"
  Coale, Samuel. *John Cheever*, 12–13.

"The Country Husband"
  Coale, Samuel. *John Cheever*, 28–33.
  Kane, Thomas S., and Leonard J. Peters. *Some Suggestions . . .*, 42–44.

"The Death of Justina"
  Coale, Samuel. *John Cheever*, 23–28.

"The Enormous Radio"
  Coale, Samuel. *John Cheever*, 40–43.
  Haas, Rudolf. "John Cheever, 'The Enormous Radio,'" in Freese, Peter, Ed. . . .
    Interpretationen, 140–151.

"The Fourth Alarm"
  Cassill, R. V. *Instructor's Handbook* . . ., 31–32.

"Goodbye, My Brother"
  Coale, Samuel. *John Cheever*, 61–64.

"The Housebreaker of Shady Hill"
  Coale, Samuel. *John Cheever*, 17–20.

"The Music Teacher"
  Coale, Samuel. *John Cheever*, 36–37.

"O Youth and Beauty"
  Coale, Samuel. *John Cheever*, 15–17.
  Moore, Stephen C. "The Hero on the 5:42: John Cheever's Short Fiction,"
    Western Hum R, 30 (1976), 148–149.

"The Scarlet Moving Van"
  Coale, Samuel. *John Cheever*, 20–23.
  Moore, Stephen C. "The Hero on the 5:42 . . .," 150–152.

"The Seaside House"
  Coale, Samuel. *John Cheever*, 37–40.

"The Swimmer"
  Coale, Samuel. *John Cheever*, 43–47.
  Kimmey, John L., Ed. *Experience and Expression* . . ., 159–160.
  Moore, Stephen C. "The Hero on the 5:42 . . .," 149–150.

"A Vision of the World"
  Coale, Samuel. *John Cheever*, 51–54.

"The World of Apples"
  Coale, Samuel. *John Cheever*, 58–60.

"The Wrysons"
  Coale, Samuel. *John Cheever*, 13–15.

ANTON CHEKHOV

"Agafya"
Hahn, Beverly. *Chekhov* . . ., 216–218.

"Anna on the Neck"
  Golubkov, V. V. "Čexov's Lyrico-Dramatic Stories," in Hulanicki, Leo, and
    David Savignac, Eds. and Trans. *Anton Čexov* . . ., 148–158.

"Anyuta"
Hahn, Beverly. *Chekhov* . . . , 213–214.

"Ariadna"
Rayfield, Donald. *Chekhov* . . . , 146–148.

"At Home"
Pospelov, G. N. "The Style of Čexov's Tales," in Hulanicki, Leo, and David
Savignac, Eds. and Trans. *Anton Čexov* . . . , 128–129.

"An Attack of Nerves"
Senderovich, Marena. "The Symbolic Structure of Chekhov's Story 'An Attack
of Nerves,'" in Debreczeny, Paul, and Thomas Eekman, Eds. *Chekhov's Art
of Writing* . . . , 11–26.

"The Beauties"
Hahn, Beverly. *Chekhov* . . . , 102–105.

"Big Volodya and Little Volodya"
Kane, Thomas S., and Leonard J. Peters. *Some Suggestions* . . . , 58–59.

"The Bishop"
Rayfield, Donald. *Chekhov* . . . , 232–237.

"The Darling"
Bayuk, Milla. "The Submissive Wife Stereotype in Anton Chekhov's
'Darling,'" *Coll Lang Assoc J*, 20 (1977), 533–539.
Cassill, R. V. *Instructor's Handbook* . . . , 36–38.
Hahn, Beverly. *Chekhov* . . . , 230–232.
Lakšin, V. "An Incomparable Artist," in Hulanicki, Leo, and David Savignac,
Eds. and Trans. *Anton Čexov* . . . , 100–101.

"Dreams"
Hahn, Beverly. *Chekhov* . . . , 63–64.

"A Dreary Story" [same as "A Tedious Tale"]
Hahn, Beverly. *Chekhov* . . . , 156–177.
Rayfield, Donald. *Chekhov* . . . , 88–92.

"The Duel"
Hahn, Beverly. *Chekhov* . . . , 178–200.
Rayfield, Donald. *Chekhov* . . . , 120–126.

"Easter Eve"
Hahn, Beverly. *Chekhov* . . . , 71–80.

"Enemies"
Hahn, Beverly. *Chekhov* . . . , 80–91.

"A Gentleman Friend"
Šklovskij, Viktor. "A. P. Čexov," in Hulanicki, Leo, and David Savignac, Eds.
and Trans. *Anton Čexov* . . . , 74–76.

"Gooseberries"
*Gullason, Thomas A. "The Short Story: An Underrated Art," in May, Charles
E., Ed. *Short Story Theories*, 25–28.
Kane, Thomas S., and Leonard J. Peters. *Some Suggestions . . .*, 57–58.
Šklovskij, Viktor. "A. P. Čexov," 76–78.

"The Grasshopper" [same as "The Flutterer"; originally titled "The Philistines"
and then "A Great Man"]
Golubkov, V. V. "Čexov's Lyrico-Dramatic Stories," 141–148.
Hahn, Beverly. *Chekhov . . .*, 232–234.

"Gusev"
Lantz, Kenneth A. "Chekhov's 'Gusev': A Study," *Stud Short Fiction,* 15
(1978), 55–61.

"Happiness"
Hahn, Beverly. *Chekhov . . .*, 105–112.

"A Horse Name"
Šklovskij, Viktor. "A. P. Čexov," 73–74.

"The House with the Mezzanine"
Dobin, E. S. "The Nature of Detail," in Hulanicki, Leo, and David Savignac,
Eds. and Trans. *Anton Čexov . . .*, 46–47.
Pospelov, G. N. "The Style of Čexov's Tales," 120–121.
Rayfield, Donald. *Chekhov . . .*, 158–162.

"The Huntsman"
Hahn, Beverly. *Chekhov . . .*, 47–49.

"In the Ravine"
Debreczeny, Paul. "The Device of Conspicuous Silence in Tolstoj, Čexov, and
Faulkner," in Terras, Victor, Ed. *American Contributions . . .*, II, 128–137.
Rayfield, Donald. *Chekhov . . .*, 181–185.

"Ionych"
Derman, A. "Structural Features in Čexov's Poetics," in Hulanicki, Leo, and
David Savignac, Eds. and Trans. *Anton Čexov . . .*, 110–111.
Katsell, Jerome H. "Character Change in Čexov's Short Stories," *Slavic & East
European J,* 18 (1974), 381–382.
Rayfield, Donald. *Chekhov . . .*, 195–197.

"The Kiss"
Kane, Thomas S., and Leonard J. Peters. *Some Suggestions . . .*, 55–56.
*Perrine, Laurence. *Instructor's Manual . . . "Story . . .,"* 8–9; *Instructor's
Manual . . . "Literature . . .,"* 8–9.
*_____, Ed. *Story and Structure*, 219–222.

"The Lady with the Dog" [same as "The Lady with the Pet Dog"]
Cassill, R. V. *Instructor's Handbook . . .*, 33–34.
Hahn, Beverly. *Chekhov . . .*, 252–263.
Katsell, Jerome H. "Character Change . . .," 380–381.
Rayfield, Donald. *Chekhov . . .*, 197–200.

"Lights"
Hahn, Beverly. *Chekhov* . . . , 113–132.

"Misery" [same as "The Lament"]
Hahn, Beverly. *Chekhov* . . . , 59–63.

"A Misfortune"
Hahn, Beverly. *Chekhov* . . . , 219–223.

"My Life"
Rayfield, Donald. *Chekhov* . . . , 163–169.

"On the Cart"
Golubkov, V. V. "Čexov's Lyrico-Dramatic Stories," 160–167.

"The Party"
Hahn, Beverly. *Chekhov* . . . , 237–251.

"Peasants"
Hahn, Beverly. *Chekhov* . . . , 153–154.
Rayfield, Donald. *Chekhov* . . . , 177–182.

"Sorrow"
Hahn, Beverly. *Chekhov* . . . , 49–51.

"The Steppe"
Hahn, Beverly. *Chekhov* . . . , 97–102.
Katsell, Jerome H. "Čexov's 'The Steppe' Revisited," *Slavic & East European J*, 22 (1978), 313–323.
Rayfield, Donald. *Chekhov* . . . , 72–75.
Šklovskij, Viktor. "A. P. Čexov," 79–83.

"The Student"
Derman, A. "The Essence of Čexov's Creative Approach," in Hulanicki, Leo, and David Savignac, Eds. and Trans. *Anton Čexov* . . . , 29–31.
Martin, David W. "*Realia* and Chekhov's 'The Student,'" *Canadian-Am Slavic Stud*, 12 (1978), 266–273.

"The Teacher of Literature"
Šklovskij, Viktor. "A. P. Čexov," 49–51.

"Three Years"
Hahn, Beverly. *Chekhov* . . . , 201–205.

"An Upheaval"
Hahn, Beverly. *Chekhov* . . . , 45–47.

"Vanka"
Hahn, Beverly. *Chekhov* . . . , 65–68.

"A Visit to Friends"
Cassill, R. V. *Instructor's Handbook* . . . , 35–36.

"Ward No. 6"
    Hahn, Beverly. *Chekhov* . . ., 148–152.

"A Woman's Kingdom"
    Hahn, Beverly. *Chekhov* . . ., 267–283.

CHARLES W. CHESNUTT

"Cicely's Dream"
    Elder, Arlene A. *The "Hindered Hand"* . . ., 169–170.

"The Conjurer's Revenge"
    Elder, Arlene A. *The "Hindered Hand"* . . ., 158–159.

"The Goophered Grapevine"
    Elder, Arlene A. *The "Hindered Hand"* . . ., 153–155.
    Hemenway, Robert. "The Functions of Folklore in Charles Chesnutt's *The Conjure Woman*," *J Folklore Institute*, 13 (1976), 288–291.

"The Gray Wolf's Ha'nt"
    Elder, Arlene A. *The "Hindered Hand"* . . ., 161–162.
    Hemenway, Robert. "The Functions of Folklore . . .," 291–292.

"Her Virginia Mammy"
    Elder, Arlene A. *The "Hindered Hand"* . . ., 165.

"Hot-Foot Hannibal"
    Elder, Arlene A. *The "Hindered Hand"* . . ., 162–163.
    Hemenway, Robert. "The Functions of Folklore . . .," 292–295.

"Mars Jeems's Nightmare"
    Elder, Arlene A. *The "Hindered Hand"* . . ., 156–158.

"A Matter of Principle"
    Elder, Arlene A. *The "Hindered Hand"* . . ., 165–166.

"The Passing of Grandison"
    Elder, Arlene A. *The "Hindered Hand"* . . .," 168–169.

"Po' Sandy"
    Elder, Arlene A. *The "Hindered Hand"* . . ., 155.

"The Sheriff's Children"
    Elder, Arlene A. *The "Hindered Hand"* . . ., 170–172.
    Selke, Hartmut K. "Charles Waddell Chesnutt: 'The Sheriff's Children,'" in Bruck, Peter, Ed. *The Black American Short Story* . . ., 27–36.

"Sis' Becky's Pickaninny"
    Elder, Arlene A. *The "Hindered Hand"* . . ., 159–161.
    Hemenway, Robert. "The Functions of Folklore . . .," 294–296.

"The Web of Circumstance"
Elder, Arlene A. *The "Hindered Hand"* . . ., 172–173.

"The Wife of His Youth"
Elder, Arlene A. *The "Hindered Hand"* . . ., 164–165.

CH'IEN CHUNG-SHU

"Cat"
Hsia, C. T. *A History* . . ., 437–439.

"Inspiration"
Hsia, C. T. *A History* . . ., 434–436.

"Souvenir"
Hsia, C. T. *A History* . . ., 439–441.

KATE CHOPIN

"Désirée's Baby"
Berzon, Judith R. *Neither White Nor Black* . . ., 102–103.
Wolff, Cynthia G. "Kate Chopin and the Fiction of Limits: 'Désirée's Baby,'"
Southern Lit J, 10 (1978), 123–133.

WALTER VAN TILBURG CLARK

"The Anonymous"
Wilner, Herbert. "Walter Van Tilburg Clark," *Western R,* 20 (1956), 109–110.

"The Buck in the Hills"
Eisinger, Chester. "The Fiction of Walter Van Tilburg Clark: Man and Nature in
the West," *Southwest R,* 44 (1959), 223–224; rpt. in his *Fiction of the Forties,*
320–321.

"Hook"
Eisinger, Chester. ". . . Man and Nature in the West," 224; rpt. in his *Fiction of
the Forties,* 321–322.
Wilner, Herbert. ". . . Clark," 104–106.

"The Indian Well"
Wilner, Herbert. ". . . Clark," 107–108.

"The Portable Phonograph"
Wilner, Herbert. ". . . Clark," 108–109.

"The Rapids"
Wilner, Herbert. ". . . Clark," 108.

"The Watchful Gods"
Eisinger, Chester. ". . . Man and Nature in the West," 225–226; rpt. in his
Fiction of the Forties, 323.

"The Wind and the Snow of Winter"
Wilner, Herbert. ". . . Clark," 107.

ARTHUR C. CLARKE

"A Meeting with Medusa"
Slusser, George E. *The Space Odyssey* . . ., 18–23.

"The Nine Billion Names of God"
Slusser, George E. *The Space Odyssey* . . ., 15.

"The Star"
Cassill, R. V. *Instructor's Handbook* . . ., 39–40.
Moskowitz, Sam. *Strange Horizons* . . ., 15–16.
Slusser, George E. *The Space Odyssey* . . ., 15–16.

"Summertime on Icarus"
Slusser, George E. *The Space Odyssey* . . ., 16–18.

JOHN COLLIER

"Wet Saturday"
Kane, Thomas S., and Leonard J. Peters. *Some Suggestions* . . ., 14–15.

RICHARD CONNELL

"The Most Dangerous Game"
*Perrine, Laurence. *Instructor's Manual* . . . *"Story* . . .," 1–2; *Instructor's
Manual* . . . *"Literature* . . .," 1–2.

JOSEPH CONRAD

"Amy Foster"
Beidler, Peter G. "Conrad's 'Amy Foster' and Chaucer's Prioress," *Nineteenth-
Century Fiction,* 30 (1975), 111–115.
Pinsker, Sanford. " 'Amy Foster': A Reconsideration," *Conradiana,* 9 (1977),
179–186.

"The End of the Tether"
Bruss, Paul S. " 'The End of the Tether': Teleological Diminishing in Conrad's
Early Metaphor of Navigation," *Stud Short Fiction,* 13 (1976), 311–320.
Tucker, Martin. *Joseph Conrad,* 42–45.
Young, Gloria L. "Chance and the Absurd in Conrad's 'The End of the Tether'
and 'Freya of the Seven Isles,' " *Conradiana,* 7 (1976), 254–256.

"Falk"
  Tanner, Tony. "'Gnawed Bones' and 'Artless Tales' — Eating and Narrative in
    Conrad," in Sherry, Norman, Ed. . . . *A Commemoration,* 17–36.

"Freya of the Seven Isles"
  Young, Gloria L. "Chance and the Absurd . . .," 256–259.

"Heart of Darkness"
  Cassill, R. V. *Instructor's Handbook* . . ., 43–48.
  Daleski, H. M. *Joseph Conrad* . . ., 51–76.
  Dolan, Paul J. *Of War and War's Alarms* . . ., 96–102.
  Ellis, James. "Kurtz's Voice: The Intended as 'The Horror!'" *Engl Lit Transi-
    tion,* 19 (1976), 105–110.
  Friedman, Alan W. *Multivalence* . . ., 115–123.
  Fwasatadi, Wabeno. "'Heart of Darkness': Le Voyage de Marlow vers l'in-
    terieur," *Cahiers de Littérature et de Linguistique Appliquée,* 7–8 (1975),
    85–92.
  Geary, Edward A. "An Ashy Halo: Woman as Symbol in 'Heart of Darkness,'"
    Stud Short Fiction, 13 (1976), 499–506.
  Gekoski, R. A. *Conrad* . . ., 72–90.
  Glassman, Peter J. *Language and Being* . . ., 198–249.
  Godshalk, William L. "Kurtz as Diabolical Christ," *Discourse,* 12 (1969),
    100–107.
  Goonetilleke, D. C. R. A. *Developing Countries* . . ., 101–118.
  Gutierrez, Donald. "Uroboros and the Serpent in Conrad's 'Heart of Dark-
    ness,'" *Nantucket R,* [n. v.] (Spring, 1976), 40–45.
  Harold, Brent. "The Intrinsic Sociology in Fiction," *Mod Fiction Stud,* 23
    (1977), 597–599.
  Henricksen, Bruce. "'Heart of Darkness' and the Gnostic Myth," *Mosaic,* 11,
    iv (1978), 35–44.
  McClure, John A. "The Rhetoric of Restraint in 'Heart of Darkness,'"
    Nineteenth-Century Fiction, 32 (1977), 310–326.
  McIntyre, Allan J. "Psychology and Symbol: Correspondences Between 'Heart
    of Darkness' and 'Death in Venice,'" *Hartford Stud Lit,* 7 (1975), 216–235.
  McLauchlan, Juliet. "The 'Something Human' in 'Heart of Darkness,'"
    Conradiana, 9 (1977), 115–125.
  Ong, Walter J. "Truth in Conrad's Darkness," *Mosaic,* 11 (1977), 151–163.
  Renner, Stanley. "Kurtz, Christ, and the Darkness of 'Heart of Darkness,'"
    Renascence, 28 (1975), 95–104.
  Sams, Larry M. "Heart of Darkness: The Meaning Around the Nutshell," *Int'l
    Fiction R,* 5 (1978), 129–133.
  Tucker, Martin. *Joseph Conrad,* 28–36.
  Watt, Ian. "Impressionism and Symbolism in 'Heart of Darkness,'" in Sherry,
    Norman, Ed. . . . *A Commemoration,* 37–53; rpt. *Southern R,* 13 (1977),
    96–113.
  Watts, Cedric. *Conrad's "Heart of Darkness"* . . ., 48–151.

"The Informer"
  Gekoski, R. A. *Conrad* . . ., 138–140.

"Karain"
  Gekoski, R. A. *Conrad* . . ., 47–50.

Herbert, Wray C. "Conrad's Psychic Landscape: The Mythic Element in 'Karain,'" *Conradiana,* 8 (1976), 225–232.

"The Lagoon"

Hulseberg, Richard A. "'The Lagoon,'" in Dietrich, R. F., and Roger H. Sundell. *Instructor's Manual . . .,* 3rd ed., 93–96.

Rice, Thomas J. "'The Lagoon': Malay and Pharisee," *Christianity & Lit,* 25, iv (1976), 25–33.

"An Outpost of Progress"

Gekoski, R. A. *Conrad . . .,* 44–47.

Goonetilleke, D. C. R. A. *Developing Countries . . .,* 99–101.

Hilson, J. C., and D. Timms. "Conrad's 'An Outpost of Progress' or, The Evil Spirit of Civilization," *Cahiers Victoriens et Edouardiens,* 2 (1975), 113–128.

Watts, Cedric. *Conrad's "Heart of Darkness" . . .,* 33–36.

"The Return"

Birdseye, Lewis E. "The Curse of Consciousness: A Study of Conrad's 'The Return,'" *Conradiana,* 9 (1977), 171–178.

Gekoski, R. A. *Conrad . . .,* 50–55.

"The Secret Sharer"

*Abcarian, Richard, and Marvin Klotz. *Instructor's Manual . . .,* 2nd ed., 5–6.

Burgess, C. F. *The Fellowship . . .,* 88–89.

Daleski, H. M. *Joseph Conrad . . .,* 171–183.

Dilworth, Thomas R. "Conrad's Secret Sharer at the Gates of Hell," *Conradiana,* 9 (1977), 203–218.

Goonetilleke, D. C. R. A. *Developing Countries . . .,* 36–38.

*Howe, Irving, Ed. *Classics of Modern Fiction . . .,* 2nd ed., 273–283.

Kane, Thomas S., and Leonard J. Peters. *Some Suggestions . . .,* 49–50.

Rosenman, John B. "The L-Shaped Room in 'The Secret Sharer,'" *Claflin Coll R,* 1, i (1976), 4–8.

Tucker, Martin. *Joseph Conrad,* 47–49.

Watts, Cedric. "The Mirror Tale: An Ethico-Structural Analysis of Conrad's 'The Secret Sharer,' " *Critical Q,* 19, iii (1977), 25–37.

"The Shadow Line"

Burgess, C. F. *The Fellowship . . .,* 122–124.

Goonetilleke, D. C. R. A. *Developing Countries . . .,* 38–40.

Gutierrez, Donald. "Fathers and Sons: Conrad's 'The Shadow Line' as an Initiation Rite of Passage," *Univ Dayton R,* 12, iii (1976), 101–106.

Schwarz, Daniel. "Achieving Self-Command: Theme and Value in Conrad's 'The Shadow Line,'" *Renascence,* 24 (1977), 131–141.

Tucker, Martin. *Joseph Conrad,* 49–51.

"Typhoon"

Daleski, H. M. *Joseph Conrad . . .,* 104–112.

Goonetilleke, D. C. R. A. *Developing Countries . . .,* 46–51.

Tucker, Martin. *Joseph Conrad,* 40–42.

"Youth"
  Burgess, C. F. *The Fellowship* . . ., 62–64.
  Goonetilleke, D. C. R. A. *Developing Countries* . . ., 35–36.
  Lindsay, Clarence B. "Conrad's 'Youth': The Harmony of Past and Present,"
    Crit R, 19 (1977), 106–113.
  *Perrine, Laurence. *Instructor's Manual* . . . *"Story* . . .," 12; *Instructor's Manual* . . . *"Literature* . . .," 12.
  Tucker, Martin. *Joseph Conrad*, 38–40.

BENJAMIN CONSTANT

"Adolphe"
  Baguley, David. "The Role of Letters in Constant's 'Adolphe,'" *Forum Mod Lang Stud*, 11 (1975), 29–35.
  Booker, John T. "The Implied *narrataire* in 'Adolphe,'" *French R*, 51 (1978), 666–673.
  Hyslop, Lois B. "'Adolphe': 'Aimer' or 'Être aimé'?" *French R*, 50 (1977), 572–578.
  Mercken-Spaas, Godelieve. "The Gaze and Threat of Death in Constant's 'Adolphe,'" *Neophilologus*, 59 (1975), 352–356.
  _____. "The Metaphor of Space in Constant's 'Adolphe,'" *Nineteenth-Century French Stud*, 5 (1977), 186–195.
  _____. *Alienation in Constant's "Adolphe"* . . ., *passim*.
  Verhoeff, Han. "'Adolphe' en parole," *Revue d'Histoire Littéraire de la France*, 75 (1975), 48–66.

ROBERT COOVER

"The Babysitter"
  Cassill, R. V. *Instructor's Handbook* . . ., 49–51.

"The Elevator"
  Pütz, Manfred. "Robert Coover, 'The Elevator,' " in Freese, Peter, Ed. . . . *Interpretationen*, 280–288.

JULIO CORTÁZAR

"All Fires the Fire"
  Carrillo, German D. "Emociones y fragmentaciones: técnicas cuentísticas de Julio Cortázar en 'Todos los fuegos el fuego,'" in Giacoman, Helmy F., Ed. *Homenaje a Julio Cortázar* . . ., 319–328.
  Curutchet, Juan C. "Julio Cortázar, cronista de las *Eras imaginarias:* Para una interpretación de 'Todos los fuegos el fuego,'" in Lagmanovich, David, Ed. *Estudios* . . . *Cortázar*, 83–98.
  Davis, Deborah. "'All Fires the Fire' by Julio Cortázar," *Review 73*, 9 (Fall, 1973), 69–70.
  González Echevarría, Roberto. "*Los reyes*: Cortázar's Mythology of Writing," in Alazraki, Jaime, and Ivar Ivask, Eds. *The Final Island* . . ., 67–68.

Gyurko, Lanin A. "Cyclic Time and Blood Sacrifice in Three Stories by Cortázar," *Revista Hispánica Moderna*, 35 (1969), 341–348.
Lagmanovich, David. "Estructura de un cuento de Julio Cortázar: 'Todos los fuegos el fuego,'" in Giacoman, Helmy F., Ed. *Homenaje a Julio Cortázar* ..., 375–387.
Luchting, Wolfgang A. "'Todos los fuegos el fuego,'" in Giacoman, Helmy F., Ed. *Homenaje a Julio Cortázar* ..., 351–363.
Mignolo, Walter. "Conexidad, coherencia, ambigüedad: 'Todos los fuegos el fuego,'" *Hispamerica*, 14 (1976), 3–26.

"At Your Service"
Garfield, Evelyn P. *Julio Cortázar*, 44–46.

"Axolotl"
Pagés Larraya, Antonio. "Perspectivas de 'Axolotl,' cuento de Julio Cortázar," in Giacoman, Helmy F., Ed. *Homenaje a Julio Cortázar* ..., 457–480.
Planells, Antonio. "Comunicación por metamorfosis: 'Axolotl' de Julio Cortázar," *Explicación de Textos Literarios*, 6, ii (1978), 135–141.
Reedy, Daniel R. "Through the Looking-Glass: Aspects of Cortázar's Epiphanies of Reality," *Bull Hispanic Stud*, 54 (1977), 129–131.

"The Band"
Gyurko, Lanin A. "Self-Deception and Self-Confrontation in Cortázar," *Southern Hum R*, 8 (1974), 361–365.

"Bestiary"
Garfield, Evelyn P. *Julio Cortázar*, 20–22.
Reedy, Daniel R. "Through the Looking-Glass ...," 125–127.

"Blow-up" [same as "Las babas del diablo"]
Carvalho, Ilka Valle de. "Surrealismo cortazariano: 'Las babas del diablo,'" *Minas Gerais, Suplemento Literário*, 23 (April, 1977), 4.
D'Lugo, Marvin. "'Las babas del diablo': In Pursuit of Cortázar's 'Reel' World," *Revista de Estudios Hispánicos*, 11 (1977), 395–409.
Garfield, Evelyn P. *Julio Cortázar*, 40–44.
Goldstein, Melvin. "Antonioni's 'Blow-up': From Crib to Camera," *Am Imago*, 32 (1975), 240–263.
Grossvogel, David I. "'Blow-up': The Forms of an Esthetic Itinerary," *Diacritics*, 11, iii (1972), 49–54.
Kester, Gary. "'Blow-up': Cortázar's and Antonioni's," *Latin Am Lit R*, 9 (1976), 7–10.
Reedy, Daniel R. "The Symbolic Reality of Cortázar's 'Las babas del diablo,'" *Hispánica Moderna*, 36 (1970–1971), 224–237.
Samuels, Charles T. "Sorting Things Out in 'Blow-up,'" *Review 72*, 7 (Winter, 1972), 22–23.

"Los buenos servicios"
Borello, Rodolfo A. "'Los buenos servicios' o la ambigüedad de las vidas ajenas," in Lagmanovich, David, Ed. *Estudios ... Cortázar*, 41–57.

"Cefalea"
Garfield, Evelyn P. *Julio Cortázar*, 19–20.

Gyurko, Lanin A. "Hallucination and Nightmare in Two Stories by Cortázar,"
Mod Lang R, 67 (1972), 550–562.

"Circe"
Gyurko, Lanin A. "The Bestiary and the Demonic in Two Stories by Cortázar,"
Revue des Langues Vivantes, 39 (1973), 112–130.

"Continuity of Parks"
Garfield, Evelyn P. *Julio Cortázar,* 32.
Rabkin, Eric S. *The Fantastic* . . ., 39–41.

"The Distances"
Alazraki, Jaime. "Doubles, Bridges and Quests for Identity: 'Lejano' Revisited," in Alazraki, Jaime, and Ivar Ivask, Eds. *The Final Island* . . ., 73–83.
Garfield, Evelyn P. *Julio Cortázar,* 27–29.

"End of the Game"
Anderson Imbert, Enrique. "Julio Cortázar: 'Final del juego,'" *Revista Iberoamericana,* 23 (1958), 173–175.

"The Gates of Heaven"
Garfield, Evelyn P. *Julio Cortázar,* 26–27.

"Homage to a Young Witch"
Francescato, Martha P. "The New Man (But Not the New Woman)," in Alazraki, Jaime, and Ivar Ivask, Eds. *The Final Island* . . ., 138–139.

"House Taken Over"
Garfield, Evelyn P. *Julio Cortázar,* 18–19.
Gyurko, Lanin A. "Hallucination and Nightmare . . .," 550–562.
Quintão, Maria do Carmo. "Poder Entorpecente da Palavra ou a Fala do Tricô em 'Casa Tomado' de Julio Cortázar," *Minas Gerais, Suplemento Literário,* 1 (July, 1978), 9.

"Instrucciones para John Howell"
Petrich, Perla. " 'Instrucciones para John Howell': Iniciación al extrañamiento," in Lagmanovich, David, Ed. *Estudios . . . Cortázar,* 139–162.

"The Isle at Noon"
Reedy, Daniel R. "Through the Looking-Glass . . .," 131–132.

"Neck of the Little Black Cat"
Garfield, Evelyn P. *"Octaedro: Eight Phases of Despair,"* in Alazraki, Jaime, and Ivar Ivask, Eds. *The Final Island* . . ., 123.

"The Night Face Up"
Garfield, Evelyn P. *Julio Cortázar,* 31–32.
Gyurko, Lanin A. "Cyclic Time and Blood Sacrifice . . .," 348–355.
Serra, Edelweis. "Conjuncion de realidad y fantasía en 'La noche boca arriba,'" in Yates, Donald A., Ed. *Otros mundos otros fuegos* . . ., 121–127.
_____. "El arte del cuento: 'La noche boca arriba,'" in Lagmanovich, David, Ed. *Estudios . . . Cortázar,* 163–177.

"Nurse Cora"
Garfield, Evelyn P. *Julio Cortázar*, 68–69.

"Omnibus"
Garfield, Evelyn P. *Julio Cortázar*, 25–26.
Gyurko, Lanin A. "The Bestiary and the Demonic . . .," 112–130.

"The Other Heaven"
Garfield, Evelyn P. *Julio Cortázar*, 72–73.

"The Phases of Severo"
Garfield, Evelyn P. *"Octaedro* . . .," 125–127.

"A Place Called Kindberg"
Garfield, Evelyn P. *"Octaedro* . . .," 123–124.
Gyurko, Lanin A. "Self-Deception . . .," 365–372.

"The Pursuer"
Alazraki, Jaime. "Introduction: Toward the Last Square of the Hopscotch," in
   Alazraki, Jaime, and Ivar Ivask, Eds. *The Final Island* . . ., 12–13.
Garfield, Evelyn P. *Julio Cortázar*, 46–49.
González Echevarría, Roberto. *"Los reyes*: Cortázar's Mythology . . .," 68–70.
Holsten, Ken. "Three Characters and a Theme in Cortázar," *Revista de Estudios
   Hispánicos*, 9 (1975), 121–125.
Veiravé, Alfredo. "Aproximaciones a 'El perseguidor,'" in Lagmanovich,
   David, Ed. *Estudios . . . Cortázar*, 191–218.

"Reunion"
Menton, Seymour. . . . *Cuban Revolution*, 255–258.

"The River"
Garfield, Evelyn P. *Julio Cortázar*, 35–37.
Hozven, Roberto. "Interpretacion de 'El río,' cuento de Julio Cortázar," in
   Giacoman, Helmy F., Ed. *Homenaje a Julio Cortázar* . . ., 405–425.

"Secret Weapons"
Reedy, Daniel R. "Through the Looking-Glass . . .," 127–129.

"The Southern Throughway"
Garfield, Evelyn P. *Julio Cortázar*, 64–68.

"Torito"
Garfield, Evelyn P. *Julio Cortázar*, 33–35.

"A Yellow Flower"
Sosnowski, Saul. "'Una flor amarilla,' vindicación de vidas fracasadas," in
   Lagmanovich, David, Ed. *Estudios . . . Cortázar*, 179–190.

MARK COSTELLO

"Murphy's Xmas"
Cassill, R. V. *Instructor's Handbook* . . ., 51–53.

JAMES GOULD COZZENS

"Eyes to See"
  Shepherd, Allen. " 'The New Aquist of True Incredible Experience': Point of View and Theme in James Gould Cozzens' 'Eyes to See,' " *Stud Short Fiction*, 13 (1976), 378–381.

HUBERT CRACKANTHORPE

"Anthony Garstin's Courtship"
  Crackanthorpe, David. *Hubert Crackanthorpe* . . ., 148–152.

"A Commonplace Chapter"
  Crackanthorpe, David. *Hubert Crackanthorpe* . . ., 87–94.

"A Dead Woman"
  Crackanthorpe, David. *Hubert Crackanthorpe* . . ., 72–75.

"Étienne Mattou"
  Crackanthorpe, David. *Hubert Crackanthorpe* . . ., 115–116.

"Gaston Lalanne's Child"
  Crackanthorpe, David. *Hubert Crackanthorpe* . . ., 116–118.

"In Cumberland" [originally "Study in Sentiment"]
  Crackanthorpe, David. *Hubert Crackanthorpe* . . ., 100–102.

"Lisa-la-Folle"
  Crackanthorpe, David. *Hubert Crackanthorpe* . . ., 112–113.

"Modern Melodrama"
  Crackanthorpe, David. *Hubert Crackanthorpe* . . ., 96–97.

"Profiles"
  Crackanthorpe, David. *Hubert Crackanthorpe* . . ., 65–68.

"Saint-Pé"
  Crackanthorpe, David. *Hubert Crackanthorpe* . . ., 114–115.

"The Struggle for Life"
  Crackanthorpe, David. *Hubert Crackanthorpe* . . ., 70–71.

"Trevor Perkins"
  Crackanthorpe, David. *Hubert Crackanthorpe* . . ., 152–155.

"The Turn of the Wheel"
  Crackanthorpe, David. *Hubert Crackanthorpe* . . ., 155–156.

"The White Maize"
  Crackanthorpe, David. *Hubert Crackanthorpe* . . ., 113–114.

"Yew Trees and Peacocks"
Crackanthorpe, David. *Hubert Crackanthorpe* . . ., 106–107.

STEPHEN CRANE

"The Blue Hotel"
Cassill, R. V. *Instructor's Handbook* . . ., 56–57.
Ellis, James. "The Game of High-Five in 'The Blue Hotel,' " *Am Lit,* 49 (1977), 440–442.
Robertson, Jamie. "Stephen Crane, Eastern Outsider in the West and Mexico," *Western Am Lit,* 13 (1978), 255–257.
Wolford, Chester L. "The Eagle and the Crow: High Tragedy and Epic in 'The Blue Hotel,' " *Prairie Schooner,* 51 (1977), 260–274.

"The Bride Comes to Yellow Sky"
*Abcarian, Richard, and Marvin Klotz. *Instructor's Manual* . . ., 2nd ed., 6–7.
Burns, Shannon, and James A. Levernier. "Androgyny in Stephen Crane's 'The Bride Comes to Yellow Sky,' " *Research Stud,* 45 (1977), 236–243.
––––––. "Crane's 'The Bride Comes to Yellow Sky,' " *Explicator,* 37, i (1978), 36–37.
Kane, Thomas S., and Leonard J. Peters. *Some Suggestions* . . ., 12–13.
*Monteiro, George. " 'The Bride Comes to Yellow Sky,' " in Dietrich, R. F., and Roger H. Sundell. *Instructor's Manual* . . ., 3rd ed., 64–76.
Robertson, Jamie. "Stephen Crane, Eastern Outsider . . .," 251–252.
*Welty, Eudora. "The Reading and Writing of Short Stories," in May, Charles E., Ed. *Short Story Theories,* 166–168.

"An Experiment in Misery"
Bonner, Thomas. "Crane's 'An Experiment in Misery,' " *Explicator,* 34 (1976), Item 56.
Johnson, Clarence O. "Crane's 'Experiment in Misery,' " *Explicator,* 35 (Summer, 1977), 20–21.

"The Five White Mice"
Mayer, Charles W. "Two Kids in the House of Chance: Crane's 'The Five White Mice,' " *Research Stud,* 44 (1976), 52–57.
Robertson, Jamie. "Stephen Crane, Eastern Outsider . . .," 248–251.

"A Little Pilgrim" [same as "A Little Pilgrimage"]
Sojka, Gregory S. "Stephen Crane's 'A Little Pilgrim': Whilomville's Young Martyr," *Notes Mod Am Lit,* 3, i (1978), Item 3.

"Maggie: A Girl of the Streets"
Begiebing, Robert J. "Stephen Crane's 'Maggie': The Death of the Self," *Am Imago,* 34 (1977), 50–71.
Mavrocordato, Alexandre. " 'Maggie,' allegorie du coeur," *Études Anglaises,* 31 (1978), 38–51.

"The Monster"
Foster, Malcolm. "The Black Crepe Veil: The Significance of Stephen Crane's 'The Monster,' " *Int'l Fiction R,* 3 (1976), 87–91.

Spofford, William K. "Crane's 'The Monster,' " *Explicator,* 36, ii (1978), 5–7.
Tenenbaum, Ruth B. "The Artful Monstrosity of Crane's 'Monster,' " *Stud Short Fiction,* 14 (1977), 403–405.

"Moonlight on the Snow"
Robertson, Jamie. "Stephen Crane, Eastern Outsider . . .," 254–255.

"One Dash—Horses"
Johnson, Glen M. " 'One Dash—Horses': A Model of 'Realistic' Irony," *Mod Fiction Stud,* 23 (1977), 571–578.
Robertson, Jamie. "Stephen Crane, Eastern Outsider . . .," 247–248.

"The Open Boat"
Cassill, R. V. *Instructor's Handbook . . .,* 54–55.
Dow, Eddy. "Cigars, Matches, and Men in 'The Open Boat,' " *RE/Artes Liberales,* 2, i (1975), 47–49.
Stappenbeck, Herb. "Crane's 'The Open Boat,' " *Explicator,* 34 (1976), Item 41.

"The Third Violet"
Andrews, William L. "Art and Success: Another Look at Stephen Crane's 'The Third Violet,' " *Wascana R,* 13, i (1978), 71–82.

"Three Miraculous Soldiers"
Nagel, James. "Stephen Crane and the Narrative Method of Impressionism," *Stud Novel,* 10 (1978), 79–83.

"Twelve O'Clock"
Robertson, Jamie. "Stephen Crane, Eastern Outsider . . .," 252–254.

"The Upturned Face"
Witherington, Paul. "Public and Private Order in Stephen Crane's 'The Upturned Face,' " *Markham R,* 6 (1977), 70–71.

ROBERT CREELEY

"The Book"
Ford, Arthur L. *Robert Creeley,* 100–101.

"The Grace"
Ford, Arthur L. *Robert Creeley,* 95–99.

"The Unsuccessful Husband"
Ford, Arthur L. *Robert Creeley,* 99–100.

ELEANOR DARK

"Urgent Call"
Day, A. Grove. *Eleanor Dark,* 31.

"Water in Moko Creek"
Day, A. Grove. *Eleanor Dark*, 32.

"Wheels"
Day, A. Grove. *Eleanor Dark*, 29.

"Wind"
Day, A. Grove. *Eleanor Dark*, 29–30.

H. L. DAVIS

"Extra Gang"
Bryant, Paul T. *H.L. Davis*, 51–52.

"Homestead Orchard"
Bryant, Paul T. *H.L. Davis*, 55–56.

"The Kettle of Fire"
Bryant, Paul T. *H.L. Davis*, 57–59.

"Old Man Isbell's Wife"
Bryant, Paul T. *H.L. Davis*, 49–50.

"Open Winter"
Bryant, Paul T. *H.L. Davis*, 52–55.

"Shiloh's Waters"
Bryant, Paul T. *H.L. Davis*, 50–51.

RICHARD HARDING DAVIS

"The Deserter"
Shepherd, Allen. " 'The Best War Story [Richard Harding Davis] Ever Knew':
'The Deserter' Concluded," *Markham R*, 5 (1976), 39–40.

DAZAI OSAMU

"Appeal to the Authorities"
Ueda, Makoto. *Modern Japanese Writers . . .*, 149–150.

SIDONIE DE LA HOUSSAYE

"The Adventures of Françoise and Suzanne"
Perret, J. John. "Strange True Stories of Louisiana: History or Hoax?" *Southern
Stud*, 16 (1977), 45–50.

"Alix de Morainville"
Perret, J. John. "Strange True Stories . . .," 50–52.

"The Young Aunt with White Hair"
Perret, J. John. "Strange True Stories . . .," 43–45.

MAZO DE LA ROCHE [MAZO ROCHE]

"A Boy in the House"
Hendrick, George. *Mazo de la Roche,* 128–129.

"Buried Treasure"
Hendrick, George. *Mazo de la Roche,* 44–45.

"D'Ye Ken John Peel?"
Hendrick, George. *Mazo de la Roche,* 45–46.

"The Son of a Miser: How Noel Caron of St. Loo Proved That He Was No Pinch-Penny"
Hendrick, George. *Mazo de la Roche,* 40–41.

"The Spirit of the Dance"
Hendrick, George. *Mazo de la Roche,* 41–42.

"The Thief of St. Loo: An Incident in the Life of Antoine O'Neill, Honest Man"
Hendrick, George. *Mazo de la Roche,* 39–40.

SUZANNE DESCHEVAUX-DUMESNIL

"F---"
Bair, Deirdre. *Samuel Beckett,* 386–387.

VLADAN DESNICA

"Florjanović"
Pribić, Nikola. "The Motif of Death in Vladan Desnica's Prose," in Terras, Victor, Ed. *American Contributions . . .,* II, 650–651.

"Oko"
Pribić, Nikola. "The Motif of Death . . .," 653–654.

"Summer Vacation During the Winter"
Pribić, Nikola. "The Motif of Death . . .," 652–653.

JESÚS DÍAZ RODRÍGUEZ

"El cojo"
Menton, Seymour. . . . *Cuban Revolution,* 198–199.

"No hay Dios que resista esto"
Menton, Seymour. . . . *Cuban Revolution,* 200–201.

"No matarás"
Menton, Seymour. . . . *Cuban Revolution,* 201–202.

"El polvo a la mitad"
Menton, Seymour. . . . *Cuban Revolution,* 199–200.

ISAK DINESEN [BARONESS KAREN BLIXEN]

"The Cardinal's Third Tale"
Burstein, Janet H. "Two Locked Caskets: Selfhood and 'Otherness' in the Works
of Isak Dinesen," *Texas Stud Lit & Lang,* 20 (1978), 628–629.

"A Consolatory Tale"
Burstein, Janet H. "Two Locked Caskets . . .," 621–622.

"The Ring"
Burstein, Janet H. "Two Locked Caskets . . .," 629–630.

"Sorrow-Acre"
Cassill, R. V. *Instructor's Handbook . . .,* 59–61.

DING LING

"A Certain Night"
Feuerwerker, Yi-tsi M. "The Changing Relationship Between Literature and
Life: Aspects of the Writer's Role in Ding Ling," in Goldman, Merle, Ed.
Modern Chinese Literature . . ., 284–288.

"Diary of Miss Sophie"
Feuerwerker, Yi-tsi M. "The Changing Relationship . . .," 290–293.

JOSÉ DONOSO

"Santelices"
Fraser, Howard M. "Witchcraft in Three Stories of José Donoso," *Latin Am Lit
R,* 4, vii (1975), 3–8.

"Summering"
Fraser, Howard M. "Witchcraft . . .," 3–8.

"Walk"
Fraser, Howard M. "Witchcraft . . .," 3–8.

FYODOR DOSTOEVSKY

"Bobok"
Phillips, Roger W. "Dostoevskij's 'Bobok': Dream of a Timid Man," *Slavic &
East European J,* 18 (1974), 132–142.

"The Double"
Calder, Angus. *Russia Discovered* . . ., 114–115.
Frank, Joseph. *Dostoevsky* . . ., 295–312.
Guerard, Albert J. *The Triumph of the Novel* . . ., 33–36.
Hingley, Ronald. *Dostoyevsky* . . ., 50–52.

"The Dream of a Ridiculous Man"
Holquist, Michael. *Dostoevsky* . . ., 155–164.
Krag, Erik. *Dostoevsky* . . ., 243–246.
Phillips, Roger W. "Dostoevsky's 'Dream of a Ridiculous Man': A Study in Ambiguity," *Criticism*, 17 (1975), 355–363.

"The Eternal Husband"
de Jonge, Alex. . . . *Age of Intensity*, 174–175.

"The Gambler"
de Jonge, Alex. . . . *Age of Intensity*, 166–168.
Krag, Erik. *Dostoevsky* . . ., 105–114.

"A Gentle Creature"
de Jonge, Alex. . . . *Age of Intensity*, 148–149.
Holquist, Michael. *Dostoevsky* . . ., 148–155.
Krag, Erik. *Dostoevsky* . . ., 236–243.

"The Grand Inquisitor"
Jones, Malcolm V. *Dostoevsky* . . ., 180–185.
Sutherland, Stewart R. "Dostoyevsky and the Grand Inquisitor: A Study in Atheism," *Yale R*, 66 (1976), 364–373.

"An Honest Thief"
Frank, Joseph. *Dostoevsky* . . ., 327–328.

"The Landlady"
Frank, Joseph. *Dostoevsky* . . ., 334–342.
Krag, Erik. *Dostoevsky* . . ., 39–44.

"A Little Hero"
Krag, Erik. *Dostoevsky* . . ., 61–64.

"Mr. Prokharchin"
Frank, Joseph. *Dostoevsky* . . ., 313–318.
Krag, Erik. *Dostoevsky* . . ., 35–39.

"Notes from Underground"
Annas, Julia. "Action and Character in Dostoyevsky's 'Notes from Underground,'" *Philosophy & Lit*, 1 (1977), 257–275.
Beatty, Joseph. "From Rebellion and Alienation to Salutary Freedom: A Study in 'Notes from Underground,'" *Soundings*, 61 (1978), 182–205.
Consigny, Scott. "The Paradox of Textuality: Writing as Entrapment and Deliverance in 'Notes from Underground,'" *Canadian-Am Slavic Stud*, 12 (1978), 341–352.
de Jonge, Alex. . . . *Age of Intensity*, 171–172.

Holquist, Michael. *Dostoevsky* . . ., 54–74.

*Howe, Irving, Ed. *Classics of Modern Fiction* . . ., 2nd ed., 3–12.

Jacks, Robert L. "Tolstoj's 'Kreutzer Sonata' and Dostoevskij's 'Notes from Underground,'" in Terras, Victor, Ed. *American Contributions* . . ., II, 284–291.

Jones, Malcolm V. *Dostoevsky* . . ., 55–66.

Krag, Erik. *Dostoevsky* . . ., 94–104.

McKinney, David M. " 'Notes from Underground': A Dostoevskean Faust," *Canadian-Am Slavic Stud*, 12 (1978), 189–229.

Nisly, Paul W. "A Modernist Impulse: 'Notes from Underground' as Model," *Coll Lit*, 4 (1977), 152–158.

Weisberg, Richard. "An Example Not to Follow: *Ressentiment* and the Underground Man," *Mod Fiction Stud*, 21 (1976), 553–563.

*Wellek, René. "Masterpieces of Nineteenth-Century Realism and Naturalism," in Mack, Maynard, *et al.*, Eds. . . . *World Masterpieces*, II, 4th ed., 720–723.

"A Novel in Nine Letters"

Frank, Joseph. *Dostoevsky* . . ., 322–323.

"The Peasant Marey"

Cassill, R. V. *Instructor's Handbook* . . ., 61–62.

Jackson, Robert L. "The Triple Vision: Dostoevsky's 'The Peasant Marey,'" *Yale R*, 67 (1978), 225–235.

"Polzunkov"

Frank, Joseph. *Dostoevsky* . . ., 323–325.

"Uncle's Dream"

Krag, Erik. *Dostoevsky* . . ., 73–77.

"The Village of Stepanchikovo"

Krag, Erik. *Dostoevsky* . . ., 77–83.

"A Weak Heart"

Krag, Erik. *Dostoevsky* . . ., 45–47.

"White Nights"

Christensen, Jerome C. "Versions of Adolescence: Robert Bresson's *Four Nights of a Dream* and Dostoyevsky's 'White Nights,'" *Literature/Film Q*, 4 (1976), 222–224.

Frank, Joseph. *Dostoevsky* . . ., 343–346.

Holquist, Michael. *Dostoevsky* . . ., 37–43.

Krag, Erik. *Dostoevsky* . . ., 48–51.

Rosenshield, Gary. "Point of View and the Imagination in Dostoevskij's 'White Nights,'" *Slavic & East European J*, 21 (1977), 191–203.

ARTHUR CONAN DOYLE

"The Disappearance of Lady Frances Carfax"

Labianca, Dominick A., and William J. Reeves. "Drug Synergism and the Case of 'The Disappearance of Lady Frances Carfax,'" *Am Notes & Queries*, 16, v (1978), 68–70.

"A Scandal in Bohemia"
   Cassill, R. V. *Instructor's Handbook* . . ., 62–63.

"The Speckled Band"
   Rabkin, Eric S. *The Fantastic* . . ., 67–71.

THEODORE DREISER

"Butcher Rogaum's Door"
   Hakutani, Yoshinobu. "The Making of Dreiser's Early Short Stories: The
   Philosopher and the Artist," *Stud Am Fiction,* 6 (1978), 55–57.

"The Lost Phoebe"
   Graham, Don. "Psychological Veracity in 'The Lost Phoebe,'" *Stud Am Fiction,* 6 (1978), 100–106.

"Nigger Jeff"
   Hakutani, Yoshinobu. "The Making . . .," 58–60.

"The Shining Slave Makers"
   Graham, Don B. "Dreiser's Ant Tragedy: The Revision of 'The Shining Slave
   Makers,'" *Stud Short Fiction,* 14 (1977), 41–48.
   Hakutani, Yoshinobu. "The Making . . .," 51–54.

"When the Old Century Was New"
   Hakutani, Yoshinobu. "The Making . . .," 60–61.

ANNETTE VON DROSTE-HÜLSHOFF

"Die Judenbuche"
   Allerdissen, Rolf. " 'Judenbuche' und 'Patriarch': Der Baum des Gerichts bei
   Annette von Droste-Hülshoff und Charles Sealfield," in Gillespie, Gerald,
   and Edgar Lohner, Eds. *Herkommen* . . ., 201–224.
   Magill, C. P. *German Literature,* 113–114.
   Oppermann, Gerald. "Die Narbe des Friedrich Mergel: Zu Aufklärung eines
   literarischen Motivs in Annette von Droste-Hülshoffs 'Die Judenbuche,'"
   Deutsche Vierteljahrsschrift für Literaturwissenschaft und Geistesgeschichte,
   50 (1976), 449–464.
   Rölleke, Heinz. " 'Kann man das Wesen gewöhnlich aus dem namen lesen?':
   Zur Bedeutung der Judenbuche der Annette von Droste-Hülshoff,"
   Euphorion, 70 (1976), 409–414.
   Weber, Betty N. "Droste's 'Judenbuche': Westphalia in International Context,"
   Germ R, 50 (1975), 203–212.

GUADALUPE DUEÑAS

"La historia de Marquita"
   Brodman, Barbara L. C. *The Mexican Cult* . . ., 73–74.

PAUL LAURENCE DUNBAR

"The Scapegoat"
Wakefield, John. "Paul Laurence Dunbar: 'The Scapegoat,' " in Bruck, Peter,
Ed. *The Black American Short Story* . . ., 44–50.

LORD DUNSANY [EDWARD JOHN MORETON DRAXPLUNKETT]

"Two Bottles of Relish"
Perrine, Laurence. *Instructor's Manual* . . . "Story . . .," 27; *Instructor's Manual* . . . "Literature . . .," 27.

MARGUERITE DURAS

"Moderato cantabile"
Bishop, Lloyd. "The Banquet Scene in 'Moderato cantabile,' " *Romanic R,*
69 (1978), 222–235.
Zepp, Evelyn H. "Languages as Ritual in Marguerite Duras's 'Moderato
cantabile,' " *Symposium,* 30 (1976), 236–259.

FRIEDRICH DÜRRENMATT

"Christmas"
Tiusanen, Timo. *Dürrenmatt* . . ., 31–32.

"The Judge and His Executioner"
Benham, G.F. " 'Escape into Inquietude': 'Der Richter und sein Henker,' "
Revue des Langues Vivantes, 42 (1976), 147–154.

"The Torturer"
Tiusanen, Timo. *Dürrenmatt* . . ., 32–34.

"The Tunnel"
Tiusanen, Timo. *Dürrenmatt* . . ., 36–39.

MARIE VON EBNER-ESCHENBACH

"Er lasst die Hand küssen"
Dormer, Lore M. "Tribunal der Ironie: Marie von Ebner-Eschenbachs
Erzählung 'Er lasst die Hand küssen,' " *Mod Austrian Lit,* 9, ii (1976), 86–97.

HALIDE EDIP-ADIVAR

"Everyday Men: The Pumpkin-Seed Seller"
Fearey, Margaret S. "Halide Edip-Adivar's 'Everyday Men: The Pumpkin-Seed
Seller': An Analysis," *Rackham Lit Stud,* 4 (1973), 75–89.

JOSEPH VON EICHENDORFF

"From the Life of a Good-for-Nothing"
Anton, Herbert. " 'Dämonische Freiheit' in Eichendorffs Erzählung 'Aus dem Leben eines Taugenichts,' " *Aurora*, 37 (1977), 21–32.
Pickar, Gertrud B. "Eichendorff's 'Aus dem Leben eines Taugenichts': Postures of Naivete and Irony," *Lang Q*, 15, i–ii (1976), 7–13, 16.
————. " 'Aus dem Leben eines Taugenichts': Personal Landscaping in Perception and Portrayal," *Literatur in Wissenschaft und Unterricht*, 11 (1978), 23–31.
Swales, Martin. "Nostalgia as Conciliation: A Note on Eichendorff's 'Aus dem Leben eines Taugenichts' and Heine's *Der Doppelgänger*," *Germ Life & Letters*, 30 (1976), 36–41.

"The Marble Statue"
Hubbs, Valentine C. "Metamorphosis and Rebirth in Eichendorff's 'Marmorbild,' " *Germ R*, 52 (1977), 243–259.

STANLEY ELKIN

"I Look Out for Ed Wolfe"
Dittmar, Kurt. "Stanley Elkin, 'I Look Out for Ed Wolfe,' " in Freese, Peter, Ed. . . . *Interpretationen*, 252–261.

GEORGE P. ELLIOTT

"The NRACP"
Cassill, R. V. *Instructor's Handbook* . . ., 64–66.

HARLAN ELLISON

"All the Sounds"
Slusser, George E. *Harlan Ellison* . . ., 44.

"Along the Scenic Route"
Slusser, George E. *Harlan Ellison* . . ., 33–34.

"Back to the Drawing Boards"
Slusser, George E. *Harlan Ellison* . . ., 31.

"Basilisk"
Slusser, George E. *Harlan Ellison* . . ., 38–40.

"Battlefield"
Slusser, George E. *Harlan Ellison* . . ., 25–26.

"The Beast That Shouted Love at the Heart of the World"
Slusser, George E. *Harlan Ellison* . . ., 45–47.

"A Boy and His Dog"
Crow, John, and Richard Erlich. "Mythic Patterns in Ellison's 'A Boy and His Dog,' " *Extrapolation,* 18, ii (1977), 162–166.
Slusser, George E. *Harlan Ellison . . .,* 34–35.

"Catman"
Slusser, George E. *Harlan Ellison . . .,* 55–56.

"The Crackpots"
Slusser, George E. *Harlan Ellison . . .,* 24–25.

"Croatoan"
Patrouch, Joseph. "Harlan Ellison and the Formula Story," in Porter, Andrew, Ed. *The Book of Ellison,* 57–64.

"The Deathbird"
Slusser, George E. *Harlan Ellison . . .,* 56–59.

"Deeper Than the Darkness"
Slusser, George E. *Harlan Ellison . . .,* 28.

"Delusion of the Dragon Slayer"
Slusser, George E. *Harlan Ellison . . .,* 51–52.

"I Have No Mouth and I Must Scream"
Patrouch, Joseph. ". . . Formula Story," 53–56.
Slusser, George E. *Harlan Ellison . . .,* 47–49.
Warrick, Patricia. "Images of the Man-Machine Intelligence Relationship in Science Fiction," in Clareson, Thomas D., Ed. *Many Futures . . .,* 213–214.

"Knox"
Slusser, George E. *Harlan Ellison . . .,* 40–41.

"Night Vigil"
Slusser, George E. *Harlan Ellison . . .,* 27–28.

"One Life"
Slusser, George E. *Harlan Ellison . . .,* 54–55.

"Paingod"
Slusser, George E. *Harlan Ellison . . .,* 44–45.

"The Place with No Name"
Slusser, George E. *Harlan Ellison . . .,* 52–53.

"Pretty Maggie Moneyeyes"
Slusser, George E. *Harlan Ellison . . .,* 49–50.

"Punky and the Yale Men"
Slusser, George E. *Harlan Ellison . . .,* 21–22.

"Repent, Harlequin! Said the Ticktockman"
  *Abcarian, Richard, and Marvin Klotz. *Instructor's Manual* . . . , 7–8.
  Slusser, George E. *Harlan Ellison* . . . , 26–27.

"Run for the Stars"
  Slusser, George E. *Harlan Ellison* . . . , 28–29.

"Silent in Gehenna"
  Slusser, George E. *Harlan Ellison* . . . , 36–38.

"The Silver Corridor"
  Slusser, George E. *Harlan Ellison* . . . , 32–33.

"Status Quo at Troyden's"
  Slusser, George E. *Harlan Ellison* . . . , 30–31.

"Wanted in Surgery"
  Slusser, George E. *Harlan Ellison* . . . , 25.

"Worlds to Kill"
  Slusser, George E. *Harlan Ellison* . . . , 31–32.

RALPH ELLISON

"Afternoon"
  Skerrett, Joseph T. "Ralph Ellison and the Example of Richard Wright," *Stud Short Fiction,* 15 (1978), 150.

"Battle Royal"
  Howard, Daniel F., and William Plummer. *Instructor's Manual* . . . , 3rd ed., 61–62.
  Kimmey, John L. *Instructor's Manual* . . . , 17–19.

"The Birthmark"
  Skerrett, Joseph T. "Ralph Ellison . . . ," 147–148.

"A Coupla Scalped Indians"
  Doyle, Mary E. "In Need of Folk: The Alienated Protagonists of Ralph Ellison's Short Fiction," *Coll Lang Assoc J,* 19 (1975), 166–167.

"Flying Home"
  Doyle, Mary E. "In Need of Folk . . . ," 169–171.
  Ostendorf, Bernard. "Ralph Ellison, 'Flying Home,'" in Freese, Peter, Ed. . . . *Interpretationen,* 64–76.

"In a Strange Country"
  Doyle, Mary E. "In Need of Folk . . . ," 168–169.

"King of the Bingo Game"
  Cassill, R. V. *Instructor's Handbook* . . . , 67–68.
  Chaffee, Patricia. "Slippery Ground: Ralph Ellison's Bingo Player," *Negro Am Lit Forum,* 10 (1976), 23–24.

Doyle, Mary E. "In Need of Folk . . .," 171–172.
Kane, Thomas S., and Leonard J. Peters. *Some Suggestions* . . ., 38–39.
Real, Willi. "Ralph Ellison: 'King of the Bingo Game,' " in Bruck, Peter, Ed. *The Black American Short Story* . . ., 114–124.
Saunders, Pearl I. "Symbolism in Ralph Ellison's 'King of the Bingo Game,' " *Coll Lang Assoc J,* 20 (1976), 35–39.

"Mister Toussan"
Skerrett, Joseph T. "Ralph Ellison . . .," 150–152.

"That I Had the Wings"
Doyle, Mary E. "In Need of Folk . . .," 167–168.
Skerrett, Joseph T. "Ralph Ellison . . .," 152–153.

GEORGE A. ENGLAND

"The Empire of the Air"
Moskowitz, Sam. *Strange Horizons* . . ., 233–234.

"June 6, 2016"
Moskowitz, Sam. *Strange Horizons* . . ., 76–77.

PER OLOV ENQUIST

"The Tracks in the Sea of Tranquillity"
Shideler, Ross. "The Swedish Short Story: Per Olov Enquist," *Scandinavian Stud,* 49 (1977), 243–248.

SAIT FAIK

"Love Letter"
Hickman, William C. "Sait Faik: Three Stories and an Essay," *Edebiyat: J Middle Eastern Lit,* 1, i (1976), 78–79.

"The Man Who Doesn't Know What a Tooth or a Toothache Is"
Hickman, William C. "Sait Faik . . .," 79.

"Sivriada Night"
Hickman, William C. "Sait Faik . . .," 77–78.

PHILIP JOSÉ FARMER

"The God Business"
Letson, Russell. "The Worlds of Philip José Farmer," *Extrapolation,* 5 (1977), 128.

"Son"
Letson, Russell. "The Worlds . . .," 128–129.

WILLIAM FAULKNER

"Barn Burning"
*Broer, Lawrence R. "'Barn Burning,'" in Dietrich, R.F., and Roger H. Sundell. *Instructor's Manual* . . ., 3rd ed., 55–62.
Cassill, R.V. *Instructor's Handbook* . . ., 74–76.
Cook, Sylvia J. *From Tobacco Road* . . ., 53–55.
Kennedy, X.J. *Instructor's Manual* . . ., 10–12.
Nicolet, William P. "Faulkner's 'Barn Burning,'" *Explicator,* 34 (1975), Item 25.

"The Bear"
Beck, Warren. *Faulkner* . . ., 382–478.
Hiers, John T. "Faulkner's Lord-to-God Bird in 'The Bear,'" *Am Lit,* 47 (1976), 636–637.
Jehlen, Myra. *Class and Character* . . ., 2–14.
Levins, Lynn G. *Faulkner's Heroic Design* . . ., 78–94.
Pounds, Wayne. "Symbolic Landscapes in 'The Bear': 'Rural Myth and Technological Fact,'" *Gypsy Scholar,* 4 (1977), 40–52.
*Welty, Eudora. "The Reading and Writing of Short Stories," in May, Charles E., Ed. *Short Story Theories,* 174–175.

"Black Music"
Solery, Marc. "'Black Music' ou la métamorphose du regard," *Delta,* 3 (1976), 35–43.

"Carcassonne"
Milum, Richard A. "Faulkner's 'Carcassonne': The Dream and the Reality," *Stud Short Fiction,* 15 (1978), 133–138.

"Delta Autumn"
Beck, Warren. *Faulkner* . . ., 478–537.
Jehlen, Myra. *Class and Character* . . ., 102–104.

"Dr. Martino"
Lang, Beatrice. "'Dr. Martino': The Conflict of Life and Death," *Delta,* 3 (1976), 23–32, 34.

"Dry September"
*Abcarian, Richard, and Marvin Klotz. *Instructor's Manual* . . ., 2nd ed., 8–9.
Debreczeny, Paul. "The Device of Conspicuous Silence in Tolstoj, Čexov, and Faulkner," in Terras, Victor, Ed. *American Contributions* . . ., II, 137–142.
McDermott, John V. "Faulkner's Cry for a Healing Measure: 'Dry September,'" *Arizona Q,* 32 (1976), 31–34.

"The Fire and the Hearth"
Beck, Warren. *Faulkner* . . ., 351–370.
Jehlen, Myra. *Class and Character* . . ., 105–107.

"Go Down, Moses"
Beck, Warren. *Faulkner* . . ., 571–582.
Jehlen, Myra. *Class and Character* . . ., 116–120.

"Golden Land"
Cassill, R. V. *Instructor's Handbook* . . ., 71–73.

"Knight's Gambit"
Volpe, Edmond L. "Faulkner's 'Knight's Gambit': Sentimentality and the Creative Imagination," *Mod Fiction Stud,* 24 (1978), 232–239.

"An Odor of Verbena"
Williams, David L. *Faulkner's Women* . . ., 210–214.

"Old Man"
Cumpiano, Marion W. "The Motif of Return: Currents and Counter Currents in 'Old Man' by William Faulkner," *Southern Hum R,* 12 (1978), 185–193.

"The Old People"
Beck, Warren. *Faulkner* . . ., 377–382.

"Once Aboard the Lugger"
Bonner, Thomas. " 'Once Aboard the Lugger': An Uncollected Faulkner Story," *Notes Mod Am Lit,* 3, i (1978), Item 8.

"Pantaloon in Black"
Akin, Warren. " 'The Normal Human Feelings': An Interpretation of Faulkner's 'Pantaloon in Black,' " *Stud Short Fiction,* 15 (1978), 397–401.
Beck, Warren. *Faulkner* . . ., 370–374.
Blanchard, Leonard A. "The Failure of the Natural Man: Faulkner's 'Pantaloon in Black,' " *Notes Mississippi Writers,* 8 (1976), 28–32.
Jehlen, Myra. *Class and Character* . . ., 99–102.
Rose, Alan H. *Demonic Vision* . . ., 108–111.

"Red Leaves"
Rose, Alan H. *Demonic Vision* . . ., 105–108.
Volpe, Edmond L. "Faulkner's 'Red Leaves': The Deciduation of Nature," *Stud Am Fiction,* 3 (1975), 121–131.

"A Rose for Emily"
Cassill, R. V. *Instructor's Handbook* . . ., 69–70.

"Spotted Horses"
Ilacqua, Alma A. "An Artistic Vision of Election in 'Spotted Horses,' " *Cithara,* 15, ii (1976), 33–45.
Jehlen, Myra. *Class and Character* . . ., 143–148.

"Tall Men"
Cook, Sylvia J. *From Tobacco Road* . . ., 59–62.

"That Evening Sun"
Beck, Warren. *Faulkner* . . ., 294–299.
Brown, Mary C. "Voice in 'That Evening Sun': A Study of Quentin Compson," *Mississippi Q,* 29 (1976), 347–360.
Garrison, Joseph M. "The Past and the Present in 'That Evening Sun,' " *Stud Short Fiction,* 13 (1976), 371–373.

*Perrine, Laurence. *Instructor's Manual . . . "Story . . .,"* 27–29; *Instructor's Manual . . . "Literature . . .,"* 27–29.

Rosenman, John B. "The Heaven and Hell Archetype in Faulkner's 'That Evening Sun' and Bradbury's *Dandelion Wine*," *So Atlantic Bull*, 43, ii (1978), 12–16.

"Uncle Willy"

Volpe, Edmond L. "Faulkner's 'Uncle Willy': A Childhood Fable," *Mosaic*, 12 (1978), 177–181.

"Was"

Beck, Warren. *Faulkner . . .*, 347–351.

Brumm, Ursula. "William Faulkner, 'Was,'" in Freese, Peter, Ed. . . . *Interpretationen*, 30–38.

Jehlen, Myra. *Class and Character . . .*, 114–116.

"Wash"

Cook, Sylvia J. *From Tobacco Road . . .*, 51–53.

Kane, Thomas S., and Leonard J. Peters. *Some Suggestions . . .*, 22–23.

IRVIN FAUST

"Jake Bluffstein and Adolph Hitler"

Wilz, Hans-Werner. "Irvin Faust, 'Jake Bluffstein and Adolph Hitler,'" in Freese, Peter, Ed. . . . *Interpretationen*, 237–251.

"Roar Lion Roar"

Cassill, R. V. *Instructor's Handbook . . .*, 77–79.

LESLIE FIEDLER

"The First Spade in the West"

Bluefarb, Sam. "Pictures of the Anti-Stereotype: Leslie Fiedler's Triptych, *The Last Jew in America*," *Coll Lang Assoc J*, 18 (1975), 420–421.

"The Last Jew in America"

Bluefarb, Sam. "Pictures of the Anti-Stereotype . . .," 412–416.

"The Last WASP in the World"

Bluefarb, Sam. "Pictures of the Anti-Stereotype . . .," 416–419.

RODERICK FINDLAY

"Jim and Miri"

Fitzgibbon, Tom. "Roderick Findlay: *Other Lovers*," *World Lit Written Engl*, 16 (1977), 383–384.

RUDOLF FISHER

"Common Meter"
  Friedmann, Thomas. "The Good Guys in the Black Hats: Color Coding in
  Rudolf Fisher's 'Common Meter,' " *Stud Black Lit,* 7, ii (1976), 8–9.

F. SCOTT FITZGERALD

"Absolution"
  Gallo, Rose A. *F. Scott Fitzgerald,* 92–94.

"The Baby Party"
  Kennedy, X. J., Ed. *An Introduction . . .,* 103–104.

"Babylon Revisited"
  Cassill, R. V. *Instructor's Handbook . . .,* 79–81.
  Gallo, Rose A. *F. Scott Fitzgerald,* 101–105.
  Howard, Daniel F., and William Plummer. *Instructor's Manual . . .,* 3rd ed., 43.
  Twitchell, James B. " 'Babylon Revisited': Chronology and Characters,"
  Fitzgerald/Hemingway Annual 1978, 155–159.

"The Cut-Glass Bowl"
  Gallo, Rose A. *F. Scott Fitzgerald,* 85–87.

"The Diamond as Big as the Ritz"
  Gallo, Rose A. *F. Scott Fitzgerald,* 82–85.

"Family in the Wind"
  Gallo, Rose A. *F. Scott Fitzgerald,* 99–101.

"May Day"
  Gallo, Rose A. *F. Scott Fitzgerald,* 87–90.
  Martin, Robert K. "Sexual and Group Relationships in 'May Day': Fear and
  Longing," *Stud Short Fiction,* 15 (1978), 99–101.
  Mazella, Anthony J. "The Tension of Opposites in Fitzgerald's 'May Day,' "
  Stud Short Fiction, 14 (1977), 379–385.

"The Rich Boy"
  Gallo, Rose A. *F. Scott Fitzgerald,* 94–97.

"Winter Dreams"
  Gallo, Rose A. *F. Scott Fitzgerald,* 90–92.

ZELDA SAYRE FITZGERALD

"A Couple of Nuts"
  Anderson, W. R. "Rivalry and Partnership: The Short Fiction of Zelda Sayre
  Fitzgerald," *Fitzgerald/Hemingway Annual 1977,* 37–39.

"Miss Ella"
　　Anderson, W. R. "Rivalry and Partnership . . .," 35–36.

GUSTAVE FLAUBERT

"Bouvard and Pécuchet"
　　Martin, George. "Friendship: Basic Theme of 'Bouvard et Pécuchet' and
　　　En attendant Godot," Lang Q, 14, iii–iv (1976), 43–46.
　　Terdiman, Richard. *The Dialectics of Isolation* . . ., 80–82.
　　Torrance, Robert. *The Comic Hero*, 234–239.

"Hérodias"
　　Cancalon, Elaine D. "La Symbolique de l'espace dans 'Hérodias,' " *So Atlantic
　　　Bull*, 40, i (1975), 23–28.
　　Duncan, Phillip A. "The Equation of Theme and Spatial Form in Flaubert's
　　　'Hérodias,' " *Stud Short Fiction*, 14 (1977), 129–136.
　　Issacharoff, Michael. *"Trois contes* et le problème de la non-linéarité," *Littéra-
　　　ture*, 15 (1974), 35–39.

"St. Julien"
　　Bart, B[enjamin] F. "Flaubert and Hunting: 'La Légende de Saint Julien
　　　l'Hospitalier,' " *Nineteenth-Century French Stud*, 4 (1975), 31–52.
　　Cassill, R. V. *Instructor's Handbook* . . ., 82–85.
　　Issacharoff, Michael. *"Trois contes* et . . . non-linéarité," 29–33.
　　Massey, Irving. *The Gaping Pig* . . ., 196–197.
　　Pilkington, A. E. "Point of View in Flaubert's 'La Légende de saint Julien,' "
　　　French Stud, 29 (1975), 266–279.

"A Simple Heart"
　　Issacharoff, Michael. *"Trois contes* et . . . non-linéarité," 33–35.
　　Mall, James P. "Flaubert's 'Un Coeur Simple,' Myth and Genealogy of Reli-
　　　gion," *J Australasian Univs Lang & Lit Assoc*, 47 (May, 1977), 39–48.

ANTONIO FOGAZZARO

"Eden Anto"
　　Hall, Robert A. *Antonio Fogazzaro*, 47–48.

"The Fiasco of Maestro Chieco"
　　Hall, Robert A. *Antonio Fogazzaro*, 48.

E. M. FORSTER

"Albergo Empedocle"
　　Page, Norman. . . . *Posthumous Fiction*, 28–30.

"Ansell"
　　Page, Norman. . . . *Posthumous Fiction*, 28.

"Arthur Snatchfold"
  Page, Norman. . . . *Posthumous Fiction*, 45–49.

"The Celestial Omnibus"
  *Dietrich, R. F. " 'The Celestial Omnibus,' " in Dietrich, R. F., and Roger H. Sundèll. *Instructor's Manual* . . ., 3rd ed., 5–9.

"The Classical Annex"
  Page, Norman. . . . *Posthumous Fiction*, 52–53.

"Dr. Woolacott"
  Page, Norman. . . . *Posthumous Fiction*, 42–44.

"The Eternal Moment"
  Colmer, John. *E.M. Forster* . . ., 36–37.

"The Machine Stops"
  Berman, Jeffrey. "Forster's Other Cave: The Platonic Structure of 'The Machine Stops,' " *Extrapolation*, 17 (1976), 172–181.
  Colmer, John. *E.M. Forster* . . ., 39–40.
  Howe, Irving, Ed. *Classics of Modern Fiction* . . ., 2nd ed., 233–239.

"The Obelisk"
  Page, Norman. . . . *Posthumous Fiction*, 49–51.

"The Other Boat"
  Malek, James S. "Persona, Shadow, and Society: A Reading of Forster's 'The Other Boat,' " *Stud Short Fiction*, 14 (1977), 21–27.

"The Other Side of the Hedge"
  Stape, John H. "Myth, Allusion, and Symbol in E. M. Forster's 'The Other Side of the Hedge,' " *Stud Short Fiction*, 14 (1977), 375–378.

"The Point of It"
  Swanson, Roy A. "Love Is the Function of Death: Forster, Lagerkvist, and Zamyatin," *Canadian R Comp Lit*, 3 (1976), 197–201.

"The Purple Envelope"
  Page, Norman. . . . *Posthumous Fiction*, 32–35.

"The Road from Colonus"
  Cassill, R. V. *Instructor's Handbook* . . ., 85–87.

"The Story of a Panic"
  Colmer, John. *E.M. Forster* . . ., 30–32.

"The Torque"
  Page, Norman. . . . *Posthumous Fiction*, 53–54.

"What Does It Matter?"
  Page, Norman. . . . *Posthumous Fiction*, 51–52.

JANET FRAME

"Keel and Kool"
Evans, Patrick. *Janet Frame*, 41–42.

"The Lagoon"
Evans, Patrick. *Janet Frame*, 39–40.

"The Reservoir"
Evans, Patrick. *Janet Frame*, 44–46.

"Swans"
Evans, Patrick. *Janet Frame*, 42–43.

MARY E. WILKINS FREEMAN

"Amanda and Love"
Crowley, John W. "Freeman's Yankee Tragedy: 'Amanda and Love,'"
Markham R, 5 (1976), 58–60.

BRUCE JAY FRIEDMAN

"When You're Excused, You're Excused"
Vandyke, Patricia. "Choosing One's Side with Care: The Liberating Repartee,"
Perspectives Contemp Lit, 1, i (1975), 109–111.

BRIAN FRIEL

"Among the Ruins"
Miner, Edmund J. "Homecoming: The Theme of Disillusion in Brian Friel's
Short Stories," *Kansas Q*, 9, ii (1977), 93–94.

"Foundry House"
Miner, Edmund J. "Homecoming . . .," 94–98.

CARLOS FUENTES

"Chac Mool"
Brodman, Barbara L. C. *The Mexican Cult* . . ., 69–71.
Gyurko, Lanin A. "Social Satire and the Ancient Mexican Gods in the Narrative
of Fuentes," *Ibero-Amerikanisches Archiv*, 1, ii (1975), 115–120.

"The Gods Speak" [same as "By the Mouth of the Gods"]
Brodman, Barbara L. C. *The Mexican Cult* . . ., 71–72.
Gyurko, Lanin A. "Social Satire . . .," 120–126.

"The Two Helens"
Chrzanowski, Joseph. "The Double in 'Las dos Elenas' by Carlos Fuentes,"
Romance Notes, 18 (1977), 6–10.

Gyurko, Lanin A. "The Pseudo-Liberated Woman in the Narrative of Fuentes,"
Research Stud, 44 (1976), 86–93.

JAQUES FUTRELLE

"The Flying Eye"
Moskowitz, Sam. *Strange Horizons . . .,* 232–233.

ERNEST J. GAINES

"A Long Day in November"
Puschmann-Nalenz, Barbara. "Ernest J. Gaines: 'A Long Day in November,' "
in Bruck, Peter, Ed. *The Black American Short Story . . .,* 158–168.

MAVIS GALLANT

"Acceptance of Their Ways"
Cassill, R. V. *Instructor's Handbook . . .,* 88–89.

JOHN GALSWORTHY

"The Japanese Quince"
Garbowsky, Maryanne. "Form and Meaning in 'The Japanese Quince,' " *Coll
Engl Notes* (N. J.), 4, iii (1978), 2.
*Perrine, Laurence. *Instructor's Manual . . . "Story . . .,"* 5–6; *Instructor's
Manual . . . "Literature . . .,"* 5–6.

GABRIEL GARCÍA MÁRQUEZ

"Artificial Roses"
McMurray, George R. *Gabriel García Márquez,* 50–51.

"Baltazar's Marvelous Afternoon"
McMurray, George R. *Gabriel García Márquez,* 54–57.

"Big Mama's Funeral"
Dauster, Frank. "The Short Stories of García Márquez," *Books Abroad,* 47, iii
(1973), 469.
Goetzinger, Judith. "The Emergence of Folk Myth in 'Los funerales de la Mamá
Grande,' " *Revista de Estudios Hispánicos,* 2 (1972), 237–248.
McMurray, George R. *Gabriel García Márquez,* 59–65.

"Bitter Sorrow for Three Sleepwalkers"
Vargas Llosa, Mario. "A Morbid Prehistory (The Early Stories)," *Books
Abroad,* 47, iii (1973), 456–457.

"Blancaman the Good, Vendor of Miracles"
McMurray, George R. *Gabriel García Márquez*, 120–124.
Morello Frosch, Marta. "The Common Wonders of García Márquez's Recent
Fiction," *Books Abroad*, 47, iii (1973), 499.

"Blue-dog Eyes"
Vargas Llosa, Mario. "A Morbid Prehistory . . .," 457.

"Death Constant Beyond Love"
McMurray, George R. *Gabriel García Márquez*, 115–116.
Morello Frosch, Marta. "The Common Wonders . . .," 499–500.

"Eve Inside Her Cat"
Vargas Llosa, Mario. "A Morbid Prehistory . . .," 453–454.

"The Handsomest Drowned Man in the World"
McMurray, George R. *Gabriel García Márquez*, 119–120.
Morello Frosch, Marta. "The Common Wonders . . .," 498–499.

"The Incredible and Sad Tale of Innocent Erendira and Her Heartless Grand-
mother"
McMurray, George R. *Gabriel García Márquez*, 108–113.

"The Last Voyage of the Ghost Ship"
McMurray, George R. *Gabriel García Márquez*, 124–126.
Morello Frosch, Marta. "The Common Wonders . . .," 499.

"Montiel's Widow"
McMurray, George R. *Gabriel García Márquez*, 52–54.

"Nabo"
Vargas Llosa, Mario. "A Morbid Prehistory . . .," 457–459.

"The Night of the Curlews"
Vargas Llosa, Mario. "A Morbid Prehistory . . .," 459–460.

"One Day After Saturday"
McMurray, George R. *Gabriel García Márquez*, 57–59.

"One of These Days"
McMurray, George R. *Gabriel García Márquez*, 49–50.

"The Other Rib of Death"
Vargas Llosa, Mario. "A Morbid Prehistory . . .," 455–456.

"The Sea of Lost Time"
McMurray, George R. *Gabriel García Márquez*, 113–115.
Morello Frosch, Marta. "The Common Wonders . . .," 497–498.

"Someone Has Disturbed the Roses"
Vargas Llosa, Mario. "A Morbid Prehistory . . .," 459.

"There Are No Thieves in This Town"
McMurray, George R. *Gabriel García Márquez,* 51–52.

"The Third Resignation"
Vargas Llosa, Mario. "A Morbid Prehistory . . .," 453.

"Tubal-Cain Forges a Star"
Vargas Llosa, Mario. "A Morbid Prehistory . . .," 454–455.

"Tuesday Siesta"
McMurray, George R. *Gabriel García Márquez,* 47–48.

"A Very Old Man with Enormous Wings"
McMurray, George R. *Gabriel García Márquez,* 116–119.
Morello Frosch, Marta. "The Common Wonders . . .," 496–497.

HAMLIN GARLAND

"The Silent Eaters"
Gish, Robert. *Hamlin Garland . . .,* 39–41.

ELIZABETH GASKELL

"The Heart of John Middleton"
Gérin, Winifred. *Elizabeth Gaskell . . .,* 118–119.

"The Sexton's Heart"
Gérin, Winifred. *Elizabeth Gaskell . . .,* 81–82.

WILLIAM GASS

"Icicles"
Bassoff, Bruce. "The Sacrificial World of William Gass: *In the Heart of the Heart of the Country,*" *Critique,* 18, i (1976), 42–46.
Waxman, Robert E. "Things in the Saddle: William Gass's 'Icicles' and 'Order of Insects,'" *Research Stud,* 46 (1978), 214–222.

"In the Heart of the Heart of the Country"
Bassoff, Bruce. "The Sacrificial World . . .," 47–57.

"Order of Insects"
Bassoff, Bruce. "The Sacrificial World . . .," 46–47.
Waxman, Robert E. "Things in the Saddle . . .," 214–222.

"The Pedersen Kid"
Bassoff, Bruce. "The Sacrificial World . . .," 36–42.

THÉOPHILE GAUTIER

"Arria Marcella, souvenir de Pompeii"
Grant, Richard B. *Théophile Gautier*, 125.
Knapp, Bettina. "The Greek Way versus Christianity: Two Opposed Outlooks in
Théophile Gautier's 'Arria Marcella,' " *Mod Lang Stud*, 6, i (1976), 61–73.
Wolfzettel, Friedrich. "Das romantische Motiv der steinernen Frau bei
Théophile Gautier: Eine psychoanalytische Deutung von 'Arria Marcella,' "
Neuphilologische Mitteilungen, 77 (1976), 254–269.

"Avatar"
Grant, Richard B. *Théophile Gautier*, 125–126.

"The Dead Leman"
Grant, Richard B. *Théophile Gautier*, 121–124.

"Fortunio"
Grant, Richard B. *Théophile Gautier*, 108–110.

"King Candaules"
Grant, Richard B. *Théophile Gautier*, 110–113.

"The Mummy's Foot"
Grant, Richard B. *Théophile Gautier*, 117–118.

"The Mummy's Tale"
Grant, Richard B. *Théophile Gautier*, 116–117.

"Omphale"
Grant, Richard B. *Théophile Gautier*, 120–121.

"One of Cleopatra's Nights"
Grant, Richard B. *Théophile Gautier*, 113–116.

"Spirite"
Grant, Richard B. *Théophile Gautier*, 126–130.

"The Twin Knight"
Grant, Richard B. *Théophile Gautier*, 124.

ANDRÉ GIDE

"The Immoralist"
Bettinson, Christopher. *Gide* . . ., 15–25.
Booker, John T. " 'The Immoralist' and the Rhetoric of First-Person Narration,"
Twentieth Century Lit, 2, i (1977), 5–22.
Cohn, Dorrit. *Transparent Minds* . . ., 158–161.
Meyers, Jeffrey. *Homosexuality* . . ., 32–41.
Mistacco, Vicki. "Narcissus and the Image: Symbol and Meaning in 'L'Immoraliste,' " *Kentucky Romance Q*, 23 (1976), 247–258.

Sonnenfeld, Albert. "On Readers and Reading in 'La Porte étroite' and 'L'Immoraliste,' " *Romanic R,* 67 (1976), 172–186.

"The Pastoral Symphony"
Bettinson, Christopher. *Gide* . . ., 53–66.
Leibowitz, Judith. *Narrative Purposes* . . ., 98–105.
Ugochukwu, Françoise A. "Le Thème de la nuit dans 'La Symphonie pastorale,' " *Le Français au Nigeria,* 10, iii (1975), 23–29.

"The Return of the Prodigal Son"
*Douglas, Kenneth, and Sarah N. Lawall. "Masterpieces of the Modern World," in Mack, Maynard, *et al.,* Eds. . . . *World Masterpieces,* II, 4th ed., 1246–1247.

"Strait Is the Gate"
Bettinson, Christopher. *Gide* . . ., 25–33.
Eisinger, Erica M. "The Hidden Eye: Clandestine Observation in Gide's 'La Porte étroite,' " *Kentucky Romance Q,* 24 (1977), 221–229.
Sonnenfeld, Albert. "On Readers and Reading . . .," 172–186.

ELLEN GLASGOW

"The Artless Age"
Raper, Julius R. "Invisible Things: The Short Stories of Ellen Glasgow," *Southern Lit J,* 9 (Spring, 1977), 76.

"Dare's Gift"
Raper, Julius R. "Invisible Things . . .," 81–83.

"The Difference"
Raper, Julius R. "Invisible Things . . .," 74–76.

"Jordan's End"
Raper, Julius R. "Invisible Things . . .," 87–89.

"The Past"
Raper, Julius R. "Invisible Things . . .," 83–84.

"The Professional Instinct"
Raper, Julius R. "Invisible Things . . .," 67–70.

"Romance and Sally Byrd"
Raper, Julius R. "Invisible Things . . .," 76–79.

"The Shadowy Third"
Raper, Julius R. "Invisible Things . . .," 80–81.

"Thinking Makes It So"
Raper, Julius R. "Invisible Things . . .," 73–74.

"Whispering Leaves"
Raper, Julius R. "Invisible Things . . .," 84–87.

SUSAN GLASPELL

"A Jury of Her Peers"
*Perrine, Laurence. *Instructor's Manual* . . . *"Story* . . .," 39–41; *Instructor's Manual* . . . *"Literature* . . .," 39–41.

JOHANN WOLFGANG VON GOETHE

"Fairy Tale"
Tiberia, Vincenza. "A Jungian Interpretation of Goethe's Alchemical Allegory: 'The Märchen,' " *Int'l J Symbology,* 6, ii (1975), 24–36.

NIKOLAI GOGOL

"The Carriage"
Rowe, William W. *Through Gogol's Looking Glass* . . ., 119–122.

"Christmas Eve"
Karlinsky, Simon. *The Sexual Labyrinth* . . ., 38–39.
Rowe, William W. *Through Gogol's Looking Glass* . . ., 38–46.

"Diary of a Madman"
Karlinsky, Simon. *The Sexual Labyrinth* . . ., 117–122.

"The Enchanted Place"
Rowe, William W. *Through Gogol's Looking Glass* . . ., 62–66.

"Ivan Fyodorovich Shponka and His Aunt"
Karlinsky, Simon. *The Sexual Labyrinth* . . ., 44–48.
Rowe, William W. *Through Gogol's Looking Glass* . . ., 55–61.

"The Lost Letter"
Rowe, William W. *Through Gogol's Looking Glass* . . ., 32–35.

"The May Night, or The Drowned Maiden"
Rowe, William W. *Through Gogol's Looking Glass* . . ., 26–31.

"The Nevsky Prospect"
Hughes, Olga R. "The Apparent and the Real in Gogol's 'Nevskij Prospekt,' " *California Slavic Stud,* 8 (1975), 77–91.
Karlinsky, Simon. *The Sexual Labyrinth* . . ., 114–117.
Rowe, William W. *Through Gogol's Looking Glass* . . ., 93–99.

"The Nose"
Berger, Willy R. "Drei phantastische Erzählungen: Chamissos 'Peter Schlemihl,' E.T.A. Hoffmanns 'Abenteur der Silvester-Nacht,' und Gogols 'Die Nase,' " *Arcadia,* [n. v.], Special Issue (1978), 106–138.
Karlinsky, Simon. *The Sexual Labyrinth* . . ., 123–130.
Massey, Irving. *The Gaping Pig* . . ., 62–65.
Rowe, William W. *Through Gogol's Looking Glass* . . ., 100–106.

"Old-World Landowners" [same as "Old-Fashioned Landowners"]
Karlinsky, Simon. *The Sexual Labyrinth* . . ., 114–117.
Poggioli, Renato. *The Oaten Flute* . . ., 241–246.
Rowe, William W. *Through Gogol's Looking Glass* . . ., 67–72.
Woodward, James B. "Allegory and Symbol in Gogol's Second Idyll," *Mod Lang R,* 73 (1978), 351–367.

"The Overcoat"
Hippisley, Anthony. "Gogol's 'The Overcoat': A Further Interpretation," *Slavic & East European J,* 20 (1976), 121–129.
Karlinsky, Simon. *The Sexual Labyrinth* . . ., 135–144.
Massey, Irving. *The Gaping Pig* . . ., 65–73.
Proffitt, Edward. "Gogol's 'Perfectly True' Tale: 'The Overcoat' and Its Mode of Closure," *Stud Short Fiction,* 14 (1977), 35–40.
Rowe, William W. *Through Gogol's Looking Glass* . . ., 113–118.
Waszink, Paul M. "Mythical Traits in Gogol's 'The Overcoat,' " *Slavic & East European J,* 22 (1978), 287–300.

"The Portrait"
Rowe, William W. *Through Gogol's Looking Glass* . . ., 107–112.

"The Quarrel Between Ivan Ivanovich and Ivan Nikoforovich"
Fiene, Donald M. " 'The Story of How Ivan Ivanovich Quarreled with Ivan Nikiforovich,' " *Explicator,* 34 (1976), Item 55.
Karlinsky, Simon. *The Sexual Labyrinth* . . ., 67–77.
Rowe, William W. *Through Gogol's Looking Glass* . . ., 84–92.

"Rome"
Rowe, William W. *Through Gogol's Looking Glass* . . ., 129–134.

"St. John's Eve"
Rowe, William W. *Through Gogol's Looking Glass* . . ., 22–25.

"The Sorochintsy Fair"
Rowe, William W. *Through Gogol's Looking Glass* . . ., 14–21.

"Taras Bulba"
Karlinsky, Simon. *The Sexual Labyrinth* . . ., 77–86.
Rowe, William W. *Through Gogol's Looking Glass* . . ., 73–77.

"The Terrible Vengeance"
Rowe, William W. *Through Gogol's Looking Glass* . . ., 47–54.

"Viy"
Karlinsky, Simon. *The Sexual Labyrinth* . . ., 86–103.
Rowe, William W. *Through Gogol's Looking Glass* . . ., 78–83.

MEÏR GOLDSCHMIDT

"Aron and Esther"
Ober, Kenneth H. *Meïr Goldschmidt,* 100.

"Avrohmehe Nattergal"
 Ober, Kenneth H. *Meïr Goldschmidt*, 115–117.

"The Battle of Marengo"
 Ober, Kenneth H. *Meïr Goldschmidt*, 117.

"Bewitched, No. 1"
 Ober, Kenneth H. *Meïr Goldschmidt*, 109–110.

"A Christmas in the Country"
 Ober, Kenneth H. *Meïr Goldschmidt*, 105.

"The Fickle Girl on Graahede"
 Ober, Kenneth H. *Meïr Goldschmidt*, 114–115.

"God's Angel from Rørvig"
 Ober, Kenneth H. *Meïr Goldschmidt*, 107.

"The Last Lucifer Match"
 Ober, Kenneth H. *Meïr Goldschmidt*, 103–104.

"Maser"
 Ober, Kenneth H. *Meïr Goldschmidt*, 108–109.

"Paolo and Giovanna"
 Ober, Kenneth H. *Meïr Goldschmidt*, 106–107.

"The Photographs and Mephistopheles"
 Ober, Kenneth H. *Meïr Goldschmidt*, 104–105.

"Poison"
 Ober, Kenneth H. *Meïr Goldschmidt*, 110–111.

NADINE GORDIMER

"Livingstone's Companion"
 Wade, Michael. *Nadine Gordimer*, 183–190.

"The Train from Rhodesia"
 *Gullason, Thomas A. "The Short Story: An Underrated Art," in May, Charles
  E., Ed. *Short Story Theories*, 28–29.

MAXIM GORKY

"The Hermit"
 Cassill, R. V. *Instructor's Handbook . . .*, 89–91.

JEREMIAS GOTTHELF [ALBERT BITZIUS]

"The Black Spider"
 Magill, C. P. *German Literature*, 114–115.

WILLIAM GOYEN

"The Children of Old Somebody"
Paul, Jay S. " 'Marvelous Reciprocity': The Fiction of William Goyen,"
Critique, 19, ii (1977), 82.

"The Enchanted Nurse"
Paul, Jay S. " 'Marvelous Reciprocity' . . .," 78–80.

"The Grasshopper's Burden"
Paul, Jay S. " 'Marvelous Reciprocity' . . .," 81–82.

"The Moss Rose"
Paul, Jay S. " 'Marvelous Reciprocity' . . .," 86.

"Nests in a Stone Image"
Paul, Jay S. " 'Nests in a Stone Image': Goyen's Surreal Gethsemane," *Stud
Short Fiction,* 15 (1978), 415–420.

"Old Wildfoot"
Paul, Jay S. " 'Marvelous Reciprocity' . . .," 82–83.

"Pore Perrie"
Paul, Jay S. " 'Marvelous Reciprocity' . . .," 87–88.

"The Rescue"
Paul, Jay S. " 'Marvelous Reciprocity' . . .," 80–81.

GRAHAM GREENE

"The Basement Room"
Kane, Thomas S., and Leonard J. Peters. *Some Suggestions* . . ., 38–39.

"The Blue Film"
Kimmey, John L. *Instructor's Manual* . . ., 4–5.

"The Destructors"
*Perrine, Laurence. *Instructor's Manual* . . . *"Story* . . .," 5; *Instructor's Manual
* . . . *"Literature* . . .," 5.

GERALD GRIFFIN

"The Barber of Bantry"
Cronin, John. *Gerald Griffin* . . ., 113–114.

"The Black Birds and the Yellow Hammers"
Cronin, John. *Gerald Griffin* . . ., 119–120.

"Card Drawing"
Cronin, John. *Gerald Griffin* . . ., 43–44.

"The Great House"
   Cronin, John. *Gerald Griffin* . . ., 114–115.

"The Half-Sir"
   Cronin, John. *Gerald Griffin* . . ., 44–48.

"A Night at Sea"
   Cronin, John. *Gerald Griffin* . . ., 115–116.

"Sir Dowling O'Hartigan"
   Cronin, John. *Gerald Griffin* . . ., 116–117.

"Touch My Honour, Touch My Life"
   Cronin, John. *Gerald Griffin* . . ., 116.

"The Village Ruin"
   Cronin, John. *Gerald Griffin* . . ., 117–118.

GEORGE GRIFFITH

"The Lord of Labour"
   Moskowitz, Sam. *Strange Horizons* . . ., 215–216.

FRANZ GRILLPARZER

"The Poor Player"
   Browning, Robert M. "Language and the Fall from Grace in Grillparzer's 'Spielmann,'" *Seminar: J Germ Stud,* 12 (1976), 215–235.
   Hunter-Lougheed, Rosemarie. "Das Motiv der Gewissenhaftigkeit; Oder die Gefehr, ins 'Wilde und Unaufhaltsame' zu geraten: Zu Grillparzers Novelle 'Der Arme Spielmann,'" *Österreich in Geschichte und Literatur,* 22 (1978), 279–289.
   _____. "Das Thema der Liebe in 'Armen Spielmann,'" *Jahrbuch der Grillparzer-Gesellschaft,* 13 (1978), 49–62.
   Magill, C. P. *German Literature,* 117–118.
   Reeve, W. C. "Proportion and Disproportion in Grillparzer's 'Der arme Spielmann,'" *Germ R,* 53 (1978), 41–49.
   Swales, Martin. *The German "Novelle,"* 114–132.

ALEXANDR GRIN

"Scarlet Sails"
   Scherr, Barry. "Alexandr Grin's 'Scarlet Sails' and the Fairy Tale," *Slavic & East European J,* 20 (1976), 387–399.

GURAZADA APPARAO

"Kanyaka"
   Sriramamurty, G. "The Stories of Gurazada," *Indian Lit,* 17, i–ii (1974), 239.

"Reform"
Sriramamurty, G. "The Stories of Gurazada," 240.

NICOMEDES GUZMÁN

"A Coin in the River"
Pearson, Lon. *Nicomedes Guzmán* . . ., 29–30.

JAMES HALL

"The War Belt"
Barnett, Louise K. *The Ignoble Savage* . . ., 101–102.

EDMOND HAMILTON

"The Man Who Evolved"
Carter, Paul A. *The Creation* . . ., 145–147.

KNUT HAMSUN [KNUT PEDERSEN]

"Under the Autumn Star"
Updike, John. "A Primal Modern," *New Yorker,* 52 (May 31, 1976), 116–118.

MARTIN A. HANSEN

"The Birds"
Ingwersen, Faith and Niels. *Martin A. Hansen,* 107–108.
Vowles, Richard B. "Martin A. Hansen and the Uses of the Past," *Am-Scandinavian R,* 46 (1958), 36–37.

"The Bridegroom's Oak"
Ingwersen, Faith and Niels. *Martin A. Hansen,* 135–136.

"Early Morning"
Ingwersen, Faith and Niels. *Martin A. Hansen,* 100–101.

"The Easter Bell"
Ingwersen, Faith and Niels. *Martin A. Hansen,* 73–78.

"The Gardener, the Beast, and the Child"
Ingwersen, Faith and Niels. *Martin A. Hansen,* 136–139.

"Haavn"
Ingwersen, Faith and Niels. *Martin A. Hansen,* 133–134.

"The Homecoming"
Ingwersen, Faith and Niels. *Martin A. Hansen,* 136–137.

"The Man from the Earth"
  Ingwersen, Faith and Niels. *Martin A. Hansen,* 108–109.

"The Messenger"
  Ingwersen, Faith and Niels. *Martin A. Hansen,* 134–135.

"The Midsummer Festival"
  Ingwersen, Faith and Niels. *Martin A. Hansen,* 78–84.
  Vowles, Richard B. ". . . Uses of the Past," 35–36.

"Night in March"
  Ingwersen, Faith and Niels. *Martin A. Hansen,* 105–106.

"The Owl"
  Ingwersen, Faith and Niels. *Martin A. Hansen,* 99–100.

"The Righteous One"
  Ingwersen, Faith and Niels. *Martin A. Hansen,* 132–133.

"Sacrifice"
  Ingwersen, Faith and Niels. *Martin A. Hansen,* 101–103.

"September Fog"
  Ingwersen, Faith and Niels. *Martin A. Hansen,* 89–95.

"The Soldier and the Girl"
  Ingwersen, Faith and Niels. *Martin A. Hansen,* 106–107.

"The Thornbush"
  Ingwersen, Faith and Niels. *Martin A. Hansen,* 95–99.

"Tirad"
  Ingwersen, Faith and Niels. *Martin A. Hansen,* 131–132.

"The Waiting Room"
  Ingwersen, Faith and Niels. *Martin A. Hansen,* 103–105.

THOMAS HARDY

"A Mere Interlude"
  Larkin, Peter. "Irony and Fulfillment in Hardy's 'A Mere Interlude,' " *J 1890's Soc,* 9 (1978), 16–22.

"Old Mrs. Chundle"
  Pinion, F. B. *Thomas Hardy . . . ,* 69–70.

"On the Western Circuit"
  Brady, Kristin. "Conventionality as Narrative Technique in Hardy's 'On the Western Circuit,' " *J 1890's Soc,* 2 (1978), 22–30.

"The Romantic Adventures of a Milkmaid"
Pinion, F. B. *Thomas Hardy . . .*, 63–65.

GEORGE WASHINGTON HARRIS

"Frustrating a Funeral"
Rose, Alan H. *Demonic Vision . . .*, 68–71.

"Old Skissim's Middle Boy"
Rose, Alan H. *Demonic Vision . . .*, 65–68.

BRET HARTE

"Tennessee's Partner"
May, Charles E. "Bret Harte's 'Tennessee's Partner': The Reader Euchred," *So Dakota R*, 15 (Spring, 1977), 109–118.

LESLIE P. HARTLEY

"Conrad and the Dragon"
Jones, Edward T. *L. P. Hartley*, 43–44.

"The Crossways"
Jones, Edward T. *L. P. Hartley*, 44–45.

"Fall in at the Double"
Jones, Edward T. *L. P. Hartley*, 55–56.

"The Killing Bottles"
Jones, Edward T. *L. P. Hartley*, 46–47.

"Pains and Pleasures"
Jones, Edward T. *L. P. Hartley*, 56–57.

"Please Do Not Touch"
Jones, Edward T. *L. P. Hartley*, 49–51.

"The Prayer"
Jones, Edward T. *L. P. Hartley*, 54–55.

"The Pylon"
Jones, Edward T. *L. P. Hartley*, 53–54.

"Someone in the Lift"
Jones, Edward T. *L. P. Hartley*, 52–53.

"A Summons"
Jones, Edward T. *L. P. Hartley*, 51–52.

GERHART HAUPTMANN

"Carnival"
Hammer, A.E. "A Note on the Denouement of Gerhart Hauptmann's 'Fasching,' " *New Germ Stud*, 4 (1976), 87–89.
Turner, David. "Setting the Record Straight on Hauptmann's 'Fasching,' " *New Germ Stud*, 4 (1976), 157–159.

"Signalman Thiel"
Leibowitz, Judith. *Narrative Purposes* . . ., 37–38.

NATHANIEL HAWTHORNE

"Alice Doane's Appeal"
Hennelly, Mark M. " 'Alice Doane's Appeal': Hawthorne's Case Against the Artist," *Stud Am Fiction*, 6 (1978), 125–140.
Markus, Manfred. "Hawthorne's 'Alice Doane's Appeal': An Anti-Gothic Tale," *Germanische-Romanische Monatsschrift*, 25 (1975), 338–349.

"The Ambitious Guest"
D'Avenzo, Mario L. "The Ambitious Guest in the Hands of an Angry God," *Engl Lang Notes*, 14, i (1976), 38–42.

"The Artist of the Beautiful"
Baym, Nina. *The Shape* . . ., 110–111.
Billy, Ted. "Time and Transformation in 'The Artist of the Beautiful,' " *Am Transcendental Q*, 29 (1976), 33–35.
Dauber, Kenneth. *Rediscovering Hawthorne*, 81–86.
*Franklin, H. Bruce. *Future Perfect* . . ., 2nd ed., 15–18.
Liebman, Sheldon W. "Hawthorne's Romanticism: 'The Artist of the Beautiful,' " *ESQ: J Am Renaissance*, 22 (1976), 85–95.

"The Birthmark"
Baxter, David J. " 'The Birthmark' in Perspective," *Nathaniel Hawthorne J*, [n. v.] (1975), 232–240.
Cassill, R. V. *Instructor's Handbook* . . ., 93–95.
*Franklin, H. Bruce. *Future Perfect* . . ., 2nd ed., 8–14.
Jones, Madison. "Variations on a Hawthorne Theme," *Stud Short Fiction*, 15 (1978), 282–283.
Napier, Elizabeth R. "Aylmer as 'Scheidekünstler': The Pattern of Union and Separation in Hawthorne's 'The Birthmark,' " *So Atlantic Bull*, 41, iv (1976), 32–35.
Staal, Arie. *Hawthorne's Narrative Art*, 27–30.
Van Leer, David M. "Aylmer's Library: Transcendental Alchemy in Hawthorne's 'The Birthmark,' " *ESQ: J Am Renaissance*, 22 (1976), 211–220.

"The Devil in Manuscript"
Dauber, Kenneth. *Rediscovering Hawthorne*, 56–60.

"Drowne's Wooden Image"
Baym, Nina. *The Shape* . . ., 111–112.

Richardson, Robert D. *Myth and Literature* . . ., 179–181.
Staal, Arie. *Hawthorne's Narrative Art*, 37–41.

"Earth's Holocaust"
Hostetler, Norman H. " 'Earth's Holocaust': Hawthorne's Parable of the Imaginative Process," *Kansas Q*, 7, iv (1975), 85–89.

"Edward Randolph's Portrait"
Dauber, Kenneth. *Rediscovering Hawthorne*, 72–75.

"Endicott and the Red Cross"
Baym, Nina. *The Shape* . . ., 78–80.
Newberry, Frederick. "The Demonic in 'Endicott and the Red Cross,' " *Papers Lang & Lit*, 13 (1977), 251–259.
Shaw, Peter. "Hawthorne's Ritual Typology of the American Revolution," *Prospects*, 3 (1977), 487–489.

"Ethan Brand"
Baym, Nina. *The Shape* . . ., 117–118.
Hennelly, Mark. "Hawthorne's *Opus Alchymicum*: 'Ethan Brand,' " *ESQ:J Am Renaissance*, 22 (1976), 96–106.

"Fancy's Show Box"
Baym, Nina. *The Shape* . . ., 66–68.

"Feathertop"
Estrin, Mark W. "Narrative Ambivalence in Hawthorne's 'Feathertop,' " *J Narrative Technique*, 5 (1975), 164–173.

"The Gray Champion"
Dauber, Kenneth. *Rediscovering Hawthorne*, 53–56.
Newberry, Frederick. " 'The Gray Champion': Hawthorne's Ironic Criticism of Puritan Rebellion," *Stud Short Fiction*, 13 (1976), 363–370.
Shaw, Peter. "Hawthorne's Ritual Typology . . .," 489–491.

"The Haunted Mind"
Baym, Nina. *The Shape* . . ., 64–66.

"The Hollow of the Three Hills"
Dauber, Kenneth. *Rediscovering Hawthorne*, 48–51.
Pandeya, Prabhat K. "The Drama of Evil in 'The Hollow of the Three Hills,' " *Nathaniel Hawthorne J*, [n.v.] (1975), 177–181.
Staal, Arie. *Hawthorne's Narrative Art*, 21–22.
Staggs, Kenneth W. "The Structure of Nathaniel Hawthorne's 'Hollow of the Three Hills,' " *Linguistics in Lit*, 2, i (1977), 1–18.

"Howe's Masquerade"
Dauber, Kenneth. *Rediscovering Hawthorne*, 70–72.

"Lady Eleanore's Mantle"
Dauber, Kenneth. *Rediscovering Hawthorne*, 75–78.

Gross, Seymour L. "Hawthorne's 'Lady Eleanore's Mantle' as History," *J Engl & Germ Philol,* 54 (1955), 549–554; rpt. Henning, Lawson, *et al.,* Eds. *Studies . . .,* 89–94.

Staal, Arie. *Hawthorne's Narrative Art,* 61–62.

"The Maypole of Merry Mount"
Feeney, Joseph J. "The Structure of Ambiguity in Hawthorne's 'The Maypole of Merry Mount,' " *Stud Am Fiction,* 3 (1975), 211–216.
Richardson, Robert D. *Myth and Literature . . .,* 182–184.
Shaw, Peter. "Hawthorne's Ritual Typology . . .," 484–487.

"The Minister's Black Veil"
Altschuler, Glenn C. "The Puritan Dilemma in 'The Minister's Black Veil,' " *Am Transcendental Q,* 24, Supp. 1 (1974), 25–27.

"Mr. Higginbotham's Catastrophe"
Duban, James. "The Sceptical Context of Hawthorne's 'Mr. Higginbotham's Catastrophe,' " *Am Lit,* 48 (1976), 292–301.
Staal, Arie. *Hawthorne's Narrative Art,* 41–44.

"My Kinsman, Major Molineux"
Adams, Joseph D. "The Societal Initiation and Hawthorne's 'My Kinsman, Major Molineux': The Night-Journey Motif," *Engl Stud Coll,* 1 (1976), 1–19.
Dolan, Paul J. *Of War and War's Alarms . . .,* 16–35.
*Hoffman, Daniel. "Yankee Bumpkin and Scapegoat King," in Timko, Michael, Ed. *38 Short Stories,* 2nd ed., 661–671.
Kozikowski, Stanley J. " 'My Kinsman, Major Molineux' as Mock-Heroic," *Am Transcendental Q,* 31 (1976), 20–21.
*Lesser, Simon O. "Hawthorne's 'My Kinsman, Major Molineux,' " in Sprich, Robert, and Richard W. Noland, Eds. *The Whispered Meaning . . .,* 44–53.
Miller, Edwin H. " 'My Kinsman, Major Molineux': The Playful Art of Nathaniel Hawthorne," *ESQ: J Am Renaissance,* 24 (1978), 145–151.
Murphy, Denis M. "Poor Robin and Shrewd Ben: Hawthorne's Kinsman," *Stud Short Fiction,* 15 (1978), 185–190.
Nilsen, Helge N. "Hawthorne's 'My Kinsman, Major Molineux': Society and the Individual," in Seyersted, Brita, Ed. *Norwegian Contributions . . .,* 123–136.
Nitsche, J.C. "House Symbolism in Hawthorne's 'My Kinsman, Major Molineux,' " *Am Transcendental Q,* 38 (1978), 167–175.
Shaw, Peter. "Fathers, Sons, and the Ambiguities of Revolution in 'My Kinsman, Major Molineux,' " *New England Q,* 49 (1976), 559–576.
_____. "Hawthorne's Ritual Typology . . .," 491–492.
Staal, Arie. *Hawthorne's Narrative Art,* 49–51, 57–59.

"Old Esther Dudley"
Baym, Nina. *The Shape . . .,* 76–78.
Dauber, Kenneth. *Rediscovering Hawthorne,* 78–81.

"Peter Goldthwaite's Treasure"
Spengemann, William C. *The Adventurous Muse . . .,* 174–176.
Staal, Arie. *Hawthorne's Narrative Art,* 25–27.

"The Prophetic Pictures"
   Staal, Arie. *Hawthorne's Narrative Art,* 44–46.

"Rappaccini's Daughter"
   Aoyama, Yoshitaka. " 'Rappaccini's Daughter': The Garden as 'Neutral Territory,' " *Sophia Engl Stud,* 1 (1976), 37–52.
   Ayo, Nicholas. "The Labyrinthine Ways of 'Rappaccini's Daughter,' " *Research Stud,* 42 (1974), 56–69.
   Bales, Kent. "Sexual Exploitation and the Fall from Natural Virtue in Rappaccini's Garden," *ESQ: J Am Renaissance,* 24 (1978), 133–144.
   Baym, Nina. *The Shape . . . ,* 106–109.
   Brenzo, Richard. "Beatrice Rappaccini: A Victim of Male Love and Horror," *Am Lit,* 48 (1976), 152–164.
   Dauber, Kenneth. *Rediscovering Hawthorne,* 25–36.
   *Franklin, H. Bruce. *Future Perfect . . . ,* 2nd ed., 18–23.
   Fryer, Judith. *The Faces of Eve . . . ,* 40–47.
   Jones, Madison. "Variations . . . ," 280–282.
   Norford, Don P. "Rappaccini's Garden of Allegory," *Am Lit,* 50 (1978), 167–186.
   Predmore, Richard L. "The Hero's Test in 'Rappaccini's Daughter,' " *Engl Lang Notes,* 15 (1978), 284–291.
   Staal, Arie. *Hawthorne's Narrative Art,* 59–61.

"Roger Malvin's Burial"
   Barnett, Louise K. *The Ignoble Savage . . . ,* 151–153.
   Byers, John R. "The Geography and Framework of Hawthorne's 'Roger Malvin's Burial,' " *Tennessee Stud Lit,* 21 (1976), 11–20.
   Carlson, Patricia A. "Images and Structure in Hawthorne's 'Roger Malvin's Burial,' " *So Atlantic Bull,* 41, iv (1976), 3–9.
   Fishman, Burton J. "Imagined Redemption in 'Roger Malvin's Burial,' " *Stud Am Fiction,* 5 (1977), 257–262.
   Hertenstein, Rod. "A Mythical Reading of 'Roger Malvin's Burial,' " in Baldanza, Frank, Ed. *Itinerary 3 . . . ,* 39–48.
   Scheick, William J. "The Hieroglyphic Rock in Hawthorne's 'Roger Malvin's Burial,' " *ESQ: J Am Renaissance,* 24 (1978), 72–76.
   Spengemann, William C. *The Adventurous Muse . . . ,* 153–160.
   Staal, Arie. *Hawthorne's Narrative Art,* 54–56.

"Wakefield"
   Dauber, Kenneth. *Rediscovering Hawthorne,* 60–65.
   Gatta, John. " 'Busy and Selfish London': The Urban Figure in Hawthorne's 'Wakefield,' " *ESQ: J Am Renaissance,* 23 (1977), 164–172.
   Kane, Thomas S., and Leonard J. Peters. *Some Observations . . . ,* 18–19.
   Kimmey, John L. *Instructor's Manual . . . ,* 23–24.
   Perry, Ruth. "The Solitude of Hawthorne's 'Wakefield,' " *Am Lit,* 49 (1978), 613–619.
   Weldon, Robert F. "Wakefield's Second Journey," *Stud Short Fiction,* 14 (1977), 69–74.

"The Wedding Knell"
   Baym, Nina. *The Shape . . . ,* 73–74.

"Young Goodman Brown"
Cargas, Harry J. "The Arc of Rebirth in 'Young Goodman Brown,'" *New Laurel R*, 4, i–ii (1975), 5–7.
Cassill, R. V. *Instructor's Handbook* . . ., 91–92.
*Fogle, Richard H. "Ambiguity and Clarity in Hawthorne's 'Young Goodman Brown,'" in Dietrich, R. F., and Roger H. Sundell. *Instructor's Manual* . . ., 3rd ed., 24–37.
Jones, Madison. "Variations . . .," 278–280.
Levy, Leo B. "The Problem of Faith in 'Young Goodman Brown,'" *J Engl & Germ Philol*, 74 (1975), 375–387.
Shriver, M. M. "'Young Goodman Brown,'" *Études Anglaises*, 30 (1977), 413–419.
Staal, Arie. *Hawthorne's Narrative Art*, 52–54.

JOHN HAY

"The Blood Seedling"
Gale, Robert L. *John Hay*, 85.

"The Foster-Brother"
Gale, Robert L. *John Hay*, 83–85.

"Kane and Abel"
Gale, Robert L. *John Hay*, 86.

"Shelby Cabell"
Gale, Robert L. *John Hay*, 82–83.

FRIEDRICH HEBBEL

"The Cow"
Lütkehaus, Ludger. "Pantragische Liquidation oder soziale Katastrophe?: Hebbels Erzählung 'Die Kuh,'" *Hebbel-Jahrbuch* (1975), 182–196.

HEINRICH HEINE

"The Baths of Lucca"
Grubačic, Slobodan. *Heines Erzählprosa* . . ., 59–78.

"Florentine Night"
Fancelli, Maria. "Heine minores: Le 'Florentinische Nächte,'" *Studi Germanici*, 11 (1973), 51–70.
Grubačic, Slobodan. *Heines Erzählprosa* . . ., 97–113.

"From the Memoirs of Herr von Schnabelewopski"
Grubačic, Slobodan. *Heines Erzählprosa* . . ., 79–96.

"Die Harzreise"
Grubačic, Slobodan. *Heines Erzählprosa* . . ., 9–24.

"The Journey from Munich to Genoa"
Grubačic, Slobodan. *Heines Erzählprosa . . .*, 25–40.

"The Rabbi of Bacherach"
Grubačic, Slobodan. *Heines Erzählprosa . . .*, 114–132.

WILLIAM HEINESEN

"The Winged Darkness"
Brønner, Hedin. "The Short Story in the Faroe Isles," *Scandinavian Stud*, 49 (1977), 173–177.

ROBERT A. HEINLEIN

"And He Built a Crooked House"
Slusser, George E. *The Classical Years . . .*, 14–15.

"By His Bootstraps"
Slusser, George E. *The Classical Years . . .*, 16–17.

"Common Sense"
Slusser, George E. *The Classical Years . . .*, 34–35.

"Coventry"
Carter, Paul A. *The Creation . . .*, 219–221.
Slusser, George E. *The Classical Years . . .*, 28–30.

"Gentlemen, Be Seated"
Slusser, George E. *The Classical Years . . .*, 20–21.

"The Green Hills of Earth"
Slusser, George E. *The Classical Years . . .*, 19–20.

" '—If This Goes On' "
Slusser, George E. *The Classical Years . . .*, 24–28.

"Life-Line"
Slusser, George E. *The Classical Years . . .*, 10–12.

"Magic, Inc." [originally titled "The Devil Makes the Law"]
Slusser, George E. *The Classical Years . . .*, 30–32.

"The Man Who Travelled in Elephants"
Slusser, George E. *The Classical Years . . .*, 23.

"Misfit"
Slusser, George E. *The Classical Years . . .*, 12–13.

"Requiem"
Slusser, George E. *The Classical Years . . .*, 13–14.

"Searchlight"
Slusser, George E. *The Classical Years* . . ., 23–24.

"Sky Lift"
Slusser, George E. *The Classical Years* . . ., 22.

"Space Jockey"
Slusser, George E. *The Classical Years* . . ., 20.

"They"
Slusser, George E. *The Classical Years* . . ., 15–16.

"Universe"
Slusser, George E. *The Classical Years* . . ., 32–34.

"Waldo"
Samuelson, David N. "The Frontier Worlds of Robert A. Heinlein," in Clareson, Thomas D., Ed. *Voices for the Future* . . ., 118–119.
Slusser, George E. *The Classical Years* . . ., 35–39.

"We Also Walk Dogs"
Slusser, George E. *The Classical Years* . . ., 17–18.

"The Year of the Jackpot"
Slusser, George E. *The Classical Years* . . ., 22–23.

ERNEST HEMINGWAY

"After the Storm"
Walker, Robert G. "Irony and Allusion in Hemingway's 'After the Storm,'" *Stud Short Fiction,* 13 (1976), 374–376.

"An Alpine Idyll"
Armistead, Myra. "Hemingway's 'An Alpine Idyll,'" *Stud Short Fiction,* 14 (1977), 255–258.

"The Battler"
Kane, Thomas S., and Leonard J. Peters. *Some Suggestions* . . ., 11–12.
Nakajima, Kenji. "Nick as 'The Battler,'" *Kyushu Am Lit,* 19 (1978), 45–48.

"Big Two-Hearted River"
*Howard, Daniel F., and William Plummer. *Instructor's Manual* . . ., 3rd ed., 49–50.
Stewart, Jack F. "Christian Allusions in 'Big Two-Hearted River,'" *Stud Short Fiction,* 15 (1978), 194–196.

"The Capital of the World"
Kennedy, X. J. *Instructor's Manual* . . ., 8–9.

"Cat in the Rain"
White, Gertrude M. "We're All 'Cats in the Rain,'" *Fitzgerald/Hemingway Annual 1978,* 241–246.

"A Clean, Well-Lighted Place"
  Broer, Lawrence. "The Iceberg in 'A Clean, Well-Lighted Place,'" *Lost Generation J*, 4, ii (1976), 14–15, 21.
  _____. "'A Clean, Well-Lighted Place,'" in Dietrich, R.F., and Roger H. Sundell. *Instructor's Manual . . .*, 3rd ed., 97–103.
  Hurley, C. Harold. "The Attribution of the Waiters' Second Speech in Hemingway's 'A Clean, Well-Lighted Place,'" *Stud Short Fiction*, 13 (1976), 81–85.
  Lodge, David. *The Novel at the Crossroads . . .*, 184–202.

"The Doctor and the Doctor's Wife"
  Flora, Joseph M. "A Closer Look at the Young Nick Adams and His Father," *Stud Short Fiction*, 14 (1977), 75–78.

"The Faithful Bull"
  Johnston, Kenneth G. "The Bull and the Lion: Hemingway's Fables for Critics," *Fitzgerald/Hemingway Annual 1977*, 149–153.

"Fathers and Sons"
  Fleming, Robert E. "Hemingway's Treatment of Suicide: 'Fathers and Sons' and *For Whom the Bell Tolls*," *Arizona Q*, 33 (1977), 122–124.

"The Gambler, the Nun, and the Radio"
  Whittle, Amberys. "A Reading of Hemingway's 'The Gambler, the Nun, and the Radio,'" *Arizona Q*, 33 (1977), 173–180.

"God Rest You Merry, Gentlemen"
  Donaldson, Scott. *By Force of Will . . .*, 237–238.

"The Good Lion"
  Johnston, Kenneth G. "The Bull and the Lion . . .," 153–155.

"Hills Like White Elephants"
  Cassill, R.V. *Instructor's Handbook . . .*, 96–97.
  Elliott, Gary D. "Hemingway's 'Hills Like White Elephants,'" *Explicator*, 35 (Summer, 1977), 22–23.
  *Perrine, Laurence. *Instructor's Manual . . . "Story . . .,"* 19–20; *Instructor's Manual . . . "Literature . . .,"* 19–20.

"Indian Camp"
  Flora, Joseph M. "A Closer Look . . .," 75–78.
  Johnston, Kenneth G. "In the Beginning: Hemingway's 'Indian Camp,'" *Stud Short Fiction*, 15 (1978), 102–104.
  Kimmey, John L., Ed. *Experience and Expression . . .*, 115.
  Penner, Dick. "The First Nick Adams Story," *Fitzgerald/Hemingway Annual 1977*, 195–202.

"The Killers"
  Davis, William V. "'The Fell of Dark': The Loss of Time in Hemingway's 'The Killers,'" *Stud Short Fiction*, 15 (1978), 319–320.
  *Oliver, Clinton F. "Hemingway's 'The Killers' and Mann's 'Disorder and Early Sorrow,'" in Timko, Michael, Ed. *38 Short Stories*, 2nd ed., 677–684.

Schlepper, Wolfgang. "Hemingway's 'The Killers': An Absurd Happening,"
    Literatur in Wissenschaft und Unterricht, 10 (1977), 104–114.
Stark de Valverde, Dorothy. "An Analysis of 'The Killers' and the Work of
    Ernest Hemingway," *Revista de la Universidad de Costa Rica,* 39 (1974),
    129–137.
Stuckey, W.J. " 'The Killers' as Experience," *J Narrative Technique,* 5 (1975),
    128–135.

"The Light of the World"
Barbour, James F. " 'The Light of the World': The Real Ketchel and the Real
    Light," *Stud Short Fiction,* 13 (1976), 17–23.
———. " 'The Light of the World': Hemingway's Comedy of Errors," *Notes
    Contemp Lit,* 7, v (1977), 5–8.

"Nobody Ever Dies"
Johnston, Kenneth G. " 'Nobody Ever Dies': Hemingway's Neglected Story of
    Freedom Fighters," *Kansas Q,* 9, ii (1977), 53–58.

"The Old Man and the Sea"
Adair, William. "Eighty-Five as a Lucky Number: A Note on 'The Old Man and
    the Sea,' " *Notes Contemp Lit,* 8, i (1978), 9.
Brøgger, Fredrik C. "Love and Fellowship in Ernest Hemingway's Fiction," in
    Seyersted, Brita, Ed. *Norwegian Contributions . . . ,* 284–285.
Donaldson, Scott. *By Force of Will . . . ,* 238–240.
Gordon, David J. *Literary Art . . . ,* 192–194.
*Handy, William J. *Modern Fiction . . . ,* 94–118.
Monteiro, George. "Santiago, DiMaggio, and Hemingway's Aging Profes-
    sionals in 'The Old Man and the Sea,' " *Fitzgerald/Hemingway Annual 1975,*
    273–280.
Singh, Satyanarain. "The Psychology of Heroic Living in 'The Old Man and the
    Sea,' " *Osmania J Engl Stud,* 10 (1973), 7–16.
Sinha, Krishna N. " 'The Old Man and the Sea': An Approach to Meaning," in
    Naik, M.K., *et al.,* Eds. *Indian Studies . . . ,* 219–228.
Whitlow, Roger. "The Destruction/Prevention of the Family Relationship in
    Hemingway's Fiction," *Lit R,* 20 (Fall, 1976), 13–15.
Wilson, G.R. "Incarnation and Redemption in 'The Old Man and the Sea,' "
    Stud Short Fiction, 14 (1977), 369–373.

"On the Quai at Smyrna"
Witherington, Paul. "Word and Flesh in Hemingway's 'On the Quai at
    Smyrna,' " *Notes Mod Am Lit,* 2, iii (1978), Item 18.

"The Revolutionist"
Hunt, Anthony. "Another Turn for Hemingway's 'The Revolutionist': Sources
    and Meanings," *Fitzgerald/Hemingway Annual 1977,* 119–135.

"The Short Happy Life of Francis Macomber"
Abcarian, Richard, and Marvin Klotz. *Instructor's Manual . . . ,* 2nd ed., 10.
Bocaz, Sergio H. "Senecan Stoicism in Hemingway's 'The Short Happy Life of
    Francis Macomber,' " in Nelson, Charles, Ed. *Studies in Language . . . ,*
    81–86.

Herndon, Jerry A. "No 'Maggie's Drawers' for Margot Macomber," *Fitzgerald/Hemingway Annual 1975*, 289–291.

Lefcourt, Charles R. "The Macomber Case," *Revue des Langues Vivantes*, 43 (1977), 341–347.

Stephens, Robert O. "Macomber and the Somali Proverb: The Matrix of Knowledge," *Fitzgerald/Hemingway Annual 1977*, 137–147.

Watson, James G. " 'A Sound Basis of Union': Structural and Thematic Balance in 'The Short Happy Life of Francis Macomber,' " *Fitzgerald/Hemingway Annual 1974*, 215–228.

Whitlow, Roger. "The Destruction/Prevention . . .," 8–9.

"The Snows of Kilimanjaro"

Elai, Richard L. "Three Symbols in Hemingway's 'The Snows of Kilimanjaro,' " *Revue des Langues Vivantes*, 41 (1975), 282–285.

Kolb, Alfred. "Symbolic Structure in Hemingway's 'The Snows of Kilimanjaro,' " *Notes Mod Am Lit*, 1, i (1976), Item 4.

"Soldier's Home"

Roberts, John J. "In Defense of Krebs," *Stud Short Fiction*, 13 (1976), 515–518.

"The Three-Day Blow"

O'Brien, Matthew. "Baseball in 'The Three-Day Blow,' " *Am Notes & Queries*, 16 (1977), 24–26.

"Three Shots"

Flora, Joseph M. "A Closer Look . . .," 75–78.

"Under the Ridge"

Kvam, Wayne. "Hemingway's 'Under the Ridge,' " *Fitzgerald/Hemingway Annual 1978*, 229–236.

STEPHAN HERMLIN

"The Commandant"

Huebener, Theodore. . . . *East Germany*, 104–105.

"Journey of a Painter in Paris"

Huebener, Theodore. . . . *East Germany*, 102–103.

"The Way of the Bolsheviks"

Huebener, Theodore. . . . *East Germany*, 103–104.

JUAN LUIS HERRERO

"Isla de Pinos"

Menton, Seymour. . . . *Cuban Revolution*, 204–205.

HERMANN HESSE

"A Child's Soul"

Sorell, Walter. *Hermann Hesse* . . ., 21–24.

"Journey to the East"
  Antosik, Stanley J. "The Confession of a Cultural Elitist: Hesse's Homecoming
    in 'Die Morgenlandfahrt,' " *Germ R,* 63 (1978), 63–68.
  Derrenberger, John. "Who is Leo?: Astrology in Hermann Hesse's 'Die Mor-
    genlandfahrt,' " *Monatshefte,* 67 (1975), 167–172.
  Middleton, J.C. "Hermann Hesse's 'Morgenlandfahrt,' " *Germ R,* 32 (1957),
    299–310; rpt. Otten, Anna, Ed. *Hesse Companion,* 170–188.
  Sorell, Walter. *Hermann Hesse . . .,* 49–51.

"Klingsor's Last Summer"
  Sorell, Walter. *Hermann Hesse . . .,* 42–43.

"Siddhartha"
  Brown, Madison. "Toward a Perspective for the Indian Element in Hermann
    Hesse's 'Siddhartha,' " *Germ Q,* 49 (1976), 191–202.
  Sorell, Walter. *Hermann Hesse . . .,* 48–49.
  Ziolkowski, Theodore. . . . *Theme and Structure,* 146–177; rpt. Otten, Anna,
    Ed. *Hesse Companion,* 71–100.

GEORG HEYM

"The Lunatic Asylum"
  Blunden, Allan. "Notes on Georg Heym's Novelle 'Der Irre,' " *Germ Life &
    Letters,* 28 (1974), 107–119.

CHESTER HIMES

"Crazy in the Stir"
  Franklin, H. Bruce. *The Victim . . .,* 216–219.
  Milliken, Stephen F. *Chester Himes . . .,* 42–44.

"Da—Da—Dee"
  Milliken, Stephen F. *Chester Himes . . .,* 67–69.

"Headwaiter"
  Milliken, Stephen F. *Chester Himes . . .,* 54–55.

"He Knew"
  Milliken, Stephen F. *Chester Himes . . .,* 39–40.

"Heaven Has Changed"
  Milliken, Stephen F. *Chester Himes . . .,* 59.

"His Last Day"
  Milliken, Stephen F. *Chester Himes . . .,* 32–33.

"Lunching at the Ritzmore"
  Milliken, Stephen F. *Chester Himes . . .,* 59–60.

"Mama's Missionary Money"
  Milliken, Stephen F. *Chester Himes . . .,* 66–67.

"A Nigger"
Liston, Maureen. "Chester Himes: 'A Nigger,' '" in Bruck, Peter, Ed. *The Black American Short Story* . . ., 90–94.
Milliken, Stephen F. *Chester Himes* . . ., 52–53.

"Pork Chop Paradise"
Milliken, Stephen F. *Chester Himes* . . ., 48–50.

"Prediction"
Milliken, Stephen F. *Chester Himes* . . ., 296–297.

"Prison Mass"
Milliken, Stephen F. *Chester Himes* . . ., 33–38.

"So Softly Smiling"
Milliken, Stephen F. *Chester Himes* . . ., 58–59.

"Tang"
Milliken, Stephen F. *Chester Himes* . . ., 295–296.

"To What Red Hell?"
Franklin, H. Bruce. *The Victim* . . ., 219–222.
Milliken, Stephen F. *Chester Himes* . . ., 44–45.

"Two Soldiers"
Milliken, Stephen F. *Chester Himes* . . ., 57–58.

CHARLES FENNO HOFFMAN

"Queen Meg"
Barnett, Louise K. *The Ignoble Savage* . . ., 31–32.

ERNST THEODOR AMADEUS HOFFMANN

"The Adventure of New Year's Night"
Berger, Willy R. "Drei phantastische Erzählungen: Chamissos 'Peter Schlemihl,' E. T. A. Hoffmanns 'Abenteur der Silvester-Nacht,' und Gogols 'Die Nase,' '" *Arcadia,* [n. v.], Special Issue (1978), 106–138.

"The Automaton"
Massey, Irving. *The Uncreating Word* . . ., 36–38.

"The Baron of B."
McGlathery, James M. " 'Der Himmel Hängt Ihm Voller Geigen': E. T. A. Hoffmann's 'Rat Krespel,' 'Die Fermate,' and 'Der Baron von B.,' '" *Germ Q,* 51 (1978), 145.

"Counselor Krespel"
Birrell, Gordon. "Instruments and Infidels: The Metaphysics of Music in E. T. A. Hoffmann's 'Rat Krespel,' '" in Frank, Luanne, Ed. *Literature and the Occult* . . ., 65–71.

Heberland, Paul M. "Number Symbolism: The Father-Daughter Relationship in E. T. A. Hoffmann's 'Rat Krespel,' " *Lang Q*, 13, iii–iv (1975), 39–42.

McGlathery, James M. " 'Der Himmel . . .,' " 135–141.

"The Deserted House"

Jaroszewski, Marek, and Marek Wydmuch. "Das Phantastische in E. T. A. Hoffmanns Novelle 'Das öde Haus,' " *Germanica Wratislaviensia*, 27 (1976), 127–135.

"The Golden Pot"

Reddick, John. "E. T. A. Hoffmann's 'Der goldne Topf' and Its 'durchgehaltene Ironie,' " *Mod Lang R*, 71 (1976), 577–594.

Tatar, Maria M. "Mesmerism, Madness, and Death in E. T. A. Hoffmann's 'Der goldne Topf,' " *Stud Romanticism*, 14 (1975), 365–389.

Willinberg, Knud. "Die Kollision verschiedener Realitätsebenen als Gattungs-problem in E. T. A. Hoffmanns 'Der goldne Topf,' " *Zeitschrift für Deutsche Philologie*, 95, i (1976), 93–113.

"Mademoiselle de Scudery"

Carne, Eva-Marie. "Der dramatische Aufbau in E. T. A. Hoffmanns 'Das Fräulein von Scuderi,' " *Proceedings Pacific Northwest Conference Foreign Langs*, 26, i (1975), 98–101.

Post, Klaus D. "Kriminalgeschichte als Heilsgeschichte: Zu E. T. A. Hoffmanns Erzählung 'Das Fräulein von Scuderi,' " *Zeitschrift für Deutsche Philologie*, 95, i (1976), 132–163.

Weiss, Hermann F. " 'The Labyrinth of Crime': A Reinterpretation of E. T. A. Hoffmann's 'Das Fräulein von Scuderi,' " *Germ R*, 51 (1976), 181–189.

"The Pause"

McGlathery, James M. " 'Der Himmel . . .,' " 142–144.

"The Princess Brambilla"

Chambers, Ross. "Two Theatrical Microcosms: 'Die Prinzessin Brambilla' and 'Mademoiselle de Maupin,' " *Comp Lit*, 27 (1975), 34–46.

"The Sandman"

Aichinger, Ingrid. "E. T. A. Hoffmanns Novelle 'Der Sandmann' und die Interpretationen Sigmund Freuds," *Zeitschrift für Deutsche Philologie*, 95, i (1976), 113–132.

Hartung, Günter. "Anatomie des 'Sandmanns,' " *Weimarer Beiträge*, 23, ix (1977), 45–65.

Magill, C. P. *German Literature*, 82–83.

Mahlendorf, Ursula R. "E. T. A. Hoffmann's 'The Sandman': The Fictional Psycho-Biography of a Romantic Poet," *Am Imago*, 32 (1975), 217–239.

Massey, Irving. *The Gaping Pig* . . ., 117–120.

HUGO VON HOFMANNSTHAL

"Horseman's Story"

Bangerter, Lowell A. *Hugo von Hofmannsthal*, 37–40.

''Reitergeschichte''
  Fiedler, Theodore. ''Hofmannsthals 'Reitergeschichte' und ihre Leser: Zur
    Politik der Ironie,'' *Germanisch-Romanische Monatsschrift*, 26 (1976),
    140–163.

''Tale of the Merchant's Son and His Servant''
  Bangerter, Lowell A. *Hugo von Hofmannsthal*, 33–37.

''Under the Copper-Beech Tree''
  Hirsch, Rudolf. ''Eine Erzählung aus dem Nachlass Hugo von Hofmannsthals,''
    Mod Austrian Lit, 7, iii–iv (1974), 12–30.

''Die Wege und die Begegnungen''
  Politzer, Heinz. ''Auf der Suche nach Agur. Zu Hugo von Hofmannsthals 'Die
    Wege und die Begegnungen,' '' in Gillespie, Gerald, and Edgar Lohner, Eds.
    Herkommen und Erneuerung . . ., 319–335.

JAMES HOGG

''The Barber of Duncow''
  Gifford, Douglas. *James Hogg*, 205–206.

''The Cameronian Preacher's Tale''
  Gifford, Douglas. *James Hogg*, 208–209.

''Mary Burnet''
  Gifford, Douglas. *James Hogg*, 209–212.

''Mr. Adamson of Laverhope''
  Gifford, Douglas. *James Hogg*, 213–214.

''Tibby Hyslop's Dream''
  Gifford, Douglas. *James Hogg*, 206–208.

JOHNSON JONES HOOPER

''The 'Tallapoonsy Vollantares' Meet the Enemy''
  Rose, Alan H. *Demonic Vision* . . ., 51–53.

WILLIAM DEAN HOWELLS

''A Difficult Case''
  Crowley, John W. ''Howells' Minister in a Maze: 'A Difficult Case,' '' *Colby
    Lib Q*, 13 (1977), 278–283.

''A Sleep and a Forgetting''
  Crowley, John W., and Charles L. Crow. ''Psychic and Psychological Themes in
    Howells' 'A Sleep and a Forgetting,' '' *ESQ: J Am Renaissance*, 23 (1977),
    41–51.

EUGÈNE IONESCO

HSIAO HUNG

"At the Foot of the Mountain"
Goldblatt, Howard. *Hsiao Hung*, 91.

"The Bridge"
Goldblatt, Howard. *Hsiao Hung*, 64–65.

"A Cry in the Wilderness"
Goldblatt, Howard. *Hsiao Hung*, 88–89.

"Flight from Danger"
Goldblatt, Howard. *Hsiao Hung*, 89–90.

"Hands"
Goldblatt, Howard. *Hsiao Hung*, 62–63.

"On the Oxcart"
Goldblatt, Howard. *Hsiao Hung*, 69–70.

"Vague Expectations"
Goldblatt, Howard. *Hsiao Hung*, 90–91.

LANGSTON HUGHES

"The Blues I'm Playing"
Bruck, Peter. "Langston Hughes: 'The Blues I'm Playing,' " in Bruck, Peter,
Ed. *The Black American Short Story* . . ., 75–80.

"Father and Son"
Berzon, Judith R. *Neither White Nor Black* . . ., 83–85.

ZORA NEALE HURSTON

"Black Death"
Hemenway, Robert E. *Zora Neale Hurston* . . ., 74–79.

"Sweet"
Hemenway, Robert E. *Zora Neale Hurston* . . ., 70–73.

ALDOUS HUXLEY

"Happily Ever After"
Pritchard, William H. *Seeing Through* . . ., 33–34.

EUGÈNE IONESCO

"Rhinoceros"
Barrault, Jean-Louis. " 'Rhinoceros': Un Cauchemar burlesque," *Cahiers de la*

Compagnie, 97 (1978), 41–46.
Kane, Thomas S., and Leonard J. Peters. *Some Suggestions . . .*, 19.

WASHINGTON IRVING

"The Adventure of the German Student"
*Clendenning, John. "Irving and the Gothic Tradition," in Myers, Andrew B.,
Ed. . . . *A Century of Commentary . . .*, 386–387.

"The Legend of Sleepy Hollow"
*Clendenning, John. ". . . Gothic Tradition," 382–383.
*Guttmann, Allen. "Washington Irving and the Conservative Imagination," in
Guttmann, Allen, Ed. . . . *A Century of Commentary . . .*, 395–397.
*Hoffman, Daniel G. "Prefigurations: 'The Legend of Sleepy Hollow,' " in
Myers, Andrew B., Ed. . . . *A Century of Commentary . . .*, 343–355.
*Ringe, Donald A. "New York and New England: Irving's Criticism of American
Society," in Myers, Andrew B., Ed. . . . *A Century of Commentary . . .*,
404–407.
Roth, Martin. *Comedy and America . . .*, 161–168.
Shear, Walter. "Time in 'Rip Van Winkle' and 'The Legend of Sleepy Hol-
low,' " *Midwest Q,* 17 (1976), 158–172.

"Rip Van Winkle"
*Clendenning, John. ". . . Gothic Tradition," 385–386.
*Guttmann, Allen. ". . . Conservative Imagination," 394–395.
Plung, Daniel R. " 'Rip Van Winkle': Metempsychosis and the Quest for
Self-Reliance," *Bull Rocky Mt Mod Lang Assoc,* 31 (1977), 65–80.
*Ringe, Donald A. "New York and New England . . .," 407–410.
Roth, Martin. *Comedy and America . . .*, 155–161.
Shear, Walter. "Time in 'Rip Van Winkle' . . .," 158–172.
*Young, Philip. "Fallen from Time: Rip Van Winkle," in Myers, Andrew B., Ed.
. . . *A Century of Commentary . . .*, 458–479.

"The Spectre Bridegroom"
*Clendenning, John. ". . . Gothic Tradition," 383–384.

"The Story of the Young Robber"
*Clendenning, John. ". . . Gothic Tradition," 381.

CHRISTOPHER ISHERWOOD

"Ambrose"
Piazza, Paul. *Christopher Isherwood . . .*, 131–135.

"The Hero"
Piazza, Paul. *Christopher Isherwood . . .*, 140–141.

"On Ruegen Island"
Piazza, Paul. *Christopher Isherwood . . .*, 93–94.

MANJERI S. ISVARAN

"At His Nativity"
Parameswaran, Uma. "An Indo-English Minstrel: A Study of Manjeri Isvaran's Fiction," *Lit East & West,* 13, i–ii (1969), 45–46.

"Consummation"
Parameswaran, Uma. "An Indo-English Minstrel . . .," 60–61.

"Sivaratri"
Parameswaran, Uma. "An Indo-English Minstrel . . .," 43.

SHIRLEY JACKSON

"After You, My Dear Alphonse"
Friedman, Lenemaja. *Shirley Jackson,* 61–62.

"The Beautiful Stranger"
Friedman, Lenemaja. *Shirley Jackson,* 45–47.

"The Bus"
Friedman, Lenemaja. *Shirley Jackson,* 53–54.

"Charles"
Friedman, Lenemaja. *Shirley Jackson,* 146–147.

"The Daemon Lover" [originally "The Phantom Lover"]
Friedman, Lenemaja. *Shirley Jackson,* 50–51.

"Flower Garden"
Kane, Thomas S., and Leonard J. Peters. *Some Suggestions . . .,* 16–17.

"The Island"
Friedman, Lenemaja. *Shirley Jackson,* 47–49.

"The Little House"
Friedman, Lenemaja. *Shirley Jackson,* 56–57.

"The Lottery"
Abcarian, Richard, and Marvin Klotz. *Instructor's Manual . . .,* 2nd ed., 10–11.
Brinkmann, Horst. "Shirley Jackson, 'The Lottery,' " in Freese, Peter, Ed. . . . *Interpretationen,* 101–109.
Cassill, R. V. *Instructor's Handbook . . .,* 98–99.
Friedman, Lenemaja. *Shirley Jackson,* 63–67.
*Perrine, Laurence. *Instructor's Manual . . . "Story . . .,"* 21–22; *Instructor's Manual . . . "Literature . . .,"* 21–22.

"On the House"
Friedman, Lenemaja. *Shirley Jackson,* 58–59.

"The Possibility of Evil"
  Friedman, Lenemaja. *Shirley Jackson*, 57–58.
  Parks, John G. " 'The Possibility of Evil': A Key to Shirley Jackson's Fiction,"
    Stud Short Fiction, 15 (1978), 320–323.

"The Rock"
  Friedman, Lenemaja. *Shirley Jackson*, 74–75.

"The Summer People"
  Friedman, Lenemaja. *Shirley Jackson*, 55–56.

"The Villager"
  Friedman, Lenemaja. *Shirley Jackson*, 52–53.

"The Visit"
  Friedman, Lenemaja. *Shirley Jackson*, 73–74.

SVAVA JAKOBSDÓTTIR

"Accident"
  Magnusson, Sigurdug. "The Icelandic Short Story: Svava Jakobsdóttir," *Scandinavian Stud*, 49 (1977), 210–212.

HENRY JAMES

"Adina"
  Jones, Granville H. *Henry James's Psychology* . . ., 98–99.
  Mackenzie, Manfred. *Communities of Honor* . . ., 5–8.

"The Altar of the Dead"
  Hartsock, Mildred. "The Most Valuable Thing: James on Death," *Mod Fiction Stud*, 22 (1977), 514–515.
  Jones, Granville H. *Henry James's Psychology* . . ., 276–278.
  Wagenknecht, Edward. *Eve and Henry James* . . ., 192–198.

"The Aspern Papers"
  Crowley, John W. "The Wiles of a 'Witless' Woman: Tina in 'The Aspern Papers,' " *ESQ: J Am Renaissance*, 22 (1976), 159–168.
  Franklin, Rosemary F. "Military Metaphors and the Organic Structure of Henry James's 'The Aspern Papers,' " *Arizona Q*, 32 (1976), 327–340.
  Jones, Granville H. *Henry James's Psychology* . . ., 221–223.
  Mackenzie, Manfred. *Communities of Honor* . . ., 117–119.
  Schneider, Daniel J. "The Unreliable Narrator: James's 'The Aspern Papers' and the Reading of Fiction," *Stud Short Fiction*, 13 (1976), 43–49.
  Tremper, Ellen. "Henry James's Altering Ego: An Examination of His Psychological Double in Three Tales," *Texas Q*, 19, iii (1976), 60–64.

"The Beast in the Jungle"
  Aldaz, Anna M. "Tiger, Tiger Burning Bright: A Study of Theme and Symbol in Henry James' 'The Beast in the Jungle,' " *Instituto Tecnologico de Aeronaut-*

ica Humanidades, 12 (1976), 83–85.

Brooks, Peter. *The Melodramatic Imagination* . . ., 174–175.

Chapman, Sara S. "Stalking the Beast: Egomania and Redemptive Suffering in James's 'Major Phase,' " *Colby Lib Q,* 11 (1975), 50–66.

Crowley, Francis E. "Henry James's 'The Beast in the Jungle' and *The Ambassadors,*" *Psychoanalytic R,* 62 (1975), 154–163.

Dawson, Anthony B. "The Reader and the Measurement of Time in 'The Beast in the Jungle,' " *Engl Stud Canada,* 3 (1977), 458–465.

Haddick, Vern. "Fear and Growth: Reflections on 'The Beast in the Jungle,' " *J Otto Rank Assoc,* 9, ii (1974–75), 38–42.

Jones, Granville H. *Henry James's Psychology* . . ., 278–284.

Jones, O. P. "The Cold World of London in 'The Beast in the Jungle,' " *Stud Am Fiction,* 6 (1978), 227–235.

Krupnick, Mark L. " 'The Beast in the Jungle' and the Dilemma of Narcissus," *Southern R: Australian J Lit Stud,* 9 (1976), 113–120.

Mochi Gioli, Giovanna. " 'The Beast in the Jungle' e l'assenza del referente," *Paragone,* 314 (1976), 51–76.

Nance, William. " 'The Beast in the Jungle': Two Versions of Oedipus," *Stud Short Fiction,* 13 (1976), 433–440.

Tremper, Ellen. "Henry James's Altering Ego . . .," 64–70.

Wagenknecht, Edward. *Eve and Henry James* . . ., 197–202.

"The Beldonald Holbein"

Jones, Granville H. *Henry James's Psychology* . . ., 242–245.

"The Bench of Desolation"

Chapman, Sara S. "Stalking the Beast . . .," 60–66.

Jones, Granville H. *Henry James's Psychology* . . ., 251–254.

Leibowitz, Judith. *Narrative Purposes* . . ., 56–60.

Melicia, Joseph. "Henry James' *Winter's Tale:* 'The Bench of Desolation,' " *Stud Am Fiction,* 6 (1978), 141–156.

Springer, Mary D. . . . *Literary Character,* 45–75.

"Benvolio"

Springer, Mary D. . . . *Literary Character,* 139–159.

"The Birthplace"

Jones, Granville H. *Henry James's Psychology* . . ., 202–204.

McMurray, William. "Reality in Henry James's 'The Birthplace,' " *Explicator,* 35 (1976), 10–11.

"Broken Wings"

Jones, Granville H. *Henry James's Psychology* . . ., 250–251.

"Brooksmith"

Jones, Granville H. *Henry James's Psychology* . . ., 200–201.

"A Bundle of Letters"

Jones, Granville H. *Henry James's Psychology* . . ., 59–60.

"The Chaperon"

Jones, Granville H. *Henry James's Psychology* . . ., 116–117.

"Collaboration"
Jones, Granville H. *Henry James's Psychology* . . ., 146–147.

"Covering End"
Jones, Granville H. *Henry James's Psychology* . . ., 159–161.

"The Coxon Fund"
Jones, Granville H. *Henry James's Psychology* . . ., 239–240.

"Crapy Cornelia"
Jones, Granville H. *Henry James's Psychology* . . ., 257–258.

"Daisy Miller"
Davidson, Cathy N. " 'Circumsexualocution' in Henry James's 'Daisy Miller,' " *Arizona Q,* 32 (1976), 353–366.
Eakin, Paul J. *The New England Girl* . . ., 13–17.
Fryer, Judith. *The Faces of Eve* . . ., 97–101.
Jones, Granville H. *Henry James's Psychology* . . ., 36–39.
Wagenknecht, Edward. *Eve and Henry James* . . ., 3–20.
Wood, Carl. "Frederick Winterbourne, James's Prisoner of Chillon," *Stud Novel,* 9 (1977), 33–45.

"A Day of Days"
Jones, Granville H. *Henry James's Psychology* . . ., 156–157.

"The Death of the Lion"
Jones, Granville H. *Henry James's Psychology* . . ., 199–200.
Mack, Stanley T. "The Narrator in James's 'The Death of the Lion': A Religious Conversion of Sorts," *Thoth,* 16, i (1975–76), 19–25.

"The Diary of a Man of Fifty"
Jones, Granville H. *Henry James's Psychology* . . ., 197–198.

"Eugene Pickering"
Jones, Granville H. *Henry James's Psychology* . . ., 22–24.

"The Figure in the Carpet"
Boland, Dorothy M. "Henry James's 'The Figure in the Carpet': A Fabric of the East," *Papers Lang & Lit,* 13 (1977), 424–429.
Jones, Granville H. *Henry James's Psychology* . . ., 234–236.
Rimmon, Shlomith. *The Concept of Ambiguity* . . ., 95–115.

"Flickerbridge"
Jones, Granville H. *Henry James's Psychology* . . ., 218–221.

"Fordham Castle"
Jones, Granville H. *Henry James's Psychology* . . ., 205–206.

"Four Meetings"
Jones, Granville H. *Henry James's Psychology* . . ., 114–115.
Seamon, Roger. "Henry James's 'Four Meetings': A Study in Irritability and Condescension," *Stud Short Fiction,* 15 (1978), 155–163.

"The Friends of the Friends"
  Jones, Granville H. *Henry James's Psychology* . . ., 61–62.
  Shelden, Pamela J. " 'The Friends of the Friends': Another Twist to 'The Turn
    of the Screw,' " *Wascana R,* 2, i (1976), 3–14.

"Georgina's Reasons"
  Jones, Granville H. *Henry James's Psychology* . . ., 101–102.

"Glasses"
  Jones, Granville H. *Henry James's Psychology* . . ., 62–63.

"The Great Good Place"
  Jones, Granville H. *Henry James's Psychology* . . ., 233–234.
  McMurray, William. "Reality in James's 'The Great Good Place,' " *Stud Short
    Fiction,* 14 (1977), 82–83.

"Greville Fane"
  Jones, Granville H. *Henry James's Psychology* . . ., 19–20.

"Guest's Confession"
  Jones, Granville H. *Henry James's Psychology* . . ., 99–100.

"The Impressions of a Cousin"
  Jones, Granville H. *Henry James's Psychology* . . ., 123–124.

"In the Cage"
  Jones, Granville H. *Henry James's Psychology* . . ., 131–133.
  Norrman, Ralf. "The Intercepted Telegram Plot in Henry James's 'In the
    Cage,' " *Notes & Queries,* 24 (1977), 424–427.

"An International Episode"
  Jones, Granville H. *Henry James's Psychology* . . ., 55–56.

"John Delavoy"
  Jones, Granville H. *Henry James's Psychology* . . ., 236–237.

"The Jolly Corner"
  Byers, John R. "Alice Stapleton's Redemption of Spencer Brydon in James'
    'The Jolly Corner,' " *So Atlantic Bull,* 41, ii (1976), 90–99.
  Chapman, Sara S. "Stalking the Beast . . .," 56–60.
  Grenander, M.E. "Benjamin Franklin's Glass Armonica and Henry James'
    'Jolly Corner,' " *Papers Lang & Lit,* 11 (1975), 415–417.
  Jones, Granville H. *Henry James's Psychology* . . ., 254–257.
  *Mackenzie, Manfred. *Communities of Honor* . . ., 45–51.
  Purdy, Strother B. *The Hole in the Fabric* . . ., 49–55.
  Rosenblatt, Jason P. "Bridegroom and Bride in 'The Jolly Corner,' " *Stud Short
    Fiction,* 14 (1977), 282–284.
  Schneider, Daniel J. *The Crystal Cage* . . ., 32–33.
  Springer, Mary D. . . . *Literary Character,* 115–125.
  Tremper, Ellen. "Henry James's Altering Ego . . .," 70–74.
  Unrue, Darlene. "Henry James and the Grotesque," *Arizona Q,* 32 (1976),
    299–300.
  Wagenknecht, Edward. *Eve and Henry James* . . ., 202–207.

"Julia Bride"
  Jones, Granville H. *Henry James's Psychology* . . ., 117–119.

"The Last of the Valerii"
  Unrue, Darlene. ". . . Grotesque," 296–297.

"The Lesson of the Master"
  Barry, Peter. "In Fairness to the Master's Wife: A Re-interpretation of 'The
    Lesson of the Master,' " *Stud Short Fiction,* 15 (1978), 385–389.
  Jones, Granville H. *Henry James's Psychology* . . ., 144–146.
  Mackenzie, Manfred. *Communities of Honor* . . ., 66–70.
  Rimmon, Shlomith. *The Concept of Ambiguity* . . ., 79–94.
  Tintner, Adeline R. "Iconic Analogy in 'The Lesson of the Master': Henry
    James's Legend of St. George and the Dragon," *J Narrative Technique,* 5
    (1975), 116–127.

"The Liar"
  Jones, Granville H. *Henry James's Psychology* . . ., 196–197.

"Louise Pallant"
  Jones, Granville H. *Henry James's Psychology* . . ., 94–95.

"Madame de Mauves"
  Jones, Granville H. *Henry James's Psychology* . . ., 51–55.
  Wagenknecht, Edward. *Eve and Henry James* . . ., 21–34.

"The Madonna of the Future"
  Jones, Granville H. *Henry James's Psychology* . . ., 198–199.

"The Marriages"
  Jones, Granville H. *Henry James's Psychology* . . ., 109–110.

"Master Eustace"
  Jones, Granville H. *Henry James's Psychology* . . ., 18–19.

"Maud-Evelyn"
  Hartsock, Mildred. "The Most Valuable Thing . . .," 516.
  Jones, Granville H. *Henry James's Psychology* . . ., 135–136.

"The Middle Years"
  Babin, James L. "Henry James's 'Middle Years' in Fiction and Autobiog-
    raphy," *Southern R,* 13 (1977), 505–517.
  Lycette, Ronald L. "Perceptual Touchstones for the Jamesian Artist-Hero,"
    Stud Short Fiction, 14 (1977), 60–62.
  Mackenzie, Manfred. *Communities of Honor* . . ., 107–110.

"Mrs. Medwin"
  Jones, Granville H. *Henry James's Psychology* . . ., 238–239.

"Mrs. Temperly"
  Jones, Granville H. *Henry James's Psychology* . . ., 113–114.

"The Modern Warning"
Jones, Granville H. *Henry James's Psychology* . . ., 110–111.

"Mora Montravers"
Jones, Granville H. *Henry James's Psychology* . . ., 154–156.

"A New England Winter"
Jones, Granville H. *Henry James's Psychology* . . ., 245–246.

"Owen Wingrave"
Jones, Granville H. *Henry James's Psychology* . . ., 115–116.

"Pandora"
Mackenzie, Manfred. *Communities of Honor* . . ., 29–34.

"The Papers"
Jones, Granville H. *Henry James's Psychology* . . ., 133–135.
Stycznska, Adela. " 'The Papers': James' Satire on the Modern Publicity System," *Kwartalnik Neofilologiczny,* 22 (1975), 419–436.

"A Passionate Pilgrim"
Jones, Granville H. *Henry James's Psychology* . . ., 206–207.
Mackenzie, Manfred. *Communities of Honor* . . ., 44–45.

"Paste"
Jones, Granville H. *Henry James's Psychology* . . ., 92–93.

"The Patagonia"
Jones, Granville H. *Henry James's Psychology* . . ., 112–113.

"The Path of Duty"
Jones, Granville H. *Henry James's Psychology* . . ., 121–122.

"The Pension Beaurepas"
Jones, Granville H. *Henry James's Psychology* . . ., 59.

"The Point of View"
Jones, Granville H. *Henry James's Psychology* . . ., 59–60.
Watson, Charles N. "The Comedy of Provincialism: James's 'The Point of View,' " *Southern Hum R,* 9 (1975), 173–183.

"Poor Richard"
Jones, Granville H. *Henry James's Psychology* . . ., 63–64.

"Professor Fargo"
Jones, Granville H. *Henry James's Psychology* . . ., 24–25.

"The Pupil"
Eggenschwiler, David. "James's 'The Pupil': A Moral Tale Without a Moral," *Stud Short Fiction,* 15 (1978), 435–444.
*Howe, Irving, Ed. *Classics of Modern Fiction* . . ., 2nd ed., 179–187.

Jones, Granville H. *Henry James's Psychology* . . ., 10–12.
Mackenzie, Manfred. *Communities of Honor* . . ., 110–114.
Rucker, Mary E. "James's 'The Pupil': The Question of Moral Ambiguity,"
  Arizona Q, 32 (1976), 301–315.

"The Real Thing"
Jones, Granville H. *Henry James's Psychology* . . ., 201–202.
Leibowitz, Judith. *Narrative Purposes* . . ., 46–48.
Lester, Pauline. "James's Use of Comedy in 'The Real Thing,' " *Stud Short
  Fiction,* 15 (1978), 33–38.
Lycette, Ronald L. "Perceptual Touchstones . . .," 57–60.
*Sundell, Roger H. " 'The Real Thing,' " in Dietrich, R.F., and Roger H.
  Sundell. *Instructor's Manual* . . ., 3rd ed., 11–16.

"A Romance of Certain Old Clothes"
Mackenzie, Manfred. *Communities of Honor* . . ., 35–36.

"Rose-Agathe"
Jones, Granville H. *Henry James's Psychology* . . ., 147–148.

"Sir Edmund Orme"
Jones, Granville H. *Henry James's Psychology* . . ., 104–105.

"The Solution"
Jones, Granville H. *Henry James's Psychology* . . ., 125–126.

"The Story in It"
Gargano, James W. "James's Stories in 'The Story in It,' " *Notes Mod Am Lit,*
  1, i (1976), Item 2.

"The Story of a Year"
Jones, Granville H. *Henry James's Psychology* . . ., 60–61.

"The Tone of Time"
Jones, Granville H. *Henry James's Psychology* . . ., 204–205.

"Travelling Companions"
Jones, Granville H. *Henry James's Psychology* . . ., 58–59.

"The Tree of Knowledge"
Cassill, R.V. *Instructor's Handbook* . . ., 99–101.

"The Turn of the Screw"
Beit-Hallahmi, Benjamin. " 'The Turn of the Screw' and *The Exorcist*: Demo-
  niacal Possession and Childhood Purity," *Am Imago,* 33 (1976), 296–303.
Bengels, Barbara. "The Term of the 'Screw': Key to Imagery in Henry James's
  'The Turn of the Screw,' " *Stud Short Fiction,* 15 (1978), 323–327.
Bersani, Leo. *A Future for Astynax* . . ., 139–141.
Brooks, Peter. *The Melodramatic Imagination* . . ., 166–168.
Brown, Bernadine. " 'The Turn of the Screw': A Case of Romantic Displace-
  ment," *Nassau R,* 2, v (1974), 75–82.
Clark, Susan. "A Note on 'The Turn of the Screw': Death from Natural
  Causes," *Stud Short Fiction,* 15 (1978), 110–112.

Dyson, J. Peter. "James' 'The Turn of the Screw,' " *Explicator,* 36, iii (1978), 9.

Felman, Shoshana. "Turning the Screw of Interpretation," *Yale French Stud,* 55/56 (1977), 94–207.

Hallab, Mary Y. " 'The Turn of the Screw' Squared," *Southern R,* 13 (1977), 492–504.

Hartsock, Mildred. "The Most Valuable Thing . . .," 519.

Houston, Neal B. "A Footnote to the Death of Miles," *RE: Artes Liberales,* 3, ii (1977), 25–27.

Huntley, H. Robert. "James' 'The Turn of the Screw': Its 'Fine Machinery,' " *Am Imago,* 34 (1977), 224–237.

Jones, Granville H. *Henry James's Psychology* . . ., 12–17.

Mackenzie, Manfred. *Communities of Honor* . . ., 78–87.

Murphy, Kevin. "The Unfixable Text: Bewilderment of Vision in 'The Turn of the Screw,' " *Texas Stud Lit & Lang,* 20 (1978), 538–551.

Obuchowski, Peter A. "Technique and Meaning in James's 'The Turn of the Screw,' " *Coll Lang Assoc J,* 21 (1978), 380–389.

Purdy, Strother B. *The Hole in the Fabric* . . ., 149–159.

Rimmon, Shlomith. *The Concept of Ambiguity* . . ., 116–166.

Shelden, Pamela J. ". . . Another Twist to 'The Turn of the Screw,' " 3–14.

Springer, Mary D. . . . *Literary Character,* 89–112.

Stepp, Walter. " 'The Turn of the Screw': If Douglas Is Miles . . .," *Nassau R,* 3, ii (1976), 76–82.

Weinstein, Arnold L. *Vision and Response* . . ., 75–90.

"The Two Faces"
Jones, Granville H. *Henry James's Psychology* . . ., 93–94.

"The Velvet Glove"
Jones, Granville H. *Henry James's Psychology* . . ., 230–233.

"Washington Square"
Gargano, James W. " 'Washington Square': A Study in the Growth of an Inner Self," *Stud Short Fiction,* 13 (1976), 355–362.
Jones, Granville H. *Henry James's Psychology* . . ., 106–108.
Springer, Mary D. . . . *Literary Character,* 77–89.

JOHN E. JENKINS

"Ginx's Baby"
Kinnane, G. C. "A Popular Victorian Satire: 'Ginx's Baby' and Its Reception," *Notes & Queries,* 22 (1975), 116–117.

SARAH ORNE JEWETT

"A White Heron"
Brenzo, Richard. "Free Heron or Dead Sparrow: Sylvia's Choice in Sarah Orne Jewett's 'A White Heron,' " *Colby Lib Q,* 14 (1978), 36–41.
Ellis, James. "The World of Dreams: Sexual Symbols in 'A White Heron,' " *Nassau R,* 3, iii (1977), 3–9.

Hovet, Theodore R. "America's 'Lonely Country Child': The Theme of Separation in Sarah Orne Jewett's 'A White Heron,' " *Colby Lib Q*, 15 (1978), 166–171.

————. " 'Once Upon a Time': Sarah Orne Jewett's 'A White Heron' as a Fairy Tale," *Stud Short Fiction*, 15 (1978), 63–68.

Stevenson, Catherine B. "The Double Consciousness of the Narrator in Sarah Orne Jewett's Fiction," *Colby Lib Q*, 11 (1975), 3–6.

RICHARD MALCOLM JOHNSTON

"The Expensive Treat of Colonel Moses Grice"
Hitchcock, Bert. *Richard Malcolm Johnston*, 57–61.

"The Goosepond School"
Hitchcock, Bert. *Richard Malcolm Johnston*, 50–53.

"How Mr. Bill Williams Took the Responsibility"
Hitchcock, Bert. *Richard Malcolm Johnston*, 53–57.

"Mr. Fortner's Marital Claims"
Hitchcock, Bert. *Richard Malcolm Johnston*, 77–78.

"Mr. Neelus Peeler's Conditions"
Hitchcock, Bert. *Richard Malcolm Johnston*, 63–64.

"Mr. Williamson Slippey and His Salt"
Hitchcock, Bert. *Richard Malcolm Johnston*, 62.

GAYL JONES

"White Rat"
Cassill, R. V. *Instructor's Handbook . . .*, 102.

JAMES JOYCE

"After the Race"
Peake, C. H. *James Joyce . . .*, 23–25.

"Araby"
*Abcarian, Richard, and Marvin Klotz, Eds. *Literature . . .*, 2nd ed., 1191–1195.

Brugaletta, John J., and Mary H. Hayden. "The Motivation for Anguish in Joyce's 'Araby,' " *Stud Short Fiction*, 15 (1978), 11–17.

Cassill, R. V. *Instructor's Handbook . . .*, 103–104.

Morse, Donald E. " 'Sing a Song of Araby': Theme and Allusion in Joyce's 'Araby,' " *Coll Lit*, 5 (1978), 125–132.

Peake, C. H. *James Joyce . . .*, 19–21.

Rosowski, Susan J. "Joyce's 'Araby' and Imaginative Freedom," *Research Stud*, 44 (1976), 183–188.

Skau, Michael, and Donald L. Cassidy. "Joyce's 'Araby,' " *Explicator*, 35, ii (1976), 5–6.

"The Boarding House"
Peake, C. H. *James Joyce . . .*, 26–28.

"Clay"
Bernhart, Walter. " 'Human Nature's Intricacies' und 'Rigorous Truth': Joyces 'Clay,' Becketts 'Dante and the Lobster,' und die Individuation (I)," *Arbeiten aus Anglistik und Amerikanistik*, 1 (1976), 39–61.
Kennedy, X. J. *Instructor's Manual . . .*, 5–6.
Nebeker, H. E. "James Joyce's 'Clay': The Well-Wrought Urn," *Renascence*, 28 (1976), 123–138.
Peake, C. H. *James Joyce . . .*, 32–33.
*Sundell, Roger H. " 'Clay,' " in Dietrich, R. H., and Roger H. Sundell. *Instructor's Manual . . .*, 3rd ed., 88–92.

"Counterparts"
Benstock, Bernard. "Joyce's Rheumatics: The Holy Ghost in *Dubliners*," *Southern R*, 14 (1978), 6–7, 10.
Peake, C. H. *James Joyce . . .*, 31–32.

"The Dead"
Benstock, Bernard. "Joyce's Rheumatics . . .," 7–8, 14–15.
Cassill, R. V. *Instructor's Handbook . . .*, 106–111.
MacNicholas, John. "Comic Design in Joyce's 'The Dead,' " *Mod Brit Lit*, 1 (1976), 56–65.
Peake, C. H. *James Joyce . . .*, 45–55.

"An Encounter"
Kimmey, John L. *Instructor's Manual . . .*, 10–12.
Leatherwood, A. M. "Joyce's Mythic Method: Structure and Unity in 'An Encounter,' " *Stud Short Fiction*, 13 (1976), 71–78.
Peake, C. H. *James Joyce . . .*, 16–19.

"Eveline"
Dilworth, Thomas. "The Numina of Joyce's 'Eveline,' " *Stud Short Fiction*, 15 (1978), 456–458.
Peake, C. H. *James Joyce . . .*, 21–23.
Rollins, Ronald, and Michael Coran. "Eden as Field and Fortress: A Note on Joyce's 'Eveline,' " *Mod Brit Lit*, 3 (1978), 78–79.

"Grace"
Benstock, Bernard. "Joyce's Rheumatics . . .," 4–6.
Peake, C. H. *James Joyce . . .*, 41–44.

"Ivy Day in the Committee Room"
Peake, C. H. *James Joyce . . .*, 37–39.

"A Little Cloud"
Cassill, R. V. *Instructor's Handbook . . .*, 105–106.
Peake, C. H. *James Joyce . . .*, 28–31.

"A Mother"
   Peake, C. H. *James Joyce* . . ., 39–41.

"A Painful Case"
   Peake, C. H. *James Joyce* . . ., 33–37.
   West, Michael, and William Hendricks. "The Genesis and Significance of Joyce's Irony in 'A Painful Case,' " *Engl Lit Hist*, 44 (1977), 701–727.

"The Sisters"
   Benstock, Bernard. "Joyce's Rheumatics . . .," 2–4.
   Peake, C. H. *James Joyce* . . ., 10–16.

"Two Gallants"
   Kane, Thomas S., and Leonard J. Peters. *Some Suggestions* . . ., 27–29.

FRANZ KAFKA

"Blumfeld, An Elderly Bachelor"
   Fickert, Kurt J. "The *Doppelgänger* Motif in Kafka's 'Blumfeld,' " *J Mod Lit*, 6 (1977), 419–423.

"The Burrow"
   Sussman, Henry. "The All-Embracing Metaphor: Reflections on Kafka's 'The Burrow,' " *Glyph*, 1 (1977), 100–131.

"The Cares of a Family Man"
   Fickert, Kurt J. "Symbol and Myth: Kafka's 'A Father's Concern,' " *Germ Notes*, 6, iv (1975), 59–62.
   Sasse, Günter. "Die Sorge des Lesers: Zu Kafkas Erzählung 'Die Sorge des Hausvaters,' " *Poetica*, 10 (1978), 262–284.

"A Country Doctor"
   Birch, Joan M. "What Happened to the Doctor in Kafka's 'Ein Landarzt,' " *Mod Austrian Lit*, 9, i (1976), 13–25.
   Brancato, John J. "Kafka's 'A Country Doctor': A Tale for Our Time," *Stud Short Fiction*, 15 (1978), 173–176.
   Cohn, Dorrit. *Transparent Minds* . . ., 199–203.
   Fickert, Kurt J. "Fatal Knowledge: Kafka's 'Ein Landarzt,' " *Monatshefte*, 66 (1974), 381–386.
   Hanlin, Todd C. "Franz Kafka's 'Landarzt': 'Und heilt er nicht . . .,' " *Mod Austrian Lit*, 11, iii–iv (1978), 333–344.
   Spann, Meno. *Franz Kafka*, 125–130.
   *Timko, Michael. "Kafka's 'A Country Doctor,' Williams' 'The Use of Force,' and White's 'The Second Tree from the Corner,' " in Timko, Michael, Ed. *38 Short Stories*, 2nd ed., 692–706.

"A Fratricide"
   Wolkenfeld, Suzanne. "Psychological Disintegration in Kafka's 'A Fratricide' and 'An Old Manuscript,' " *Stud Short Fiction*, 13 (1976), 27–28.

"The Great Wall of China"
   Goodden, Christian. "The Great Wall of China: The Elaboration of an Intel-

lectual Dilemma," in Kuna, Franz, Ed. . . . *Perspectives*, 128–145.
Rolleston, James. *Kafka's Narrative Theater*, 109–111.

"A Hunger Artist"
    Cassill, R. V. *Instructor's Handbook* . . ., 113–114.
    Norris, Margot. "Sadism and Masochism in Two Kafka Stories: 'In der Straf-kolonie' and 'Ein Hungerkünstler,' " *Mod Lang Notes*, 93 (1978), 430–447.
    Perrine, Laurence. *Instructor's Manual* . . . "*Story* . . .," 42–45; *Instructor's Manual* . . . "*Literature* . . .," 42–45.
    Spann, Meno. *Franz Kafka*, 164–167.

"The Hunter Gracchus"
    Haase, Donald P. "Kafka's 'Der Jäger Gracchus': Fragment or Figment of the Imagination?" *Mod Austrian Lit*, 11, iii–iv (1978), 319–332.
    Ternes, Hans. "Franz Kafka's 'Hunter Gracchus': An Interpretation," in Sokel, Walter H., Albert A. Kipa, and Hans Ternes, Eds. *Probleme der Komparatistik* . . ., 216–223.

"In the Gallery"
    Reschke, Claus. "The Problem of Reality in Kafka's 'Auf der Galerie,' " *Germ R*, 51 (1976), 41–51.
    Spann, Meno. *Franz Kafka*, 122–124.

"In the Penal Colony"
    Dolan, Paul J. *Of War and War's Alarms* . . ., 125–144.
    Norris, Margot. "Sadism and Masochism . . .," 430–447.
    Pasley, Malcolm. " 'In the Penal Colony,' " in Flores, Angel, Ed. *The Kafka Debate* . . ., 298–303.
    Rolleston, James. *Kafka's Narrative Theater*, 88–100.
    Spann, Meno. *Franz Kafka*, 108–119.
    Steinberg, Erwin R. "The Judgment in Kafka's 'In the Penal Colony,' " *J Mod Lit*, 5 (1976), 492–514.
    Thieberger, Richard. "The Botched Ending of 'In the Penal Colony,' " in Flores, Angel, Ed. *The Kafka Debate* . . ., 304–310.

"Investigations of a Dog"
    Spann, Meno. *Franz Kafka*, 167–169.

"Josephine the Singer"
    Mahldendorf, Ursula R. "Kafka's 'Josephine the Singer or the Mousefolk': Art at the Edge of Nothingness," *Mod Austrian Lit*, 11, iii–iv (1978), 199–242.
    Nicolai, Ralf R. "Kafka's 'Josefine'—Erzählung im Lichte Dreistufigkeit," *Studi Germanici*, 12 (1974), 273–290.
    Rolleston, James. *Kafka's Narrative Theater*, 130–139.
    Sattler, Emil E. "Narrative Stance in Kafka's 'Josephine,' " *J Mod Lit*, 6 (1977), 410–418.

"The Judgment"
    Bernheimer, Charles. "Letters to an Absent Friend: A Structural Reading," in Flores, Angel, Ed. *The Problem of "The Judgment"* . . ., 146–167.
    Corngold, Stanley. "The Hermeneutic of 'The Judgment,' " in Flores, Angel, Ed. *The Problem of "The Judgment"* . . ., 39–62.

*Ellis, John M. "The Bizarre Texture of 'The Judgment,' " in Flores, Angel, Ed. *The Problem of "The Judgment"* . . ., 73–96.

Flores, Kate. "The Pathos of Fatherhood," in Flores, Angel, Ed. *The Problem of "The Judgment"* . . ., 168–192; rpt. Flores, Angel, Ed. *The Kafka Debate* . . ., 254–272.

Goldstein, Bluma. "Bachelors and Work: Social and Economic Conditions in 'The Judgment,' 'The Metamorphosis,' and *The Trial,*" in Flores, Angel, Ed. *The Kafka Debate* . . ., 148–154.

*Gray, Ronald. "Through Dream to Self-Awareness," in Flores, Angel, Ed. *The Problem of "The Judgment"* . . ., 63–72.

Levine, Robert T. "The Familiar Friend: A Freudian Approach to Kafka's 'The Judgment,' " *Lit & Psych,* 27 (1977), 164–173.

Neumann, E. "Franz Kafka: 'The Judgment'—A Depth Psychological Interpretation," *Analytische Psychologie,* 5 (1974), 252–306.

Oellers, Norbert. "Die Bestrafung der Söhne: Zu Kafkas Erzählungen 'Das Urteil,' 'Der Heizer,' und 'Die Verwandlung,' " *Zeitschrift für Deutsche Philologie,* 97, Special Issue (1978), 74–79.

Rolleston, James. *Kafka's Narrative Theater,* 42–51; rpt. Flores, Angel, Ed. *The Problem of "The Judgment"* . . ., 131–145.

Sokel, Walter H. "Perspectives and Truth in 'The Judgment,' " in Flores, Angel, Ed. *The Problem of "The Judgment"* . . ., 193–237.

Spann, Meno. *Franz Kafka,* 50–63.

Sparks, Kimberly. "Radicalization of Space in Kafka's Stories," in Kuna, Franz, Ed. . . . *Perspectives,* 121–126.

Stern, J. P. "Guilt and the Feeling of Guilt," in Flores, Angel, Ed. *The Problem of "The Judgment"* . . ., 114–132.

White, John J. "Georg Bendemann's Friend in Russia: Symbolic Correspondence," in Flores, Angel, Ed. *The Problem of "The Judgment"* . . ., 97–113.

"Metamorphosis"

Abcarian, Richard, and Marvin Klotz. *Instructor's Manual* . . ., 2nd ed., 11–13.

Cantrell, Carol H. " 'The Metamorphosis': Kafka's Study of a Family," *Mod Fiction Stud,* 23 (1977), 578–586.

Cassill, R. V. *Instructor's Handbook* . . ., 115–118.

Currie, Robert. *Genius* . . ., 147–149.

*Douglas, Kenneth, and Sarah N. Lawall. "Masterpieces of the Modern World," in Mack, Maynard, *et al.,* Eds. . . . *World Masterpieces,* II, 4th ed., 1261.

Goldstein, Bluma. "Bachelors and Work . . .," 154–159.

*Howe, Irving, Ed. *Classics of Modern Fiction* . . ., 2nd ed., 401–409.

Irwin, W. R. . . . *The Rhetoric of Fantasy,* 81–88.

Kimmey, John L. *Instructor's Manual* . . ., 30–32.

Oellers, Norbert. "Die Bestrafung . . .," 83–87.

Rolleston, James. *Kafka's Narrative Theater,* 52–68.

Spann, Meno. *Franz Kafka,* 63–74.

"The New Advocate"

Spann, Meno. *Franz Kafka,* 121–122.

"A Report to an Academy"

Emrich, Wilhelm. "Franz Kafkas 'Menschen und Tiergericht': Zu Erzählung 'Ein Bericht für eine Akademie,' " *Mod Austrian Lit,* 11, iii–iv (1978), 151–166.

Spann, Meno. *Franz Kafka,* 124–125.

"The Silence of the Sirens"
  Struc, Roman S. " 'Negative Capability' and Kafka's Protagonists," *Mod Austrian Lit,* 11, iii (1978), 100–101.

"The Stoker"
  Oellers, Norbert. "Die Bestrafung . . .," 80–83.
  Rolleston, James. *Kafka's Narrative Theater,* 18–31.

"The Village Schoolteacher"
  Rolleston, James. *Kafka's Narrative Theater,* 104–109.

KAWABATA YASUNARI

"A Man Who Does Not Smile"
  Ueda, Makoto. *Modern Japanese Writers . . .,* 216–218.

DAVID KELLER

"The Menace"
  Moskowitz, Sam. *Strange Horizons . . .,* 139–140.

"The Revolt of the Pedestrians"
  Moskowitz, Sam. *Strange Horizons . . .,* 109–110.

GOTTFRIED KELLER

"Clothes Make the Man"
  Leibowitz, Judith. *Narrative Purposes . . .,* 30–31.

"The Three Righteous Comb-Makers"
  Swales, Martin. *The German "Novelle,"* 158–179.

"A Village Romeo and Juliet"
  Dickerson, Harold D. "The Music of *This* Sphere in Keller's 'Romeo und Julia auf dem Dorfe,' " *Germ Q,* 51 (1978), 47–56.

WILLIAM MELVIN KELLEY

"The Poker Party"
  Galloway, David. "William Melvin Kelley: 'The Poker Party,' " in Bruck, Peter, Ed. *The Black American Short Story . . .,* 135–139.

DANIEL KEYES

"Flowers for Algernon"
  Perrine, Laurence. *Instructor's Manual . . . "Story . . .,"* 35–37; *Instructor's Manual . . . "Literature . . .,"* 35–37.

LEONARD KIBERA

"It's a Dog's Share in Our Kinshasa"
Roscoe, Adrian. *Uhuru's Fire* . . ., 195–197.

"Silent Song"
Roscoe, Adrian. *Uhuru's Fire* . . ., 193–194.

"The Stranger"
Roscoe, Adrian. *Uhuru's Fire* . . ., 197–200.

"The Tailor"
Roscoe, Adrian. *Uhuru's Fire* . . ., 200–201.

RUDYARD KIPLING

"Below the Mill Dam"
Wilson, Angus. *The Strange Ride* . . ., 244–245.

"The Church That Was at Antioch"
Wilson, Angus. *The Strange Ride* . . ., 337–340.

"The Comprehension of Private Copper"
Wilson, Angus. *The Strange Ride* . . ., 218–220.

"Dayspring Mishandled"
Wilson, Angus. *The Strange Ride* . . ., 336–337.

"The Dog Hervey"
Wilson, Angus. *The Strange Ride* . . ., 268–269.

"The Friendly Brook"
Wilson, Angus. *The Strange Ride* . . ., 283–284.

"The Gardener"
Newsom, G. H. "Ways of Looking at 'The Gardener,' " *Kipling J*, No. 205 (1978), 5–10.
Wilson, Angus. *The Strange Ride* . . ., 316–318.

"An Habitation Enforced"
Wilson, Angus. *The Strange Ride* . . ., 281–282.

"The House Surgeon"
Coates, John. "Religious Cross Currents in 'The House of Surgeons,' " *Kipling J*, No. 207 (1978), 2–7.
Wilson, Angus. *The Strange Ride* . . ., 268.

"In the Same Boat"
Wilson, Angus. *The Strange Ride* . . ., 268–269.

"The Madonna of the Trenches"
Wilson, Angus. *The Strange Ride* . . ., 314–315.

"The Man Who Would Be King"
Beliappa, K.C. "Kipling's 'The Man Who Would Be King': A Parable of Empire Building," *Commonwealth Q*, 2, viii (1978), 27–33.

"Mary Postgate"
Firchow, Peter E. "Kipling's 'Mary Postgate': The Barbarians and the Critics," *Études Anglaises*, 29 (1976), 27–39.
Wilson, Angus. *The Strange Ride* . . ., 309–312.

"Mrs. Bathurst"
Wilson, Angus. *The Strange Ride* . . ., 221–223.

"My Son's Wife"
Wilson, Angus. *The Strange Ride* . . ., 282–283.

"The Puzzler"
Wilson, Angus. *The Strange Ride* . . ., 251–252.

"Sea Constable"
Wilson, Angus. *The Strange Ride* . . ., 312–313.

"The Strange Ride of Morrowbie Jukes"
Goonetilleke, D.C.R.A. *Developing Countries* . . ., 137–139.
Wilson, Angus. *The Strange Ride* . . ., 71–72.

"Swept and Garnished"
Wilson, Angus. *The Strange Ride* . . ., 308–309.

"They"
Wilson, Angus. *The Strange Ride* . . ., 264–266.

"Unprofessional"
Wilson, Angus. *The Strange Ride* . . ., 332–333.

"The Vortex"
Wilson, Angus. *The Strange Ride* . . ., 252–253.

"A Wayside Comedy"
Wilson, Angus. *The Strange Ride* . . ., 72–73.

"The Wish House"
Wilson, Angus. *The Strange Ride* . . ., 286–288.

"The Woman in His Life"
Wilson, Angus. *The Strange Ride* . . ., 313–314.

HEINRICH VON KLEIST

"The Beggar Woman of Locarno"
Dyer, Denys. *The Stories of Kleist* . . ., 80–87.
Schmidt, Siegfried J. "Interpretationsanalyse von E. Staiger: Heinrich von Kleists 'Das Bettelweib von Locarno,' " in Kindt, Walther, and Siegfried J.

Schmidt, Eds. *Interpretationsanalysen* . . ., 93–104.

Schröer, Jürgen. " 'Das Bettelweib von Locarno': Zum Gespenstichen in den Novellen Heinrich von Kleists," *Germanisch-Romanische Monatsschrift*, 48 (1967), 193–207.

Werlich, Egon. "Kleists 'Bettelweib von Locarno': Versuch einer Aufwerfung des Gehalts," *Wirkendes Wort*, 15 (1965), 239–257.

"The Duel"

Dyer, Denys. *The Stories of Kleist* . . ., 170–194.

Ellis, John M. "Kleist's 'Der Zweikampf,' " *Monatshefte*, 65 (1973), 48–60.

Grawe, Christian. "Zur Deutung von Kleists Novelle 'Der Zweikampf,' " *Germanische-Romanische Monatsschrift*, 27 (1977), 416–425.

Martin, George M. "The Apparent Ambiguity of Kleist's Stories," *Germ Life & Letters*, 31 (1978), 154–155.

Mommsen, Katharina. "Kleist's Duel Story as 'Erlebnisdichtung,' " *Carleton Germ Papers*, 2 (1974), 49–66.

Oppel, Horst. "Kleists Novelle 'Der Zweikampf,' " *Deutsche Vierteljahrsschrift*, 22 (1944), 92–105.

"The Earthquake in Chile"

Dyer, Denys. *The Stories of Kleist* . . ., 13–30.

Fitschen, Irmela. "Antithetische Züge in Kleists Erzählung 'Das Erdbeben in Chili,' " *Acta Germanica*, 8 (1973), 43–58.

Graham, Ilse. . . . *Quest for the Symbol*, 159–167.

Johnson, Richard L. "Kleist's 'Erdbeben in Chili,' " *Seminar*, 11 (1975), 33–45.

Lorenz, Dagmar C.G. "Vater und Mutter in der Sozialstruktur von Kleists 'Erdbeben in Chili,' " *Études Germaniques*, 33 (1978), 270–281.

Lucas, R.S. "Studies in Kleist," *Deutsche Vierteljahrsschrift*, 44 (1970), 145–170.

Martin, George M. "The Apparent Ambiguity . . .," 145–147.

Thayer, Terence K. "Kleist's Don Fernando and 'Das Erdbeben in Chili,' " *Colloquia Germanica*, 11 (1978), 263–288.

"The Engagement in Santo Domingo"

Dyer, Denys. *The Stories of Kleist* . . ., 31–47.

Gilman, Sander L. "The Aesthetics of Blackness in Heinrich von Kleist's 'Die Verlobung in St. Domingo,' " *Mod Lang Notes*, 90 (1975), 661–672.

Graham, Ilse. . . . *Quest for the Symbol*, 128–134.

Martin, George M. "The Apparent Ambiguity . . .," 152–154.

"The Foundling"

Dyer, Denys. *The Stories of Kleist* . . ., 48–59.

Hoffmeister, Werner. "Heinrich von Kleists 'Findling,' " *Monatshefte*, 58 (1966), 49–63.

Moore, Erna. "Heinrich von Kleists 'Findling': Psychologie des Verhängnisses," *Colloquia Germanica*, 8 (1974), 275–297.

Parkes, Ford B. "Shifting Narrative Perspectives in Kleist's 'Findling,' " *J Engl & Germ Philol*, 76 (1977), 165–176.

Reinhardt, George W. "Turbulence and Enigma in Kleist's 'Der Findling,' " *Essays Lit* (Western Illinois), 4 (1977), 265–274.

Ryder, Frank G. "Kleist's 'Findling': Oedipus *manqué?" Mod Lang Notes,* 92 (1977), 509–524.

"The Marquise of O—"
Blankenagel, J.C. "Heinrich von Kleists 'Marquise von O—,' " *Germ R,* 6 (1931), 363–372.
Blume, Bernhard. "The Marquise of O—'s Knitting: A New Look at Kleist's Novella," *Boston Univ J,* 26, ii (1978), 45–49.
Cohn, Dorrit. "Kleist's 'Marquise von O—': The Problem of Knowledge," *Monatshefte,* 67 (1975), 129–144.
Dyer, Denys. *The Stories of Kleist* . . . , 60–79.
Gelus, Marjorie. "Laughter and Joking in the Works of Heinrich von Kleist," *Germ Q,* 50 (1977), 453–458.
Politzer, Heinz. "Der Fall der Frau Marquise: Beobachtungen zu Kleists 'Die Marquise von O—,' " *Deutsche Vierteljahrsschrift,* 51 (1977), 98–128.
Swales, Erika. "The Beleaguered Citadel: A Study of Kleist's 'Die Marquise von O—,' " *Deutsche Vierteljahrsschrift,* 51 (1977), 129–147.
Weiss, Hermann F. "Precarious Idylls, The Relationship Between Father and Daughter in Heinrich von Kleist's 'Die Marquise von O—,' " *Mod Lang Notes,* 91 (1976), 538–542.

"Michael Kohlhaas"
Anstett, Jean-Jacques. "A propos de 'Michael Kohlhaas,' " *Études Germaniques,* 14 (1959), 150–156.
Dyer, Denys. *The Stories of Kleist* . . . , 107–150.
Gelus, Marjorie. "Laughter and Joking . . . ," 458–459.
Graham, Ilse. . . . *Quest for the Symbol,* 213–223.
Hoverland, Lilian. "Heinrich von Kleists 'Michael Kohlhaas' jenseits der Gerechtigkeit," *Colloquia Germanica,* 9 (1975), 269–290.
Lucas, R.S. "Studies in Kleist," 120–145.
Martin, George M. "The Apparent Ambiguity . . . ," 147–152.
Meyer-Benfey, H. "Die innere Geschichte des 'Michael Kohlhaas,' " *Euphorion,* 15 (1908), 99–140.
Passage, C.E. " 'Michael Kohlhaas': Form Analysis," *Germ R,* 30 (1955), 181–197.
Paulin, Harry W. "Kohlhaas and Family," *Germ R,* 52 (1977), 171–182.
Stahleder, Helmuth. "Dramatische Szenenbildung und ihre Elemente in Heinrich von Kleists 'Michael Kohlhaas,' " *Literatur und Wissenschaft und Unterricht,* 9 (1976), 167–181.

"St. Cecilia or the Power of Music"
Dyer, Denys. *The Stories of Kleist* . . . , 92–106.
Edel, Edmund. "Heinrich von Kleists 'Die Heilige Cäcilie oder die Gewalt der Musik': Eine Legende," *Wirkendes Wort,* 19 (1969), 105–115.
Graham, Ilse. . . . *Quest for the Symbol,* 196–201.

KŌDA ROHAN

"The Bearded Man"
Mulhern, Chieko I. *Kōda Rohan,* 121–124.

"Destiny"
Mulhern, Chieko I. *Kōda Rohan,* 143–148.

"Encounter with a Skull"
Mulhern, Chieko I. *Kōda Rohan,* 46–50.

"Love Bodhisattva"
Mulhern, Chieko I. *Kōda Rohan,* 39–43.

"Snowflakes Dancing"
Mulhern, Chieko I. *Kōda Rohan,* 45–46.

"A Sword"
Mulhern, Chieko I. *Kōda Rohan,* 57–58.

"Viewing of a Painting"
Mulhern, Chieko I. *Kōda Rohan,* 88–89.

WILLIAM KOTZWINKLE

"Follow the Eagle"
Cassill, R. V. *Instructor's Handbook . . .,* 119–120.

ALEXANDER KUPRIN

"At the Circus"
Luker, Nicholas. *Alexander Kuprin,* 57–59.

"The Bracelet of Garnets"
Luker, Nicholas. *Alexander Kuprin,* 127–129.

"Delirium"
Luker, Nicholas. *Alexander Kuprin,* 117–118.

"Emerald"
Luker, Nicholas. *Alexander Kuprin,* 121–123.

"The Enquiry"
Luker, Nicholas. *Alexander Kuprin,* 26–28.

"In the Dark"
Luker, Nicholas. *Alexander Kuprin,* 25–26.

"The Jewess"
Luker, Nicholas. *Alexander Kuprin,* 65–66.

"The Last Debut"
Luker, Nicholas. *Alexander Kuprin,* 22–24.

"Off the Street"
Luker, Nicholas. *Alexander Kuprin,* 66–67.

"A Quiet Life"
Luker, Nicholas. *Alexander Kuprin*, 67–68.

"The River of Life"
Luker, Nicholas. *Alexander Kuprin*, 114–116.

"Staff-Captain Rybnikow"
Luker, Nicholas. *Alexander Kuprin*, 113–114.

"The Swamp"
Luker, Nicholas. *Alexander Kuprin*, 59–62.

ALEX LA GUMA

"Coffee for the Road"
Roscoe, Adrian. *Uhuru's Fire* . . ., 241.

"The Gladiators"
Roscoe, Adrian. *Uhuru's Fire* . . ., 245–247.

"A Matter of Taste"
Roscoe, Adrian. *Uhuru's Fire* . . ., 242–245.

PÄR LAGERKVIST

"Father and I"
Sjöberg, Leif. *Pär Lagerkvist*, 18–19.

"The Hangman"
Sjöberg, Leif. *Pär Lagerkvist*, 21–25.

RING LARDNER

"Alibi Ike"
Yardley, Jonathan. *Ring* . . ., 188–189.

"A Caddy's Diary"
Messenger, Christian. "Southwest Humorists and Ring Lardner—Sports in American Literature," *Illinois Q*, 39 (Fall, 1976), 16.

"Champion"
Messenger, Christian. "Southwest Humorists . . .," 13–14.

"The Golden Honeymoon"
Yardley, Jonathan. *Ring* . . ., 249–251.

"Haircut"
Kane, Thomas S., and Leonard J. Peters. *Some Suggestions* . . ., 21–22.
*Perrine, Laurence. *Instructor's Manual* . . . *"Story* . . .," 17–18; *Instructor's Manual* . . . *"Literature* . . .," 17–18.

''I Can't Breathe''
    Yardley, Jonathan. *Ring* . . ., 311–312.

''Insomnia''
    Yardley, Jonathan. *Ring* . . ., 351–353.

''My Roomy''
    Messenger, Christian. ''Southwest Humorists . . .,'' 12–13.

''Some Like Them Cold''
    Yardley, Jonathan. *Ring* . . ., 247–249.

MARY LAVIN

''An Akoulina of the Irish Midlands''
    Peterson, Richard F. *Mary Lavin*, 93–94.

''At Sallygap''
    Dunleavy, Janet E. ''The Fiction of Mary Lavin: Universal Sensibility in a
        Particular Milieu,'' *Irish Univ R*, 7 (1977), 225–229.
    Peterson, Richard F. *Mary Lavin*, 25–29.

''The Becker Wives''
    Peterson, Richard F. *Mary Lavin*, 39–40.

''Bridal Sheets''
    Dunleavy, Janet E. ''The Fiction of Mary Lavin . . .,'' 234–236.

''The Cuckoo-Spit''
    Peterson, Richard F. *Mary Lavin*, 111–117.

''A Cup of Tea''
    Peterson, Richard F. ''The Circle of Truth: The Stories of Katherine Mansfield
        and Mary Lavin,'' *Mod Fiction Stud*, 24 (1978), 392–393.
    _____ . *Mary Lavin*, 36–37.

''A Gentle Soul''
    Peterson, Richard F. *Mary Lavin*, 82–83.

''The Great Wave''
    Peterson, Richard F. *Mary Lavin*, 101–103.

''The Green Grave and the Black Grave''
    Dunleavy, Janet E. ''The Fiction of Mary Lavin . . .,'' 232–234.
    Peterson, Richard F. *Mary Lavin*, 101–103.

''Happiness''
    Peterson, Richard F. *Mary Lavin*, 122–124.

''A Happy Death''
    Peterson, Richard F. *Mary Lavin*, 40–43.

"Heart of Gold"
   Peterson, Richard F. *Mary Lavin*, 113.

"In a Café"
   Peterson, Richard F. *Mary Lavin*, 109–111.

"In the Middle of the Fields"
   Peterson, Richard F. *Mary Lavin*, 111–112.

"The Little Prince"
   Peterson, Richard F. *Mary Lavin*, 96–98.

"The Lost Child"
   Peterson, Richard F. *Mary Lavin*, 127–132.

"Love Is for Lovers"
   Peterson, Richard F. *Mary Lavin*, 28–29.

"Loving Memory"
   Peterson, Richard F. *Mary Lavin*, 98–99.

"A Memory"
   Dunleavy, Janet E. "The Fiction of Mary Lavin . . .," 229–232.
   Peterson, Richard F. *Mary Lavin*, 138–142.

"Miss Holland"
   Peterson, Richard F. *Mary Lavin*, 32–33.

"A Mock Auction"
   Peterson, Richard F. *Mary Lavin*, 119–122.

"My Vocation"
   Peterson, Richard F. *Mary Lavin*, 90–91.

"The New Gardener"
   Peterson, Richard F. *Mary Lavin*, 124–125.

"An Old Boot"
   Peterson, Richard F. *Mary Lavin*, 95–96.

"One Evening"
   Peterson, Richard F. *Mary Lavin*, 125–126.

"One Summer"
   Peterson, Richard F. *Mary Lavin*, 117–119.

"The Pastor of Six Mile Bush"
   Peterson, Richard F. *Mary Lavin*, 80–81.

"The Patriot Son"
   Peterson, Richard F. *Mary Lavin*, 91–92.

"A Pure Accident"
Peterson, Richard F. *Mary Lavin*, 126–127.

"The Sand Castle"
Dunleavy, Janet E. "The Fiction of Mary Lavin . . .," 224–225.

"Sarah"
Peterson, Richard F. *Mary Lavin*, 29–31.

"The Small Bequest"
Peterson, Richard F. *Mary Lavin*, 79–80.

"Story with a Pattern"
Peterson, Richard F. *Mary Lavin*, 76–78.

"Sunday Brings Sunday"
Peterson, Richard F. *Mary Lavin*, 37–39.

"Tom"
Peterson, Richard F. *Mary Lavin*, 16–17.

"Tomb of an Ancestor"
Peterson, Richard F. *Mary Lavin*, 132–133.

"A Tragedy"
Peterson, Richard F. *Mary Lavin*, 88–90.

"Trastevere"
Peterson, Richard F. *Mary Lavin*, 133–136.

"What's Wrong with Aubretia?"
Peterson, Richard F. *Mary Lavin*, 107–108.

"The Widow's Son"
Peterson, Richard F. *Mary Lavin*, 83–85.

"The Will"
Peterson, Richard F. *Mary Lavin*, 34–35.

"A Woman Friend"
Peterson, Richard F. *Mary Lavin*, 81–82.

"The Yellow Beret"
Peterson, Richard F. *Mary Lavin*, 104–106.

D. H. LAWRENCE

"The Blind Man"
Langbaum, Robert. *The Mysteries* . . ., 292–293.
Pinion, F. B. *A D. H. Lawrence Companion* . . ., 230–231.
Wheeler, Richard R. "Intimacy and Irony in 'The Blind Man,' " *D.H. Lawrence R,* 9 (1976), 236–253.

"The Border Line"
Pinion, F. B. *A D.H. Lawrence Companion* . . ., 240–241.

"The Captain's Doll"
Leavis, F. R. *Thought, Word and Creativity* . . ., 94–121.
Pinion, F. B. *A D.H. Lawrence Companion* . . ., 234–235.

"The Christening"
Harris, Janice H. "Insight and Experiment in D. H. Lawrence's Early Short
Fiction," *Philol Q,* 55 (1976), 422–425.
Pinion, F. B. *A D.H. Lawrence Companion* . . ., 224.

"Daughters of the Vicar"
Harris, Janice H. "Insight and Experiment . . .," 425–427.
Howe, Marguerite B. *The Art* . . ., 32–33.
Pinion, F. B. *A D.H. Lawrence Companion* . . ., 220–221.

"The Fox"
Langbaum, Robert. *The Mysteries* . . ., 269–272.
Pinion, F. B. *A D.H. Lawrence Companion* . . ., 233–234.
Ruderman, Judith G. " 'The Fox' and the Devouring Mother," *D.H. Lawrence
R,* 10 (1977), 251–269.
Wolkenfeld, Suzanne. " 'The Sleeping Beauty' Retold: D.H. Lawrence's 'The
Fox,' " *Stud Short Fiction,* 14 (1977), 345–352.

"The Horse Dealer's Daughter" [originally "The Miracle"]
Abcarian, Richard, and Marvin Klotz. *Instructor's Manual* . . ., 2nd ed., 13–14.
Cassill, R. V. *Instructor's Handbook* . . ., 120–123.
Kane, Thomas S., and Leonard J. Peters. *Some Suggestions* . . ., 36–37.
Pinion, F. B. *A D.H. Lawrence Companion* . . ., 230.

"Jimmy and the Desperate Woman"
Pinion, F. B. *A D.H. Lawrence Companion* . . ., 241.

"The Ladybird"
Pinion, F. B. *A D.H. Lawrence Companion* . . ., 235–236.

"The Last Laugh"
Pinion, F. B. *A D.H. Lawrence Companion* . . ., 241–242.

"Love Among the Haystacks"
Pinion, F. B. *A D.H. Lawrence Companion* . . ., 225–226.

"The Lovely Lady"
Pinion, F. B. *A D.H. Lawrence Companion* . . ., 247–248.

"The Man Who Died"
Hinz, Evelyn J., and John J. Teunissen. "Savior and Cock: Allusion and Icon in
Lawrence's 'The Man Who Died,' " *J Mod Lit,* 5 (1976), 279–296.
MacDonald, Robert A. "The Union of Fire and Water: An Examination of the
Imagery of 'The Man Who Died,' " *D.H. Lawrence R,* 10 (1977), 34–51.
Pinion, F. B. *A D.H. Lawrence Companion* . . ., 246–247.

"The Man Who Loved Islands"
  Pinion, F. B. *A D. H. Lawrence Companion* . . ., 243–244.
  Willbern, David. "Malice in Paradise: Isolation and Projection in 'The Man Who Loved Islands,' " *D. H. Lawrence R,* 10 (1977), 223–241.

"New Eve and Old Adam"
  Pinion, F. B. *A D. H. Lawrence Companion* . . ., 227–228.

"Odour of Chrysanthemums"
  Harris, Janice H. "Insight and Experiment . . .," 420–422.
  *Howard, Daniel F., and William Plummer. *Instructor's Manual* . . ., 3rd ed., 36.
  Kalnins, Mara. "D. H. Lawrence's 'Odour of Chrysanthemums': The Three Endings," *Stud Short Fiction,* 13 (1976), 471–479.
  Pinion, F. B. *A D. H. Lawrence Companion* . . ., 219–220.

"The Overtone"
  Pinion, F. B. *A D. H. Lawrence Companion* . . ., 236.

"The Princess"
  Pinion, F. B. *A D. H. Lawrence Companion* . . ., 236–237.

"The Prussian Officer" [originally "Honour and Arms"]
  Humma, John B. "Melville's 'Billy Budd' and Lawrence's 'The Prussian Officer,' " *Essays Lit,* 1, i (1974), 83–88.
  Pinion, F. B. *A D. H. Lawrence Companion* . . ., 227.

"The Rocking-Horse Winner"
  Cassill, R. V. *Instructor's Handbook* . . ., 126–127.
  Humma, John B. "Pan and 'The Rocking-Horse Winner,' " *Essays Lit,* 5 (1978), 53–60.
  Koban, Charles. "Allegory and the Death of the Heart in 'The Rocking-Horse Winner,' " *Stud Short Fiction,* 15 (1978), 391–396.
  *Perrine, Laurence. *Instructor's Manual* . . . "Story . . .," 35; *Instructor's Manual* . . . "Literature . . .," 35.
  *Snodgrass, W. D. " 'The Rocking-Horse Winner,' " in Dietrich, R. F., and Roger H. Sundell. *Instructor's Manual* . . ., 3rd ed., 104–112.

"St. Mawr"
  Goonetilleke, D. C. R. A. *Developing Countries* . . ., 174–179.
  Langbaum, Robert. *The Mysteries* . . ., 273–279.
  *Leavis, F. R. "The Novel as Dramatic Poem: 'St. Mawr,' " in Hazell, Stephen, Ed. *The English Novel* . . ., 85–101.
  Pinion, F. B. *A D. H. Lawrence Companion* . . ., 238–240.
  Scholtes, M. " 'St. Mawr': Between Degeneration and Regeneration," *Dutch Q R,* 5 (1975), 253–269.

"Second Best"
  Harris, Janice H. "Insight and Experiment . . .," 431–433.
  Pinion, F. B. *A D. H. Lawrence Companion* . . ., 222–223.

"The Shades of Spring"
  Pinion, F. B. *A D. H. Lawrence Companion* . . ., 225.

"The Shadow in the Rose Garden"
Chua, Cheng Lok. "Lawrence's 'The Shadow in the Rose Garden,' " *Explicator*, 37, i (1978), 23–24.

"Sun"
Pinion, F. B. *A D. H. Lawrence Companion* . . ., 244–245.

"The Thimble"
Pinion, F. B. *A D. H. Lawrence Companion* . . ., 228–229.

"Things"
Kimmey, John L., Ed. *Experience and Expression* . . ., 194–195.

"Tickets, Please"
Cassill, R. V. *Instructor's Handbook* . . ., 123–125.
Wheeler, Richard P. " 'Cunning in His Overthrow': Give and Take in 'Tickets, Please,' " *D. H. Lawrence R*, 10 (1977), 242–250.

"The Virgin and the Gipsy"
Pinion, F. B. *A D. H. Lawrence Companion* . . ., 245–246.

"Wintry Peacock"
Pinion, F. B. *A D. H. Lawrence Companion* . . ., 232–233.

"The Witch à la Mode"
Pinion, F. B. *A D. H. Lawrence Companion* . . ., 221–222.

"The Woman Who Rode Away"
Goonetilleke, D. C. R. A. *Developing Countries* . . ., 181–184.
Pinion, F. B. *A D. H. Lawrence Companion* . . ., 237–238.
Rose, Shirley. "Physical Trauma in D. H. Lawrence's Short Fiction," *Contemp Lit*, 16 (1975), 75–76.

HENRY LAWSON

"The Bush Undertaker"
Dobrex, Livio. "The Craftsmanship of Lawson Revisited," *Australian Lit Stud*, 7 (1976), 378–381.

"The Drover's Wife"
Dobrex, Livio. ". . . Lawson Revisited," 375–378.

"The Green Lady"
Dobrex, Livio. ". . . Lawson Revisited," 383–387.

CAMARA LAYE

"Les Yeux de la Statue"
King, Adele. "Camara Laye," in King, Bruce, and Kolawole Ogungbesan, Eds. *A Celebration* . . ., 119.

JEAN-MARIE GUSTAVE LE CLÉZIO

"A Day in Old Age"
  Waelti-Walters, Jennifer R. "Narrative Movement in J.M.G. Le Clézio's 'Fever,'" *Stud Short Fiction,* 14 (1977), 250–251.

"Fever"
  Oxenhandler, Neal. "Nihilism in Le Clézio's 'La Fièvre,'" in Tetel, Marcel, Ed. *Symbolism . . .,* 264–273.
  Waelti-Walters, Jennifer R. "Narrative Movement . . .," 247–249.

"Martin"
  Cagnon, Maurice, and Stephen Smith. " 'Martin': A Portrait of the Artist as a Young Hydrocephalic," *Int'l Fiction R,* 2 (1975), 64–67.
  Waelti-Walters, Jennifer R. "Narrative Movement . . .," 249–250.

URSULA LE GUIN

"The New Atlantis"
  Cassill, R. V. *Instructor's Handbook . . .,* 128–129.

"Nine Lives"
  Remington, Thomas J. "A Touch of Difference, A Touch of Love: Theme in Three Stories by Ursula K. Le Guin," *Extrapolation,* 18, i (1976), 28–30.

"Vaster Than Empires and More Slow"
  Remington, Thomas J. "A Touch of Difference . . .," 34–40.
  Watson, Ian. "The Forest as Metaphor for Mind: 'The Word for World is *Forest*' and 'Vaster Than Empires and More Slow,' " *Sci-Fiction Stud,* 2 (1975), 232–236.

"The Word for World is *Forest*"
  Remington, Thomas J. "A Touch of Difference . . .," 30–33.
  Watson, Ian. "The Forest as Metaphor . . .," 231–232.

FRITZ LEIBER

"The Man Who Made Friends with Electricity"
  Favier, Jacques. "Space and Settor in Short Science Fiction," in Johnson, Ira and Christiane, Eds. *Les Américanistes . . .,* 198–199.

STANISLAW LEM

"In Hot Pursuit"
  Warrick, Patricia. "Images of the Man-Machine Relationship in Science Fiction," in Clareson, Thomas D., Ed. *Many Futures . . .,* 205–206.

MIKHAIL LERMONTOV

"Taman"
Calder, Angus. *Russia Discovered* . . ., 44–45.

NIKOLAI LESKOV

"Administrative Grace"
McLean, Hugh. *Nikolai Leskov* . . ., 622–625.

"The Alexandrite"
McLean, Hugh. *Nikolai Leskov* . . ., 475–478.

"The Amazon"
Ansberg, Aleksej B. "Frame Story and First Person Story in N. S. Leskov,"
Scando-Slavica, 3 (1957), 60.

"Ancient Psychopaths"
McLean, Hugh. *Nikolai Leskov* . . ., 416–417.

"Antukà"
McLean, Hugh. *Nikolai Leskov* . . ., 612–613.

"An Apparition in the Engineers' Castle"
McLean, Hugh. *Nikolai Leskov* . . ., 381–382.

"The Battle-axe"
McLean, Hugh. *Nikolai Leskov* . . ., 152–161.

"The Beauteous Aza"
McLean, Hugh. *Nikolai Leskov* . . ., 574–577.

"Boyarin Nikita Yurievich"
McLean, Hugh. *Nikolai Leskov* . . ., 185–186.

"Boyarinya Marfa Andreyevna"
McLean, Hugh. *Nikolai Leskov* . . ., 187–188.

"Brahmadatta and Radovan"
McLean, Hugh. *Nikolai Leskov* . . ., 560–561.

"The Bugbear"
McLean, Hugh. *Nikolai Leskov* . . ., 441–444.

"A Case That Was Dropped"
McLean, Hugh. *Nikolai Leskov* . . ., 96–99.

"The Cattle-Pen"
McLean, Hugh. *Nikolai Leskov* . . ., 451–455.

"Christ Visits a Muzhik"
McLean, Hugh. *Nikolai Leskov* . . . , 541–545.

"The Co-Functionaries: A Bucolic Tale on a Historical Canvas"
McLean, Hugh. *Nikolai Leskov* . . . , 474–475.

"The Darner" [originally titled "The Moscow Ace"]
McLean, Hugh. *Nikolai Leskov* . . . , 379–380.

"The Dead Estate"
McLean, Hugh. *Nikolai Leskov* . . . , 463–464.

"Deception" [originally titled "The Featherbrains"]
McLean, Hugh. *Nikolai Leskov* . . . , 384–385.

"The Enchanted Pilgrim"
Ansberg, Aleksej B. "Frame Story . . . ," 64–66.
McLean, Hugh. *Nikolai Leskov* . . . , 242–255.
Wehrle, Albert J. "Paradigmatic Aspects of Leskov's 'The Enchanted Pilgrim,' " *Slavic & East European J,* 20 (1976), 371–378.

"An Enigmatic Incident in an Insane Asylum"
McLean, Hugh. *Nikolai Leskov* . . . , 473–474.

"Episcopal Justice"
McLean, Hugh. *Nikolai Leskov* . . . , 309–313.

"The Felon of Ashkelon"
McLean, Hugh. *Nikolai Leskov* . . . , 579–582.

"Figura"
McLean, Hugh. *Nikolai Leskov* . . . , 547–549.

"Fish Soup Without Fish"
McLean, Hugh. *Nikolai Leskov* . . . , 428–429.

"The Hour of God's Will"
McLean, Hugh. *Nikolai Leskov* . . . , 550–553.

"The Improvisers"
McLean, Hugh. *Nikolai Leskov* . . . , 613–614.

"In a Coach"
McLean, Hugh. *Nikolai Leskov* . . . , 103–104.

"Interesting Men"
McLean, Hugh. *Nikolai Leskov* . . . , 478–481.

"Iron Will"
McLean, Hugh. *Nikolai Leskov* . . . , 322–326.

"The Tale of Theodore the Christian and His Friend Abraham the Hebrew"
McLean, Hugh. *Nikolai Leskov* . . ., 429–435.

"The Toupee Artist"
McLean, Hugh. *Nikolai Leskov* . . ., 438–441.

"The Unbaptized Priest"
McLean, Hugh. *Nikolai Leskov* . . ., 313–317.

"The Unmercenary Engineers"
McLean, Hugh. *Nikolai Leskov* . . ., 464–467.

"Vexation of Spirit"
McLean, Hugh. *Nikolai Leskov* . . ., 556–557.

"White Eagle"
McLean, Hugh. *Nikolai Leskov* . . ., 376–378.

"The Wild Beast"
McLean, Hugh. *Nikolai Leskov* . . ., 385–388.

"A Winter's Day"
McLean, Hugh. *Nikolai Leskov* . . ., 614–620.

"Yid Somersault"
McLean, Hugh. *Nikolai Leskov* . . ., 422–425.

DORIS LESSING

"The Ant Heap"
Singleton, Mary A. *The City* . . ., 27–30.

"The Black Madonna"
Cassill, R. V. *Instructor's Handbook* . . ., 130–131.

"Dialogue"
Singleton, Mary A. *The City* . . ., 63–64.

" 'Leopard' George"
Singleton, Mary A. *The City* . . ., 22–27.

"The Old Chief Mshlanga"
Singleton, Mary A. *The City* . . ., 41–42.

"The Second Hut"
Singleton, Mary A. *The City* . . ., 60–61.

"A Sunrise on the Veld"
Singleton, Mary A. *The City* . . ., 22–23.

"The Temptation of Jack Orkney"
  Singleton, Mary A. *The City . . .*, 141–144.

"To Room Nineteen"
  Abcarian, Richard, and Marvin Klotz. *Instructor's Manual . . .*, 2nd ed., 14–15.

"Two Potters"
  Singleton, Mary A. *The City . . .*, 66–68.

HENRY CLAY LEWIS

"The Curious Widow"
  Rose, Alan H. *Demonic Vision . . .*, 28–31.

"Stealing a Baby"
  Rose, Alan H. *Demonic Vision . . .*, 31–33.

"A Struggle for Life"
  Rose, Alan H. *Demonic Vision . . .*, 34–38.

O. F. LEWIS

"Alma Mater"
  Perrine, Laurence. *Instructor's Manual . . . "Story . . .,"* 33–34; *Instructor's Manual . . . "Literature . . .,"* 33–34.

RICHARD O. LEWIS

"The Fate Changer"
  Carter, Paul A. *The Creation . . .*, 96–99.

SINCLAIR LEWIS

"The Hidden People"
  Light, Martin. *The Quixotic Vision . . .*, 54–55.

"Young Man Axelbrod"
  Light, Martin. *The Quixotic Vision . . .*, 55–56.
  Perrine, Laurence. *Instructor's Manual . . . "Story . . .,"* 31–33; *Instructor's Manual . . . "Literature . . .,"* 31–33.

WYNDHAM LEWIS

"Beau Sejour"
  Materer, Timothy. *Wyndham Lewis . . .*, 37–39.

"Bestre"
Materer, Timothy. *Wyndham Lewis* . . ., 39–40.

"Brotcotnaz"
Materer, Timothy. *Wyndham Lewis* . . ., 41–43.

"Cantleman's Spring Mate"
Materer, Timothy. *Wyndham Lewis* . . ., 71–73.

"The Death of the Ankou"
Materer, Timothy. *Wyndham Lewis* . . ., 43–44.

"The French Poodle"
Materer, Timothy. *Wyndham Lewis* . . ., 69–70.

JONAS LIE

"The Nordfjord Horse"
Lyngstrad, Sverre. *Jonas Lie,* 34–35.

"The Søndmøre Boat" [same as "The Eight-Oared Boat"]
Lyngstrad, Sverre. *Jonas Lie,* 35–36.

ROBERT LINDNER

"The Jet-Propelled Couch"
Moskowitz, Sam. *Strange Horizons* . . ., 107–108.

LING SHU-HUA

"Embroidered Pillows"
Hsia, C. T. *A History* . . ., 79–80.

"The Eve of the Mid-Autumn Festival"
Hsia, C. T. *A History* . . ., 80–82.

"Little Liu"
Hsia, C. T. *A History* . . ., 82–83.

LO HUA-SHENG [HSÜ TI-SHAN]

"The Vain Labors of a Spider"
Hsia, C. T. *A History* . . ., 85–87.

"Yü-kuan"
Hsia, C. T. *A History* . . ., 87–92.

JACK LONDON

"All Gold Canyon"
  Labor, Earle. "From 'All Gold Canyon' to *The Acorn Planter*: Jack London's
  Agrarian Vision," *Western Am Lit*, 11 (1976), 95–97.

"The Call of the Wild"
  Mann, John S. "The Theme of the Double in 'The Call of the Wild,' " *Markham
  R*, 8 (1978), 1–5.
  Spinner, Jonathan H. "A Syllabus for the 20th Century: Jack London's 'The Call
  of the Wild,' " *Jack London Newsletter*, 7 (1974), 73–78.

"A Piece of Steak"
  Hatchel, Linda. "Animal Imagery in London's 'A Piece of Steak,' " *Jack
  London Newsletter*, 8 (1975), 119–121.

"The Red One"
  Collins, Billy G. "Jack London's 'The Red One,' " *Jack London Newsletter*,
  10, i (1977), 1–6.
  Jorgenson, Jens P. "Jack London's 'The Red One': A Freudian Approach,"
  Jack London Newsletter, 8 (1975), 101–103.
  Riber, Jorgen. "Archetypal Patterns in 'The Red One,' " *Jack London News-
  letter*, 8 (1975), 104–106.

"To Build a Fire"
  Kimmey, John L. *Instructor's Manual* . . ., 1–2.
  May, Charles E. " 'To Build a Fire': Physical Fiction and Metaphysical
  Critics," *Stud Short Fiction*, 15 (1978), 19–24.

"Told in the Drooling Ward"
  Graham, Don. "Jack London's Tale Told by a High-Grade Feeb," *Stud Short
  Fiction*, 15 (1978), 429–433.

"The Wife of a King"
  Tavernier-Courbin, Jacqueline. " 'The Wife of a King': A Defense," *Jack
  London Newsletter*, 10, i (1977), 34–38.

AUGUSTUS BALDWIN LONGSTREET

"The Mother and Her Child"
  Rose, Alan H. *Demonic Vision* . . ., 22–23.

H. P. LOVECRAFT

"At the Mountain of Madness"
  Schweitzer, Darrell. *The Dream Quest* . . ., 41–42.

"The Call of Cthulku"
  Schweitzer, Darrell. *The Dream Quest* . . ., 30–32.

"The Colour Out of Space"
  Schweitzer, Darrell. *The Dream Quest* . . ., 34–35.

"Dagon"
  Schweitzer, Darrell. *The Dream Quest* . . ., 6–7.

"Dreams in the Witch House"
  Schweitzer, Darrell. *The Dream Quest* . . ., 44–45.

"The Dunwich Horror"
  Schweitzer, Darrell. *The Dream Quest* . . ., 38–39.

"The Haunter of the Dark"
  Schweitzer, Darrell. *The Dream Quest* . . ., 50–51.

"He"
  Schweitzer, Darrell. *The Dream Quest* . . ., 28–29.

"The Horror at Red Hook"
  Schweitzer, Darrell. *The Dream Quest* . . ., 29–30.

"The Nameless City"
  Schweitzer, Darrell. *The Dream Quest* . . ., 23.

"The Other Gods"
  Schweitzer, Darrell. *The Dream Quest* . . ., 17.

"The Outsider"
  Schweitzer, Darrell. *The Dream Quest* . . ., 22–23.

"Pickman's Model"
  Schweitzer, Darrell. *The Dream Quest* . . ., 33–34.

"The Picture in the House"
  Schweitzer, Darrell. *The Dream Quest* . . ., 20–21.

"Polaris"
  Schweitzer, Darrell. *The Dream Quest* . . ., 12–13.

"The Rats in the Walls"
  Schweitzer, Darrell. *The Dream Quest* . . ., 25–26.

"The Shadow out of Time"
  Schweitzer, Darrell. *The Dream Quest* . . ., 48–49.

"The Shadow over Innsmouth"
  Schweitzer, Darrell. *The Dream Quest* . . ., 43–44.

"The Shunned House"
  Schweitzer, Darrell. *The Dream Quest* . . ., 27–28.

"The Temple"
Schweitzer, Darrell. *The Dream Quest* . . ., 9–10.

"The Thing on the Doorstep"
Schweitzer, Darrell. *The Dream Quest* . . ., 47–48.

"Through the Gates of the Silver Key"
Schweitzer, Darrell. *The Dream Quest* . . ., 45–46.

"The Tomb"
Schweitzer, Darrell. *The Dream Quest* . . ., 7–8.

"The Whisperer in Darkness"
Schweitzer, Darrell. *The Dream Quest* . . ., 39–40.

MALCOLM LOWRY

"The Bravest Boat"
*Dodson, Daniel B. "Malcolm Lowry," in Stade, George, Ed. *Six Contemporary British Novelists,* 152–153.

"Elephant and Colosseum"
*Dodson, Daniel B. "Malcolm Lowry," 154–155.

"The Forest Path to the Spring"
*Dodson, Daniel B. "Malcolm Lowry," 156–158.

"Gin and Goldenrod"
*Dodson, Daniel B. "Malcolm Lowry," 155–156.

"The Present Estate of Pompeii"
*Dodson, Daniel B. "Malcolm Lowry," 155.

"Strange Comforts Afforded by the Profession"
*Dodson, Daniel B. "Malcolm Lowry," 153–154.

"Through the Panama"
*Dodson, Daniel B. "Malcolm Lowry," 151–152.

LU HSÜN [LU XUN, also CHOU SHU-JEN]

"Benediction"
Hsia, C. T. *A History* . . ., 39–40.

"Brothers"
Lyell, William A. *Lu Hsün's Vision* . . ., 188–196.

"Diary of a Madman"
Fokkema, Douwe W. "Lu Xun: The Impact of Russian Literature," in Goldman, Merle, Ed. *Modern Chinese Literature* . . ., 95–97.

Hsia, C. T. *A History* . . ., 32–33.

"Divorce"
Hsia, C. T. *A History* . . ., 44–45.
Lyell, William A. *Lu Hsün's Vision* . . ., 215–218.

"Dragon Boat Festival"
Lyell, William A. *Lu Hsün's Vision* . . ., 172–176.

"A Happy Family"
Lyell, William A. *Lu Hsün's Vision* . . ., 194–199.

"In a Restaurant"
Hsia, C. T. *A History* . . ., 40–42.

"K'ung I-chi"
Hsia, C. T. *A History* . . ., 33–34.

"Medicine"
Doleželová-Velingerová, Milena. "Lu Xun's 'Medicine,' " in Goldman, Merle, Ed. *Modern Chinese Literature* . . ., 221–231.
Hanan, Patrick. "The Technique of Lu Hsün's Fiction," *Harvard J Asiatic Stud,* 34 (1974), 53–96.
Hsia, C. T. *A History* . . ., 34–36.
Lyell, William A. *Lu Hsün's Vision* . . ., 276–280.

"The New Year's Sacrifice"
Lyell, William A. *Lu Hsün's Vision* . . ., 141–145.

"Remorse"
Lyell, William A. *Lu Hsün's Vision* . . ., 203–209.

"Soap"
Hsia, C. T. *A History* . . ., 42–44.
Lyell, William A. *Lu Hsün's Vision* . . ., 155–160.

"Storm in a Teacup"
Lyell, William A. *Lu Hsün's Vision* . . ., 211–215.

"The True Story of Ah Q"
Hsia, C. T. *A History* . . ., 37–38.
Lyell, William A. *Lu Hsün's Vision* . . ., 227–246.

"Upstairs in the Wineshop"
Lyell, William A. *Lu Hsün's Vision* . . ., 179–182.

"A Warning to the People"
Lyell, William A. *Lu Hsün's Vision* . . ., 264–267.

"The White Light"
Lyell, William A. *Lu Hsün's Vision* . . ., 149–155.

HARRIS M. LYON

"The 2000th Christmas"
Moskowitz, Sam. *Strange Horizons* . . ., 38–39.

CARSON McCULLERS

"The Ballad of the Sad Café"
Gray, Richard. *The Literature of Memory* . . ., 267–272.

"The Jockey"
Cassill, R. V. *Instructor's Handbook* . . ., 132.

"The Sojourners"
Howard, Daniel F., and William Plummer. *Instructor's Manual* . . ., 3rd ed., 64.

"A Tree, A Rock, A Cloud"
Popp, Klaus-Jürgen. "Carson McCullers, 'A Tree, a Rock, a Cloud,' " in
Freese, Peter, Ed. . . . *Interpretationen*, 48–53.

CLAUDE McKAY

"Brownskin Blues"
Giles, James R. *Claude McKay*, 110–112.

"Highball"
Giles, James R. *Claude McKay*, 116.

"The Little Sheik"
Giles, James R. *Claude McKay*, 122–123.

"Mattie and Her Sweetman"
Giles, James R. *Claude McKay*, 116–117.

"Near-White"
Berzon, Judith R. *Neither White Nor Black* . . ., 148–149.
Giles, James R. *Claude McKay*, 114–115.

"The Prince of Porto Rico"
Giles, James R. *Claude McKay*, 112–113.

"The Strange Burial of Sue"
Giles, James R. *Claude McKay*, 119–121.

"When I Pounded the Pavement"
Giles, James R. *Claude McKay*, 117–118.

JAMES ALAN McPHERSON

"Gold Coast"
Kimmey, John L. *Instructor's Manual* . . ., 8–10.

"A Solo Song: For Doc"
  Cassill, R. V. *Instructor's Handbook* . . ., 133–134.

SVEND AGE MADSEN

"Here"
  Marx, Leonie. "Literary Experimentation in a Time of Transition: The Danish Short Story After 1945," *Scandinavian Stud*, 49 (1977), 142–151.

NORMAN MAILER

"A Calculus at Heaven"
  Radford, Jean. *Norman Mailer* . . ., 76–77.

"The Man Who Studied Yoga"
  Bufithis, Philip H. *Norman Mailer*, 39–43.
  Radford, Jean. *Norman Mailer* . . ., 91–92.

"The Time of Her Time"
  Bufithis, Philip H. *Norman Mailer*, 60–61.

BERNARD MALAMUD

"Angel Levine"
  *Howard, Daniel F., and William Plummer. *Instructor's Manual* . . ., 3rd ed., 58.

"Behold the Key"
  Cohen, Sandy. *Bernard Malamud* . . ., 103–104.
  Sweet, Charles A. "Unlocking the Door: Malamud's 'Behold the Key,' " *Notes Contemp Lit*, 5, v (1975), 11–12.

"Black Is My Favorite Color"
  *Skaggs, Merrill M. " 'Black Is My Favorite Color,' " in Dietrich, R. F., and Roger H. Sundell. *Instructor's Manual* . . ., 3rd ed., 81–87.

"A Choice of Profession"
  Cohen, Sandy. *Bernard Malamud* . . ., 71.
  Hergt, Tobias. "Bernard Malamud's 'A Choice of Profession': Interpretation einer Kurzgeschichte mit Anregungen zu ihrer Behandlung im Oberstufenunterricht," *Die Neueren Sprachen*, 24 (1975), 443–453.

"The First Seven Years"
  Gittleman, Sol. *From Shtetl to Suburbia* . . ., 165–166.

"The Girl of My Dreams"
  Cohen, Sandy. *Bernard Malamud* . . ., 71–72.

"The Glass Blower of Venice"
  Cohen, Sandy. *Bernard Malamud* . . ., 102–103.

"Idiots First"
  *Abcarian, Richard, and Marvin Klotz. *Instructor's Manual* . . ., 2nd ed., 15.

"The Jewbird"
  Cassill, R. V. *Instructor's Handbook* . . ., 135.
  Vandyke, Patricia. "Choosing One's Side with Care: The Liberating Repartee,"
    Perspectives Contemp Lit, 1, i (1975), 107–109.

"The Lady of the Lake"
  Gittleman, Sol. *From Shtetl to Suburbia* . . ., 156–158.

"The Last Mohican"
  Benson, Jackson J. "An Introduction: Bernard Malamud and the Haunting of
    America," in Astro, Richard, and Jackson J. Benson, Eds. *The Fiction of
    Bernard Malamud,* 22–24.
  Freese, Peter. "Bernard Malamud, 'The Last Mohican,' " in Freese, Peter, Ed.
    . . . *Interpretationen,* 205–214.
  Gittleman, Sol. *From Shtetl to Suburbia* . . ., 158–161.
  Winn, H. Harbour. "Malamud's Uncas: 'Last Mohican,' " *Notes Contemp Lit,*
    5, ii (1975), 13–14.

"Life Is Better Than Death"
  Cohen, Sandy. *Bernard Malamud* . . ., 104–105.

"The Loan"
  Peterson, Tricia. "The Levels of Allegory in 'The Loan,' " *Linguistics in Lit,* 2,
    iii (1977), 41–57.

"The Magic Barrel"
  Gittleman, Sol. *From Shtetl to Suburbia* . . ., 161–164.
  Kane, Thomas S., and Leonard J. Peters. *Some Suggestions* . . ., 23–24.

"The Maid's Shoes"
  Cohen, Sandy. *Bernard Malamud* . . ., 105.

"Naked Nude"
  Cohen, Sandy. *Bernard Malamud* . . ., 98–99.

"Picture of the Artist"
  Cohen, Sandy. *Bernard Malamud* . . ., 101–102.

"A Pimp's Revenge"
  Cohen, Sandy. *Bernard Malamud* . . ., 99–101.

"The Silver Crown"
  Kimmey, John L. *Instructor's Manual* . . ., 15–17.
  *Perrine, Laurence. *Instructor's Manual* . . . "Story . . .," 12–14; *Instructor's
    Manual* . . . "Literature . . .," 12–14.

"Still Life"
  Cohen, Sandy. *Bernard Malamud* . . ., 96–98.

"Take Pity"
   Helmcke, Hans. "Bernard Malamud: 'Take Pity,'" in Busch, Frieder, and
   Renate S. Bardeleben, Eds. *Amerikanische Erzählliteratur 1950–1970*, 207–
   217.

ALBERT MALTZ

"Good-by"
   Salzman, Jack. *Albert Maltz*, 40–41.

"The Happiest Man on Earth"
   Salzman, Jack. *Albert Maltz*, 42–44.

"Incident on a Street Corner"
   Salzman, Jack. *Albert Maltz*, 41–42.

"Man on a Road"
   Salzman, Jack. *Albert Maltz*, 36–37.

"Season of Celebration"
   Salzman, Jack. *Albert Maltz*, 34–36.

"The Way Things Are"
   Salzman, Jack. *Albert Maltz*, 38–40.

PIEYRE DE MANDIARGUES

"The Tide"
   Charney, Hanna. "The Tide as Structure in 'La Marée,' " *Dada/Surrealism*, 5
   (1975), 5–10.

JOHN STREETER MANIFOLD

"Smoko with the Balkans"
   Hall, Rodney. *J.S. Manifold . . .*, 134–135.

KLAUS MANN

"Le Dernier Cri"
   Hoffer, Peter T. *Klaus Mann*, 108–109.

"The Monk"
   Hoffer, Peter T. *Klaus Mann*, 114–115.

"Three Star Hennessy"
   Hoffer, Peter T. *Klaus Mann*, 107–108.

THOMAS MANN

"Blood of the Walsungs"
Sjögren, Christine O. "The Variant Ending as a Clue to the Interpretation of Thomas Mann's 'Wälsungenblut,' " *Seminar*, 14 (1978), 97–104.

"Death in Venice"
Albright, Daniel. *Personality* . . ., 226–235.
Consigny, Scott. "Aschenbach's 'Page and a Half of Choicest Prose': Mann's Rhetoric of Irony," *Stud Short Fiction*, 14 (1977), 359–367.
Davidson, Leah. "Mid-Life Crisis in Thomas Mann's 'Death in Venice,' " *J Am Acad Psychoanalysis*, 4 (1976), 203–214.
Ezergailis, Inta M. *Male and Female* . . ., 47–71.
Farrelly, D. J. "Apollo and Dionysus Interpreted in Thomas Mann's 'Der Tod in Venedig,' " *New Germ Stud*, 3 (1975), 1–15.
Hermes, Eberhard. "Thomas Mann: 'Der Tod in Venedig' (1912): Anregungen zur Interpretation," *Der Deutschunterricht*, 29, iv (1977), 59–86.
*Howe, Irving, Ed. *Classics of Modern Fiction* . . ., 2nd ed., 325–336.
Karsunke, Yaak. " ' . . . von der albernen Sucht, besonders zu sein': Thomas Manns 'Der Tod in Venedig' wiedergelesen," *Text und Kritik*, [n. v.], Special Issue (1976), 61–69.
Kelley, Alice V. "Von Aschenbach's Phaedrus: Platonic Allusion in 'Der Tod in Venedig,' " *J Engl & Germ Philol*, 75 (1976), 228–240.
Leibowitz, Judith. *Narrative Purposes* . . ., 89–95.
McIntyre, Allan J. "Psychology and Symbol: Correspondences Between 'Heart of Darkness' and 'Death in Venice,' " *Hartford Stud Lit*, 7 (1975), 216–235.
Meyers, Jeffrey. *Homosexuality* . . ., 42–53.
Smith, Duncan. "The Education to Despair: Some Thoughts on 'Death in Venice,' " *Praxis*, 1, i (1975), 73–80.
Stewart, Walter K. " 'Der Tod in Venedig': The Path to Insight," *Germ R*, 53 (1978), 50–55.

"Disorder and Early Sorrow"
Cassill, R. V. *Instructor's Handbook* . . ., 136–138.
*Oliver, Clinton F. "Hemingway's 'The Killers' and Mann's 'Disorder and Early Sorrow,' " in Timko, Michael, Ed. *38 Short Stories*, 2nd ed., 684–692.

"Fallen"
Lindsay, T. M. "Thomas Mann's First Story, 'Gefallen,' " *Germ Life & Letters*, 28 (1974), 297–307.

"Gladius Dei"
Dolan, Paul J. *Of War and War's Alarms* . . ., 150–156.

"The Infant Prodigy"
*Perrine, Laurence. *Instructor's Manual* . . . "*Story* . . .," 41–42; *Instructor's Manual* . . . "*Literature* . . .," 41–42.

"Mario and the Magician"
Bauer, Arnold. *Thomas Mann*, 61–63.
Dolan, Paul J. *Of War and War's Alarms* . . ., 157–167.

Freese, Wolfgang. "Thomas Mann und sein Leser: Zum Verhältnis von Antifaschismus und Leseerwartung in 'Mario und der Zauberer,' " *Deutsche Vierteljahrsschrift,* 51 (1977), 659–675.

Garrin, Stephen H. "Thomas Mann's 'Mario und der Zauberer': Artistic Means and Didactic Ends," *J Engl & Germanic Philol,* 77 (1978), 92–103.

McIntyre, Allen J. "Determinism in 'Mario and the Magician,' " *Germ R,* 52 (1977), 205–216.

Orr, John. *Tragic Realism . . .,* 124–127.

Schwarz, Egon. "Fascism and Society: Remarks on Thomas Mann's Novella 'Mario and the Magician,' " *Michigan Germ Stud,* 2 (1976), 47–67.

"Tonio Kröger"
Bauer, Arnold. *Thomas Mann,* 26–27.

Bennett, Benjamin. "Casting out Nines: Structure, Parody and Myth in 'Tonio Kröger,' " *Revue des Langues Vivantes,* 42 (1976), 126–146.

O'Neill, Patrick. "Dance and Counterdance: A Note on 'Tonio Kröger,' " *Germ Life & Letters,* 29 (1976), 291–295.

"The Will to Happiness"
Wolf, Ernest M. "Der falsche Saraceni: Eine Anmerkung zu Thomas Manns Erzählung 'Der Wille zum Glücke,' " *Blätter der Thomas Mann Gesellschaft,* 16 (1977–1978), 21–31.

KATHERINE MANSFIELD [KATHERINE BEAUCHAMP]

"At Lehmann's"
Burgan, Mary. "Childbirth Trauma in Katherine Mansfield's Early Stories," *Mod Fiction Stud,* 24 (1978), 401–402.

Rohrberger, Mary H. . . . *Katherine Mansfield,* 50–51.

"At the Bay"
Burgan, Mary. "Childbirth Trauma . . .," 406–411.

Peterson, Richard F. "The Circle of Truth: The Stories of Katherine Mansfield and Mary Lavin," *Mod Fiction Stud,* 24 (1978), 388–389.

Rohrberger, Mary H. . . . *Katherine Mansfield,* 133–143.

"Bains Turcs"
Rohrberger, Mary H. . . . *Katherine Mansfield,* 80–81.

"Bank Holiday"
Rohrberger, Mary H. . . . *Katherine Mansfield,* 71–72.

"The Baron"
Rohrberger, Mary H. . . . *Katherine Mansfield,* 74–75.

"A Birthday"
Burgan, Mary. "Childbirth Trauma . . .," 400–401.

Rohrberger, Mary H. . . . *Katherine Mansfield,* 66–67.

"Carnation"
Rohrberger, Mary H. . . . *Katherine Mansfield,* 51–52.

"The Daughters of the Late Colonel"
Kleine, Don W. "Mansfield and the Orphans of Time," *Mod Fiction Stud*, 24 (1978), 423–438.
Rohrberger, Mary H. . . . *Katherine Mansfield*, 110–111.

"The Doll's House"
Delany, Paul. "Short and Simple Annals of the Poor: Katherine Mansfield's 'The Doll's House,' " *Mosaic*, 10 (1976), 7–17.
Rohrberger, Mary H. . . . *Katherine Mansfield*, 102–105.

"The Education of Audrey"
Hankin, Cherry. "Fantasy and a Sense of an Ending in the Works of Katherine Mansfield," *Mod Fiction Stud*, 24 (1978), 470.

"Die Einsame"
Hankin, Cherry. "Fantasy . . .," 468.

"The Escape"
Rohrberger, Mary H. . . . *Katherine Mansfield*, 87–88.

"The Fly"
Kane, Thomas S., and Leonard J. Peters. *Some Suggestions* . . ., 15–16.
Rohrberger, Mary H. . . . *Katherine Mansfield*, 99–100.
Zinman, Toby S. "The Snail Under the Leaf: Katherine Mansfield's Imagery," *Mod Fiction Stud*, 24 (1978), 463–464.

"Frau Brechennacher Attends a Wedding"
Burgan, Mary. "Childbirth Trauma . . .," 399–400.
Rohrberger, Mary H. . . . *Katherine Mansfield*, 121–122.

"The Garden Party"
Cassill, R. V. *Instructor's Handbook* . . ., 139–140.
Rohrberger, Mary H. . . . *Katherine Mansfield*, 93–95.
Sorkin, Adam J. "Katherine Mansfield's 'The Garden Party': Style and Social Occasion," *Mod Fiction Stud*, 24 (1978), 439–455.

"Germans at Meat"
Rohrberger, Mary H. . . . *Katherine Mansfield*, 73–74.

"How Pearl Button Was Kidnapped"
Rohrberger, Mary H. . . . *Katherine Mansfield*, 36–37.

"An Indiscreet Journey"
Rohrberger, Mary H. . . . *Katherine Mansfield*, 62–63.

"Je Ne Parle Pas Français"
Rohrberger, Mary H. . . . *Katherine Mansfield*, 112–117.

"Marriage à la Mode"
Rohrberger, Mary H. . . . *Katherine Mansfield*, 87–88.

"Miss Brill"
*Perrine, Laurence. *Instructor's Manual* . . . "Story . . .," 50–52; *Instructor's*

Manual . . . "Literature . . .," 50–52.
*Welty, Eudora. "The Reading and Writing of Short Stories," in May, Charles
E., Ed. *Short Story Theories,* 168–169.

"The Modern Soul"
Rohrberger, Mary H. . . . *Katherine Mansfield,* 76–77.

"New Dresses"
Rohrberger, Mary H. . . . *Katherine Mansfield,* 42–44.

"Pension Sequin"
Rohrberger, Mary H. . . . *Katherine Mansfield,* 78–79.

"Pictures"
Rohrberger, Mary H. . . . *Katherine Mansfield,* 69–70.

"Prelude"
Burgan, Mary. "Childbirth Trauma . . .," 403–406.
Peterson, Richard F. "The Circle of Truth . . .," 386–388.
Rohrberger, Mary H. . . . *Katherine Mansfield,* 124–133.
Zinman, Toby S. "The Snail Under the Leaf . . .," 461–462.

"The Singing Lesson"
Rohrberger, Mary H. . . . *Katherine Mansfield,* 85–86.

"The Sister of the Baroness"
Rohrberger, Mary H. . . . *Katherine Mansfield,* 75–76.

"Six Years After"
Rohrberger, Mary H. . . . *Katherine Mansfield,* 111–112.

"Spring Picture"
Rohrberger, Mary H. . . . *Katherine Mansfield,* 105–106.

"The Stranger"
Rohrberger, Mary H. . . . *Katherine Mansfield,* 86–87.

"A Suburban Fairy Tale"
Rohrberger, Mary H. . . . *Katherine Mansfield,* 41–42.
Zinman, Toby S. "The Snail Under the Leaf . . .," 461.

"Sun and Moon"
Rohrberger, Mary H. . . . *Katherine Mansfield,* 40–41.

"The Swing of the Pendulum"
Rohrberger, Mary H. . . . *Katherine Mansfield,* 54–55.

"Taking the Veil"
Rohrberger, Mary H. . . . *Katherine Mansfield,* 49–50.

"This Flower"
Rohrberger, Mary H. . . . *Katherine Mansfield,* 58–59.

"The Tiredness of Rosabel"
Rohrberger, Mary H. . . . *Katherine Mansfield,* 25–29.

"A Truthful Adventure"
Rohrberger, Mary H. . . . *Katherine Mansfield,* 81–82.

"Violet"
Rohrberger, Mary H. . . . *Katherine Mansfield,* 79–80.

"The Wind Blows"
Rohrberger, Mary H. . . . *Katherine Mansfield,* 96–98.

"The Woman at the Store"
Rohrberger, Mary H. . . . *Katherine Mansfield,* 82–83.

"The Wrong House"
Rohrberger, Mary H. . . . *Katherine Mansfield,* 37–38.

"The Young Girl"
Rohrberger, Mary H. . . . *Katherine Mansfield,* 47–49.

MAO DUN [MAO TUN or TUNG; also SHEN YEN-PING]

"Autumn Harvest"
Hsia, C. T. *A History . . .,* 163–164.

"Autumn in Kuling"
Chen, Yü-shih. "Mao Dun and the Use of Political Allegory in Fiction: A Case Study of His 'Autumn in Kuling,' " in Goldman, Merle, Ed. *Modern Chinese Literature . . .,* 273–280.

"Creation"
Berninghausen, John. "The Central Contradiction in Mao Dun's Earliest Fiction," in Goldman, Merle, Ed. *Modern Chinese Literature . . .,* 249–250.

"Spring Silkworms"
Hsia, C. T. *A History . . .,* 162–163.

"Suicide"
Berninghausen, John. "The Central Contradiction . . .," 252–253.

WILLIAM MARCH

"Aesop's Last Fable"
Kane, Thomas S., and Leonard J. Peters. *Some Suggestions . . .,* 6–7.

PESACH MARCUS

"Higher and Higher"
Gittleman, Sol. *From Shtetl to Suburbia . . .,* 136–138.

JUAN MARIN

"Black Port"
Swain, James O. *Juan Marin* . . ., 72–73.

"A Flight into Mystery"
Swain, James O. *Juan Marin* . . ., 65.

"Julian Aranda's Death"
Swain, James O. *Juan Marin* . . ., 79–80.

"Lazarus"
Swain, James O. *Juan Marin* . . ., 74.

"The Man at the Funeral"
Swain, James O. *Juan Marin* . . ., 66.

"The Man Hunt"
Swain, James O. *Juan Marin* . . ., 75–76.

"Nuptial"
Swain, James O. *Juan Marin* . . ., 66–67.

"Percival Lawrence's Crime"
Swain, James O. *Juan Marin* . . ., 79.

PAULE MARSHALL

"Barbados"
Keizs, Marcia. "Theme and Style in the Works of Paule Marshall," *Negro Am Lit Forum*, 9 (1975), 72–73.

"Brooklyn"
Keizs, Marcia. "Theme and Style . . .," 73.

"To Da-duh, In Memoriam"
Keizs, Marcia. "Theme and Style . . .," 75.

W. SOMERSET MAUGHAM

"The Outstation"
Cassill, R. V. *Instructor's Handbook* . . ., 141–142.

"Sanatorium"
Perrine, Laurence. *Instructor's Manual* . . . "*Story* . . .," 9–11; *Instructor's Manual* . . . "*Literature* . . .," 9–11.

GUY DE MAUPASSANT

"The Necklace"
Cassill, R. V. *Instructor's Handbook* . . ., 142–143.

FRANÇOIS MAURIAC

"Thérèse Desqueyroux"
> Brosman, Catherine S. "Point of View and Christian Viewpoint in 'Thérèse Desqueyroux,' " *Essays French Lit,* 11 (1974), 69–73.
> Crisafulli, Alessandro S. "The Theme of Captivity and Its Metaphorical Expression in Mauriac's 'Thérèse Desqueyroux,' " in Sola-Solé, Josep M., Alessandro S. Crisafulli, and Siegfried A. Schulz, Eds. . . . *Tatiana Fotitch,* 29–35.
> Farrell, Edith R. and Frederick. " 'Thérèse Desqueyroux': A Complete Suicide," *Lang Q,* 14, iii–iv (1976), 13–15, 18, 22.
> Monferier, Jacques. "Thérèse Desqueyroux, Phèdre et le destin," *La Revue des Lettres Modernes,* Nos. 516–522 (1977), 109–118.

HERMAN MELVILLE

"The Apple-Tree Table"
> Dillingham, William B. *Melville's Short Fiction* . . ., 341–366.
> Douglas, Ann. *The Feminization* . . ., 318–319.
> *Fisher, Marvin. *Going Under* . . ., 124–132.

"Bartleby the Scrivener"
> Abrams, Robert E. " 'Bartleby' and the Fragile Pageantry of the Ego," *Engl Lit Hist,* 45 (1978), 488–500.
> Billy, Ted. "Eros and Thanatos in 'Bartleby,' " *Arizona Q,* 31 (1975), 21–32.
> Blake, Nancy. "Mourning and Melancholia in 'Bartleby,' " *Delta,* 7 (1978), 155–168.
> Cassill, R. V. *Instructor's Handbook* . . ., 144–146.
> Davidson, Cathy N. "Courting God and Mammon: The Biographer's Impasse in 'Bartleby the Scrivener,' " *Delta,* 6 (1978), 47–59.
> Dillingham, William B. *Melville's Short Fiction* . . ., 18–55.
> Douglas, Ann. *The Feminization* . . ., 315–317.
> Emery, Allan M. "The Alternatives in Melville's 'Bartleby,' " *Nineteenth-Century Fiction,* 31 (1976), 170–187.
> *Fisher, Marvin. *Going Under* . . ., 179–199.
> Fleurdorge, Claude. " 'Bartleby': A Story of Broadway," *Delta,* 7 (1978), 65–109.
> Franklin, H. Bruce. *The Victim* . . ., 56–60.
> Gupta, R. K. " 'Bartleby': Melville's Critique of Reason," *Indian J Am Stud,* 4, i–ii (1974), 66–71.
> Joswick, Thomas P. "The 'Incurable Disorder' in 'Bartleby the Scrivener,' " *Delta,* 6 (1978), 79–93.
> Kornfeld, Milton. "Bartleby and the Presentation of Self in Everyday Life," *Arizona Q,* 31 (1975), 51–56.
> Laroque, François. "Bartleby l'idée fixe," *Delta,* 7 (1978), 143–153.
> Leavis, Q. D. "Melville: The 1853–6 Phase," in Pullin, Faith, Ed. *New Perspectives* . . ., 199–200.
> Mathews, James W. " 'Bartleby': Melville's Tragedy of Humours," *Interpretations,* 10 (1978), 41–48.
> Mottram, Eric. "Orpheus and Measured Forms: Laws, Madness and Reticence in Melville," in Pullin, Faith, Ed. *New Perspectives* . . ., 232–234.

Pinsker, Sanford. " 'Bartleby the Scrivener': Language as Wall," *Coll Lit,* 2 (1975), 17–27.

Ryan, Steven T. "The Gothic Formula of 'Bartleby,' " *Arizona Q,* 34 (1978), 311–316.

Sanderlin, Reed. "A Re-Examination of the Role of the Lawyer-Narrator in Melville's 'Bartleby,' " *Interpretations,* 10 (1978), 49–55.

Singleton, Marvin. "Melville's 'Bartleby': Over the Republic, a Ciceronian Shadow," *Canadian R Am Stud,* 6 (1975), 165–173.

Sullivan, William P. "Bartleby and Infantile Autism: A Naturalistic Explanation," *Bull West Virginia Assoc Coll Engl Teachers,* 3, ii (1976), 43–60.

Vitoux, Pierre. " 'Bartleby': Analyse du récit," *Delta,* 7 (1978), 173–187.

Zuppinger, Renaud. " 'Bartleby': Prometheus Revisited: Pour une problematique de la confiance, ou, la 'sortie du souterrain,' " *Delta,* 6 (1978), 61–77.

"The Bell Tower"

Carter, Everett. *The American Idea* . . ., 182–183.

Cohen, Hennig. "Bannadonna's Bell Ritual," *Melville Soc Extracts,* 36 (1978), 7–8.

Dillingham, William B. *Melville's Short Fiction* . . ., 208–226.

*Fisher, Marvin. *Going Under* . . ., 95–104.

*Franklin, H. Bruce. *Future Perfect* . . ., 2nd ed., 146–150.

Puk, Francine S. "The Sovereign Nature of 'The Bell-Tower,' " *Extracts,* 27 (1976), 14–15.

"Benito Cereno"

D'Avanzo, Mario L. " 'Undo It, Cut It, Quick': The Gordian Knot in 'Benito Cereno,' " *Stud Short Fiction,* 15 (1978), 192–194.

Dillingham, William B. *Melville's Short Fiction* . . ., 227–270.

Fisher, Marvin. " 'Benito Cereno': Old World Experience, New World Expectations and Third World Realities," *Forum* (Houston), 13, iii (1976), 31–36.
———. *Going Under* . . ., 104–117.

Frank, Max. "Die Farb- und Lichtsymbolik im Prosawerk Herman Melvilles," *Beihefte zum Jahrbuch für Amerikastudien,* 19 (1967), 131–136.

Franklin, H. Bruce. *The Victim* . . ., 60–62.

Gilmore, Michael T. *The Middle Way* . . ., 165–182.

Grenander, M. E. "Benito Cereno and Legal Oppression: A Szaszian Interpretation," *J Libertarian Stud,* 2 (1978), 337–342.

Johnson, Paul D. "American Innocence and Guilt: Black-White Destiny in 'Benito Cereno,' " *Phylon,* 36 (1975), 426–434.

Justman, Stewart. "Repression and Self in 'Benito Cereno,' " *Stud Short Fiction,* 15 (1978), 301–306.

Karcher, Carolyn L. "Melville and Racial Prejudice: A Re-Evaluation," *Southern R,* 12 (1976), 297–310.

Leavis, Q. D. ". . . The 1853–6 Phase," 206–208.

Roundy, Nancy. "Present Shadows: Epistemology in Melville's 'Benito Cereno,' " *Arizona Q,* 34 (1978), 344–350.

Sequeira, Isaac. "The San Dominick: The Shadow of Benito Cereno," *Osmania J Engl Stud,* 10 (1973), 1–6.

Shehan, Peter J. "Strands of the Knot: Ritual Structure in Melville's 'Benito Cereno,' " *New Laurel R,* 6, i (1976), 23–37.

Valenti, Peter L. "Images of Authority in 'Benito Cereno,' " *Coll Lang Assoc J,*

21 (1978), 367–379.

Vanderbilt, Kermit. " 'Benito Cereno': Melville's Fable of Black Complicity,"
    Southern R, 12 (1976), 311–322.

Welsh, Howard. "The Politics of Race in 'Benito Cereno,' " *Am Lit,* 46 (1975),
    556–566.

Zlatic, Thomas D. " 'Benito Cereno': Melville's 'Back-Handed-Well-Knot,' "
    Arizona Q, 34 (1978), 327–343.

"Billy Budd"

Beidler, Philip D. " 'Billy Budd': Melville's Valedictory to Emerson," *ESQ: J
    Am Renaissance,* 24 (1978), 215–228.

Branch, Watson. "Melville's 'Incompetent' World in 'Billy Budd, Sailor,' "
    Melville Soc Extracts, 34 (1978), 1–2.

Cheiken, Miriam Q. "Captain Vere: Darkness Made Visible," *Arizona Q,* 34
    (1978), 293–310.

Cifelli, Edward M. " 'Billy Budd': Boggy Ground to Build On," *Stud Short
    Fiction,* 13 (1976), 463–469.

Cohen, Hennig. "The Singing Stammerer Motif in 'Billy Budd,' " *Western
    Folklore,* 34 (1975), 54–55.

Douglas, Ann. *The Feminization . . .,* 323–326.

Floyd, Nathaniel M. " 'Billy Budd': A Psychological Autopsy," *Am Imago,* 34
    (1977), 28–49.

Frank, Max. "Die Farb- und Lichtsymbolik . . .," 137–143.

Franklin, H. Bruce. *The Victim . . .,* 67–70.

Fussell, Mary E. B. " 'Billy Budd': Melville's Happy Ending," *Stud Romanti-
    cism,* 15 (1976), 43–58.

Garner, Stanton. "Fraud as Fact in Herman Melville's 'Billy Budd,' " *San José
    Stud,* 4, ii (1978), 82–107.

Gilmore, Michael T. *The Middle Way . . .,* 182–194.

Gordon, David J. *Literary Art . . .,* 123–152.

Humma, John B. "Melville's 'Billy Budd' and Lawrence's 'The Prussian
    Officer,' " *Essays Lit,* 1, i (1974), 83–88.

Longenecker, Marlene. "Captain Vere and the Form of Truth," *Stud Short
    Fiction,* 14 (1977), 337–343.

Manlove, C. N. "An Organic Hesitancy: Theme and Style in 'Billy Budd,' " in
    Pullin, Faith, Ed. *New Perspectives . . .,* 275–300.

Marks, William S. "Melville, Opium, and 'Billy Budd,' " *Stud Am Fiction,* 6
    (1978), 33–45.

Mottram, Eric. "Orpheus and Measured Forms . . .," 242–253.

Obuchowski, Peter A. " 'Billy Budd' and the Failure of Art," *Stud Short
    Fiction,* 15 (1978), 445–452.

Reed, Walter L. "The Measured Forms of Captain Vere," *Mod Fiction Stud,* 23
    (1977), 227–235.

Reinert, Otto. " 'Secret Mines and Dubious Side': The World of 'Billy Budd,' "
    in Seyersted, Brita, Ed. *Norwegian Contributions . . .,* 183–192.

Scorza, Thomas J. "Technology, Philosophy and Political Virtue: The Case of
    'Billy Budd, Sailor,' " *Interpretation: J Pol Phil,* 5, i (1975), 91–107.

Spengemann, William C. *The Adventurous Muse . . .,* 210–211.

"Cock-A-Doodle-Doo!"

Dillingham, William B. *Melville's Short Fiction . . .,* 56–74.

Fisher, Marvin. *Going Under . . .,* 161–178.

Leavis, Q. D. ". . . The 1853–6 Phase," 200–204.

"The Encantadas"
 Dillingham, William B. *Melville's Short Fiction* . . ., 75–108.
 Fisher, Marvin. *Going Under* . . ., 28–50.
 Franzosia, John. "Darwin and Melville: Why a Tortoise?" *Am Imago,* 33
  (1976), 361–379.
 Leavis, Q. D. ". . . The 1853–6 Phase," 198.
 Roberts, David A. "Structure and Meaning in Melville's 'The Encantadas,' "
  ESQ: J Am Renaissance, 22 (1976), 234–244.

"The Fiddler"
 Dillingham, William B. *Melville's Short Fiction* . . ., 143–167.
 Leavis, Q. D. ". . . The 1853–6 Phase," 200.

"The Happy Failure"
 Dillingham, William B. *Melville's Short Fiction* . . ., 143–167.
 Fisher, Marvin. *Going Under* . . ., 155–161.

"I and My Chimney"
 Dillingham, William B. *Melville's Short Fiction* . . ., 271–295.
 Douglas, Ann. *The Feminization* . . ., 317–318.
 Fisher, Marvin. *Going Under* . . ., 199–213.
 Leavis, Q. D. ". . . The 1853–6 Phase," 209–210.

"Jimmy Rose"
 Dillingham, William B. *Melville's Short Fiction* . . ., 296–318.
 *Fisher, Marvin. *Going Under* . . ., 133–145.
 Jeffrey, David K. "Unreliable Narration in Melville's 'Jimmy Rose,' " *Arizona
  Q,* 31 (1975), 69–72.

"The Lightning-Rod Man"
 Dillingham, William B. *Melville's Short Fiction* . . ., 168–182.
 *Fisher, Marvin. *Going Under* . . ., 118–124.
 Leavis, Q. D. ". . . The 1853–6 Phase," 208–209.
 Mastriano, Mary A. "Melville's 'The Lightning-Rod Man,' " *Stud Short Fic-
  tion,* 14 (1977), 29–33.

"The Paradise of Bachelors and the Tartarus of Maids"
 Dillingham, William B. *Melville's Short Fiction* . . ., 183–207.
 *Fisher, Marvin. *Going Under* . . ., 70–94.
 Frank, Max. "Die Farb- und Lichtsymbolik . . .," 128–131.
 Franklin, H. Bruce. *The Victim* . . ., 52–56.
 Kennedy, X. J. *Instructor's Manual* . . ., 21–22.
 Leavis, Q. D. ". . . The 1853–6 Phase," 204–206.

"The Piazza"
 Avallone, C. Sherman. "Melville's 'Piazza,' " *ESQ: J Am Renaissance,* 22
  (1976), 221–233.
 Dillingham, William B. *Melville's Short Fiction* . . ., 319–340.
 *Fisher, Marvin. *Going Under* . . ., 13–28.
 Roundy, Nancy. "Fancies, Reflections and Things: Imagination as Perception in

'The Piazza,' " *Coll Lang Assoc J,* 20 (1977), 539–546.

"Poor Man's Pudding and Rich Man's Crumbs"
Dillingham, William B. *Melville's Short Fiction* . . ., 119–142.
*Fisher, Marvin. *Going Under* . . ., 61–70.

"The Two Temples"
Dillingham, William B. *Melville's Short Fiction* . . ., 104–118.
*Fisher, Marvin. *Going Under* . . ., 51–61.

PROSPER MÉRIMÉE

"The Blue Room"
Bowman, Frank P. *Prosper Mérimée* . . ., 16–17.
Smith, Maxwell A. *Prosper Mérimée,* 168–171.

"The Capture of the Redoubt"
Smith, Maxwell A. *Prosper Mérimée,* 102–105.

"Carmen"
Leibowitz, Judith. *Narrative Purposes* . . ., 39–41.
Smith, Maxwell A. *Prosper Mérimée,* 143–147.

"Colomba"
Smith, Maxwell A. *Prosper Mérimée,* 133–139.

"La Double Méprise"
Lethbridge, Robert, and Michael Tilby. "Reading Mérimée's 'La Double
Méprise,' " *Mod Lang R,* 73 (1978), 767–785.
Smith, Maxwell A. *Prosper Mérimée,* 117–123.

"The Etruscan Vase"
Smith, Maxwell A. *Prosper Mérimée,* 110–113.

"Federigo"
Smith, Maxwell A. *Prosper Mérimée,* 107–110.

"The Game of Backgammon"
Smith, Maxwell A. *Prosper Mérimée,* 113–116.

"Lokis"
Massey, Irving. *The Gaping Pig* . . ., 110–114.
Smith, Maxwell A. *Prosper Mérimée,* 171–176.

"Mateo Falcone"
Smith, Maxwell A. *Prosper Mérimée,* 98–100.

"Venus of Ille"
Bowman, Frank P. *Prosper Mérimée* . . ., 54–55.
Massey, Irving. *The Gaping Pig* . . ., 110–114.

Smith, Maxwell A. *Prosper Mérimée*, 228–233.

"The Vision of Charles XI"
Smith, Maxwell A. *Prosper Mérimée*, 100–102.

CONRAD FERDINAND MEYER

"The Amulet"
Berkhard, Marianne. *Conrad Ferdinand Meyer*, 69–74.
McCort, Dennis. "Historical Consciousness versus Action in C. F. Meyer's 'Das Amulett,' " *Symposium*, 32 (1978), 114–132.

"Angela Borgia"
Berkhard, Marianne. *Conrad Ferdinand Meyer*, 147–152.

"Gustav Adolf's Page"
Berkhard, Marianne. *Conrad Ferdinand Meyer*, 123–124.

"Der Heilige"
Berkhard, Marianne. *Conrad Ferdinand Meyer*, 86–94.
Leibowitz, Judith. *Narrative Purposes* . . ., 32–37.

"The Monk's Wedding"
Berkhard, Marianne. *Conrad Ferdinand Meyer*, 129–136.

"Die Richterin"
Berkhard, Marianne. *Conrad Ferdinand Meyer*, 137–141.

"Der Schuss von der Kanzel"
Berkhard, Marianne. *Conrad Ferdinand Meyer*, 83–85.

"The Sufferings of a Boy"
Berkhard, Marianne. *Conrad Ferdinand Meyer*, 126–129.
Swales, Martin. "Fagon's Defeat: Some Remarks on C. F. Meyer's 'Das Leiden eines Knaben,' " *Germ R*, 52 (1977), 29–43.
————. *The German "Novelle,"* 180–201.

"Die Versuchung des Pescara"
Berkhard, Marianne. *Conrad Ferdinand Meyer*, 141–147.
Stauffacher, Walter. "Der ermordete Vater: Zu einem Motiv in C.F. Meyers 'Die Versuchung des Pescara,' " *Wirkendes Wort*, 28 (1978), 191–197.

KÁLMÁN MIKSZÁTH

"The Big Spender"
Scheer, Steven C. *Kálmán Mikszáth*, 45–47.

"The First Narrative"
Scheer, Steven C. *Kálmán Mikszáth*, 42–44.

"The Golden Maid"
Scheer, Steven C. *Kálmán Mikszáth*, 31–33.

"Lapaj, the Famous Bagpiper"
Scheer, Steven C. *Kálmán Mikszáth*, 35.

"The Late Lamb"
Scheer, Steven C. *Kálmán Mikszáth*, 36–37.

"The Lottery"
Scheer, Steven C. *Kálmán Mikszáth*, 29–31.

"The Novel of Two Manors"
Scheer, Steven C. *Kálmán Mikszáth*, 36.

"Pali Szücs's Luck"
Scheer, Steven C. *Kálmán Mikszáth*, 40.

"Poor Janos Gelyi's Horses"
Scheer, Steven C. *Kálmán Mikszáth*, 37–38.

"The Queen's Skirt"
Scheer, Steven C. *Kálmán Mikszáth*, 39–40.

"The Second Narrative"
Scheer, Steven C. *Kálmán Mikszáth*, 44–45.

"That Black Stain"
Scheer, Steven C. *Kálmán Mikszáth*, 33–35.

"That Which Poisons the Soul"
Scheer, Steven C. *Kálmán Mikszáth*, 28–29.

"The Virgin Mary of Gozon"
Scheer, Steven C. *Kálmán Mikszáth*, 40–41.

"Where Has Magda Gal Gone?"
Scheer, Steven C. *Kálmán Mikszáth*, 38–39.

ARTHUR MILLER

"Monte Sant' Angelo"
Jacobson, Irving. "The Vestigial Jews on Monte Sant' Angelo," *Stud Short Fiction*, 13 (1976), 507–512.

SCHUYLER MILLER

"The Cave"
Carter, Paul A. *The Creation* . . ., 266–267.

WALTER M. MILLER

"The Big Hunger"
Samuelson, David M. "The Lost Canticles of Walter M. Miller, Jr.," *Sci-Fiction Stud,* 3 (1976), 8–9.

"Blood Bank"
Samuelson, David M. "The Lost Canticles . . .," 13–14.

"Check and Checkmate"
Samuelson, David M. "The Lost Canticles . . .," 6.

"Cold Awakening"
Samuelson, David M. "The Lost Canticles . . .," 8.

"Command Performance"
Samuelson, David M. "The Lost Canticles . . .," 17.

"Conditionally Human"
Samuelson, David M. "The Lost Canticles . . .," 17–18.

"Crucifixus Etiam"
Samuelson, David M. "The Lost Canticles . . .," 19–21.

"Dark Benediction"
Samuelson, David M. "The Lost Canticles . . .," 18–19.

"Death of a Spaceman" [same as "Memento Homo"]
Samuelson, David M. "The Lost Canticles . . .," 9.

"The Hoofer"
Samuelson, David M. "The Lost Canticles . . .," 9.

"I Made You"
Samuelson, David M. "The Lost Canticles . . .," 9–10.

"No Moon for Me"
Samuelson, David M. "The Lost Canticles . . .," 8.

"Please Me Plus"
Samuelson, David M. "The Lost Canticles . . .," 7.

"Six and Ten Are Johnny"
Samuelson, David M. "The Lost Canticles . . .," 11.

"The Soul-Empty Ones"
Samuelson, David M. "The Lost Canticles . . .," 6–7.

"The Ties That Bind"
Samuelson, David M. "The Lost Canticles . . .," 13.

"The Yokel"
Samuelson, David M. "The Lost Canticles . . .," 7–8.

MISHIMA YUKIO

"Patriotism"
   *Abcarian, Richard, and Marvin Klotz. *Instructor's Manual* . . ., 2nd ed., 16–17.
   Cassill, R. V. *Instructor's Handbook* . . ., 147–148.

IRENE MUSILLO MITCHELL

"Scenes from the Thistledown Theatre"
   Rohrberger, Mary. *Instructor's Manual* . . ., 44–45.

CATHERINE L. MOORE
[See also her pseudonyms LAWRENCE O'DONNELL and LEWIS PADGETT]

"The Bright Illusion"
   Carter, Paul A. *The Creation* . . ., 182–183.

"No Woman Born"
   Gunn, James. "Henry Kuttner, C. L. Moore, Lewis Padgett, *et al.,*" in
   Clareson, Thomas D., Ed. *Voices for the Future* . . ., 202–204.

GEORGE MOORE

"Albert Nobbs"
   Fontana, Ernest L. "Sexual Alienation in George Moore's 'Albert Nobbs,' "
   Int'l Fiction R, 4 (1977), 183–185.

"The Exile"
   Farrow, Anthony. *George Moore,* 119–120.

"Henrietta Marr" [an expansion of "Mildred Lawson"]
   Seinfelt, Frederick W. *George Moore* . . ., 150–153.

"In the Clay"
   Farrow, Anthony. *George Moore,* 114–116.

"Julia Cahill's Curse"
   Farrow, Anthony. *George Moore,* 121–122.

"A Letter to Rome"
   Farrow, Anthony. *George Moore,* 120–121.

"Liadin and Curithir"
   Seinfelt, Frederick W. *George Moore* . . ., 205–206.

"Mildred Lawson" [originally "An Art Student"; later expanded to become
   "Henrietta Marr"]
   Seinfelt, Frederick W. *George Moore* . . ., 148–150.

"Peronnik the Fool"
Seinfelt, Frederick W. *George Moore* . . ., 218–219.

"Priscilla and Emily Lofft"
Seinfelt, Frederick W. *George Moore* . . ., 135–137.

"Sarah Gwynn"
Seinfelt, Frederick W. *George Moore* . . ., 134–135.

"So on He Fares"
Seinfelt, Frederick W. *George Moore* . . ., 129–130.

"Some Parishioners"
Farrow, Anthony. *George Moore*, 117–119.

"The Way Back"
Farrow, Anthony. *George Moore*, 116–117.

"The Wedding Gown"
Seinfelt, Frederick W. *George Moore* . . ., 131.

"The Wild Goose"
Seinfelt, Frederick W. *George Moore* . . ., 189–192.

"Wilfred Holmes"
Seinfelt, Frederick W. *George Moore* . . ., 74–77.

"The Window"
Seinfelt, Frederick W. *George Moore* . . ., 130–131.

FRANK MOORHOUSE

"The American, Paul Jonson"
Harrison-Ford, Carl. "The Short Stories of Wilding and Moorhouse," *Southerly*, 33 (1973), 168–169.

"The Machine Gun"
Harrison-Ford, Carl. "The Short Stories . . .," 169–170.

MORI ŌGAI

"Sanshō the Steward" [same as "Sanshō the Bailiff"]
Rimer, J. Thomas. *Modern Japanese Fiction* . . ., 155–161.

EDUARD MÖRIKE

"Mozart on the Way to Prague"
Field, G. Wallis. "Silver and Orange: Notes on Mörike's Mozart-*Novelle*," *Seminar*, 14 (1978), 243–254.

WILLIAM MORRIS

"A Dream"
Mathews, Richard. *Worlds Beyond the World* . . ., 10–11.

"Gertha's Lovers"
Mathews, Richard. *Worlds Beyond the World* . . ., 11–12.

"Golden Wings"
Mathews, Richard. *Worlds Beyond the World* . . ., 17–18.

"The Hollow Land"
Mathews, Richard. *Worlds Beyond the World* . . ., 14–17.

"Lindenborg Pool"
Mathews, Richard. *Worlds Beyond the World* . . ., 9–10.

"The Story of the Glittering Plain"
Mathews, Richard. *Worlds Beyond the World* . . ., 34–36.

"The Story of the Unknown Church"
Mathews, Richard. *Worlds Beyond the World* . . ., 6–8.

"Svend and His Brethren"
Mathews, Richard. *Worlds Beyond the World* . . ., 12–14.

WILLARD MOTLEY

"The Almost White Boy"
Fleming, Robert E. *Willard Motley*, 33–34.

"The Boy"
Fleming, Robert E. *Willard Motley*, 25–26.

"The Boy Grows Up"
Fleming, Robert E. *Willard Motley*, 26.

EZEKIEL MPHAHLELE

"Across Down Stream"
Barnett, Ursula. *Ezekiel Mphahlele*, 41–42.

"A Ballad of Oyo"
Barnett, Ursula. *Ezekiel Mphahlele*, 88–89.

"The Barber of Bariga"
Barnett, Ursula. *Ezekiel Mphahlele*, 85–87.

"Down the Quiet Street"
Barnett, Ursula. *Ezekiel Mphahlele*, 42–43.

"Grieg on a Stolen Piano"
  Barnett, Ursula. *Ezekiel Mphahlele*, 89–95.

"He and the Cat"
  Barnett, Ursula. *Ezekiel Mphahlele*, 83–84.

"In Corner B"
  Barnett, Ursula. *Ezekiel Mphahlele*, 97–102.
  Roscoe, Leonard. *Uhuru's Fire . . .*, 230–231.

"The Leaves Were Falling"
  Barnett, Ursula. *Ezekiel Mphahlele*, 20–22.

"The Living and Dead"
  Barnett, Ursula. *Ezekiel Mphahlele*, 71–75.

"The Master of Doornvlei"
  Barnett, Ursula. *Ezekiel Mphahlele*, 77–79.

"Mrs. Plum"
  Barnett, Ursula. *Ezekiel Mphahlele*, 102–110.

"Out Brief Candle"
  Barnett, Ursula. *Ezekiel Mphahlele*, 24–25.

"A Point of Identity"
  Barnett, Ursula. *Ezekiel Mphahlele*, 95–97.

"Reef Train"
  Barnett, Ursula. *Ezekiel Mphahlele*, 40–41.

"The Suitcase"
  Barnett, Ursula. *Ezekiel Mphahlele*, 81–83.

"Tomorrow You Shall Reap"
  Barnett, Ursula. *Ezekiel Mphahlele*, 19–21.

"We'll Have Dinner at Eight"
  Barnett, Ursula. *Ezekiel Mphahlele*, 75–77.

"The Woman"
  Barnett, Ursula. *Ezekiel Mphahlele*, 79–80.

"The Woman Walks Out"
  Barnett, Ursula. *Ezekiel Mphahlele*, 80.

ALICE MUNRO

"The Dance of the Happy Shades"
  Macdonald, Rae M. "A Madman Loose in the World: The Vision of Alice
  Munro," *Mod Fiction Stud*, 22 (1976), 365–367.

"Day of the Butterfly"
Macdonald, Rae M. "A Madman Loose . . .," 367–368.

"The Time of Death"
Macdonald, Rae M. "A Madman Loose . . .," 369–370.

"Winter Wind"
Macdonald, Rae M. "A Madman Loose . . .," 373.

ROBERT MUSIL

"The Blackbird"
Mauch, Gudrun. "Das Märchen in Musils Erzählung 'Die Amsel,' " *Literatur und Kritik,* 113 (1977), 149–166.

"Grigia"
Eibl, Karl. *Robert Musil* . . ., 141–146.
Grieser, Dietmar. "Musil, 'Grigia' und das Fersental," *Das Fenster Tiroler Kulturzeitschrift,* 17 (1976), 1750–1756.
Peters, Frederick G. *Robert Musil* . . ., 107–126.

"The Perfection of Love"
Braun, Wilhelm. "Die Wassermetapher in 'Die Vollendung der Liebe,' " *Colloquia Germanica,* 10 (1976–77), 237–246.
Cohn, Dorrit. *Transparent Minds* . . ., 41–43.
Peters, Frederick G. *Robert Musil* . . ., 59–70.

"The Portuguese Lady"
Eibl, Karl. *Robert Musil* . . ., 146–150.
Peters, Frederick G. *Robert Musil* . . ., 126–145.

"The Temptation of Silent Veronica"
Peters, Frederick G. *Robert Musil* . . ., 70–104.

"Tonka"
Eibl, Karl. *Robert Musil* . . ., 150–155.
Peters, Frederick G. *Robert Musil* . . ., 145–187.
Sjögren, Christine O. "The Enigma of Musil's 'Tonka,' " *Mod Austrian Lit,* 9, iii–iv (1976), 100–113.

VLADIMIR NABOKOV

"An Affair of Honor"
Naumann, Marina T. *Blue Evenings* . . ., 126–137.

"Bachmann"
Naumann, Marina T. *Blue Evenings* . . ., 153–163.

"Benevolence"
Naumann, Marina T. *Blue Evenings* . . ., 44–50.

"Spring in Fialta"
  Bodenstein, Jürgen. "Vladimir Nabokov, 'Spring in Fialta,' " in Freese, Peter,
    Ed. . . . *Interpretationen*, 90–100.
  Lee, L. L. *Vladimir Nabokov*, 31–33.

"The Storm"
  Naumann, Marina T. *Blue Evenings* . . ., 76–81.

"Terror"
  Naumann, Marina T. *Blue Evenings* . . ., 173–181.

"The Vane Sisters"
  Ristkok, Tuuli-Ann. "Nabakov's 'The Vane Sisters': 'Once in a Thousand Years
    of Fiction,' " *Univ Windsor R*, 11, ii (1976), 27–48.

NAGAI KAFŪ

"The River Sumida"
  Rimer, J. Thomas. *Modern Japanese Fiction* . . ., 142–150.

VIDIADHAR SURAJPRASAD NAIPAUL

"A Christmas Story"
  White, Landeg. *V. S. Naipaul* . . ., 161–163.

"The Enemy"
  White, Landeg. *V. S. Naipaul* . . ., 55–58.

"Gopi"
  White, Landeg. *V. S. Naipaul* . . ., 36–37.

"Gurudeva"
  White, Landeg. *V. S. Naipaul* . . ., 43–45.

"The Mourners"
  Winser, Leigh. "Naipaul's Painters and Their Pictures," *Critique*, 18, i (1976),
    73–74.

"My Aunt Gold Teeth"
  White, Landeg. *V. S. Naipaul* . . ., 60–62.

"One out of Many"
  White, Landeg. *V. S. Naipaul* . . ., 202–205.

"Tell Me Who to Kill"
  White, Landeg. *V. S. Naipaul* . . ., 202–205.

JOHN NEAL

"Courtship"
Lease, Benjamin. *That Wild Fellow* . . ., 178–179.

"David Whicher"
Lease, Benjamin. *That Wild Fellow* . . ., 162–163, 166–167.
Sears, Donald A. *John Neal*, 94–95.

"The Haunted Man"
Lease, Benjamin. *That Wild Fellow* . . ., 170–172.

"The Ins and Outs"
Lease, Benjamin. *That Wild Fellow* . . ., 182–183.

"Otter-Bag"
Lease, Benjamin. *That Wild Fellow* . . ., 167–170.

"Robert Steele"
Sears, Donald A. *John Neal*, 108.

"The Utilitarian"
Lease, Benjamin. *That Wild Fellow* . . ., 179–180.

"The Young Phrenologist"
Lease, Benjamin. *That Wild Fellow* . . ., 180–181.

GÉRARD DE NERVAL [GÉRARD LABRUNIE]

"Sylvie"
Carroll, Robert C. "Romanesque Seduction in Nerval's 'Sylvie,' " *Nineteenth-Century French Stud*, 5 (1977), 222–235.

ANAÏS NIN

"Birth"
Spencer, Sharon. *Collage of Dreams* . . ., 71–72.

"Hedja"
Spencer, Sharon. *Collage of Dreams* . . ., 95–99.

"The Mouse"
Spencer, Sharon. *Collage of Dreams* . . ., 126–127.

"Ragtime"
Spencer, Sharon. *Collage of Dreams* . . ., 8–9.

"Stella"
Spencer, Sharon. *Collage of Dreams* . . ., 113–114.

"The Voice"
Spencer, Sharon. *Collage of Dreams* . . ., 58–61.

"Winter of Artifice"
Spencer, Sharon. *Collage of Dreams* . . ., 15–17, 26–27.

LINO NOVÁS CALVO

"La abuela reina y el sobrino Delfín"
Menton, Seymour. . . . *Cuban Revolution,* 236–237.

"Cayo Canas"
Souza, Raymond D. "Time and Terror in the Stories of Lino Novás Calvo," *Symposium,* 29 (1975), 295–297.

"Un dedo encima"
Souza, Raymond D. "Time and Terror . . .," 297.

"Nadie a quien matar"
Menton, Seymour. . . . *Cuban Revolution,* 237–238.

"The Night of Ramón Yendía"
Leal, Luis. "The Pursued Hero: 'La noche de Ramón Yendía,' " *Symposium,* 29 (1975), 255–260.

"El otro cayo"
Souza, Raymond D. "Time and Terror . . .," 297–299.

"La vaca en la azotea"
Lichtblau, Myron I. "Reality and Unreality in 'La vaca en la azotea,' " *Symposium,* 29 (1975), 261–265.

JOYCE CAROL OATES

"At the Seminary"
Allen, Mary. *The Necessary Blankness* . . ., 139.

"The Children"
Allen, Mary. *The Necessary Blankness* . . ., 149–150.

"The Dead"
Allen, Mary. *The Necessary Blankness* . . ., 150–151.
Grant, Mary K. *The Tragic Vision* . . ., 17–18.

"Did You Ever Slip on Red Blood?"
Grant, Mary K. *The Tragic Vision* . . ., 105–106.

"The Girl"
Grant, Mary K. *The Tragic Vision* . . ., 106–107.

"How I Contemplated the World from the Detroit House of Correction and Began
My Life Over Again"
Cassill, R. V. *Instructor's Handbook* . . ., 150–153.
Goetsch, Paul. "Joyce Carol Oates, 'How I Contemplated the World from the
Detroit House of Correction and Began My Life Over Again,' " in Freese,
Peter, Ed. . . . *Interpretationen*, 301–313.
Park, Sue S. "A Study in Counterpoint: Joyce Carol Oates's 'How I Contem-
plated the World from the Detroit House of Correction and Began My Life
Over Again,' " *Mod Fiction Stud*, 22 (1976), 213–224.

"The Metamorphosis"
Kimmey, John L. *Instructor's Manual* . . ., 32–34.

"Narcotic"
Grant, Mary K. *The Tragic Vision* . . ., 98–99.

"Normal Love"
Allen, Mary. *The Necessary Blankness* . . ., 144–146.

"Pastoral Blood"
Dike, Donald A. "The Aggressive Victim in the Fiction of Joyce Carol Oates,"
Greyfriar, 15 (1974), 13–14.

"Puzzle"
Allen, Mary. *The Necessary Blankness* . . ., 146–147.

"Waiting"
Grant, Mary K. *The Tragic Vision* . . ., 85–86.

"Where Are You Going, Where Have You Been?"
Allen, Mary. *The Necessary Blankness* . . ., 141–143.
Howard, Daniel F., and William Plummer. *Instructor's Manual* . . ., 3rd ed., 84.
Urbanski, Marie. "Existential Allegory: Joyce Carol Oates's 'Where Are You
Going, Where Have You Been?' " *Stud Short Fiction*, 15 (1978), 200–203.
Wegs, Joyce M. " 'Don't You Know Who I Am?': The Grotesque in Oates's
'Where Are You Going, Where Have You Been?' " *J Narrative Technique*, 5
(1975), 66–72.

FLANNERY O'CONNOR

"The Artificial Nigger"
Desmond, John F. "Mr. Head's Epiphany in Flannery O'Connor's 'The Arti-
ficial Nigger,' " *Notes Mod Am Lit*, 1, iii (1977), Item 20.
Hawkins, Peter S. "When Less Is More: Problem of Overstatement in Religious
Fiction and Criticism," *Reflection*, 76, i (1978), 20–22.
Kane, Thomas S., and Leonard J. Peters. *Some Suggestions* . . ., 51–52.
Rose, Alan H. *Demonic Vision* . . ., 124–127.

"The Barber"
  May, John R. *The Pruning Word* . . ., 24–27.

"A Circle in the Fire"
  McCown, Robert. "Flannery O'Connor and the Reality of Sin," *Catholic World,* 188 (1959), 287.

"The Comforts of Home"
  McFarland, Dorothy T. *Flannery O'Connor,* 53–56.

"The Crop"
  May, John R. *The Pruning Word* . . ., 29–31.

"The Displaced Person"
  Howe, Irving, Ed. *Classics of Modern Fiction* . . ., 2nd ed., 459–468.
  Lesgoirres, Daniel. " 'The Displaced Person' ou 'Le Christ recrucifie,' " *Delta* (Montpellier), 2 (1976), 75–87.
  McCown, Robert. ". . . Reality of Sin," 289–290.
  McFarland, Dorothy T. *Flannery O'Connor,* 30–35.
  Mayer, David R. "Flannery O'Connor and the Peacock," *Asian Folklore Stud,* 35, ii (1976), 11–14.

"The Enduring Chill"
  Aiken, David. "Flannery O'Connor's Portrait of the Artist as a Young Failure," *Arizona Q,* 32 (1976), 245–259.
  McFarland, Dorothy T. *Flannery O'Connor,* 46–48.

"Enoch and the Gorilla"
  Kimmey, John L. *Instructor's Manual* . . ., 6–8.
  May, John R. *The Pruning Word* . . ., 46–49.

"Everything That Rises Must Converge"
  Avila, Carmen. " 'Everything That Rises Must Converge,' " in Dietrich, R. F., and Roger H. Sundell. *Instructor's Manual* . . ., 3rd ed., 42–45.
  Cassill, R. V. *Instructor's Handbook* . . ., 157–159.
  Denham, Robert D. "The World of Guilt and Sorrow: Flannery O'Connor's 'Everything That Rises Must Converge,' " *Flannery O'Connor Bull,* 4 (Autumn, 1975), 42–51.
  McFarland, Dorothy T. *Flannery O'Connor,* 44–46.

"The Geranium"
  May, John R. *The Pruning Word* . . ., 21–24.

"Good Country People"
  Abcarian, Richard, and Marvin Klotz. *Instructor's Manual* . . ., 2nd ed., 17–18.
  Fleurdorge, Claude. " 'Good Country People,' ou la visite à la vieille dame: Examen d'une pratique significante," *Delta* (Montpellier), 2 (1976), 89–130.
  *Howard, Daniel F., and William Plummer. *Instructor's Manual* . . ., 3rd ed., 72.
  Kane, Thomas S., and Leonard J. Peters. *Some Suggestions* . . ., 53–55.
  McFarland, Dorothy T. *Flannery O'Connor,* 35–40.
  Pierce, Constance. "The Mechanical World of 'Good Country People,' " *Flannery O'Connor Bull,* 5 (1976), 30–38.

"A Good Man Is Hard to Find"
  Cassill, R. V. *Instructor's Handbook* . . ., 153–155.
  Ellis, James. "Watermelons and Coca-Cola in 'A Good Man Is Hard to Find,' "
    Notes Contemp Lit, 8, iii (1978), 7–8.
  McCown, Robert. ". . . Reality of Sin," 289.
  McFarland, Dorothy T. *Flannery O'Connor,* 17–22.
  Martin, Carter. "Comedy and Humor in Flannery O'Connor's Fiction,"
    Flannery O'Connor Bull, 4 (1975), 7–12.
  Portch, Stephen R. "O'Connor's 'A Good Man Is Hard to Find,' " *Explicator,*
    37, i (1978), 19–20.
  Richard, Claude. "Desir et destin dans 'A Good Man Is Hard to
    Find,' " *Delta* (Montpellier), 2 (1976), 61–73.

"Greenleaf"
  Kane, Thomas S., and Leonard J. Peters. *Some Suggestions* . . ., 52–53.
  McFarland, Dorothy T. *Flannery O'Connor,* 48–50.
  *Perrine, Laurence. *Instructor's Manual* . . . "Story . . .," 24–26; *Instructor's
    Manual* . . . "Literature . . .," 24–26.

"The Heart of the Park"
  May, John R. *The Pruning Word* . . ., 40–46.

"Judgement Day"
  McFarland, Dorothy T. *Flannery O'Connor,* 67–71.

"The Lame Shall Enter First"
  McFarland, Dorothy T. *Flannery O'Connor,* 56–60.

"The Life You Save May Be Your Own"
  Desmond, John F. "The Shifting of Mr. Shiflet: Flannery O'Connor's 'The Life
    You Save May Be Your Own,' " *Mississippi Q,* 28 (1975), 55–59.
  McCown, Robert. ". . . Reality of Sin," 288–289.
  McFarland, Dorothy T. *Flannery O'Connor,* 24–25.

"Parker's Back"
  Cassill, R. V. *Instructor's Handbook* . . ., 160–162.
  McFarland, Dorothy T. *Flannery O'Connor,* 64–67.

"The Peeler"
  May, John R. *The Pruning Word* . . ., 37–41.

"Revelation"
  McFarland, Dorothy T. *Flannery O'Connor,* 60–63.
  Tolomeo, Diane. "Flannery O'Connor's 'Revelation' and the Book of Job,"
    Renascence, 30 (1978), 78–90.

"The River"
  McCown, Robert. ". . . Reality of Sin," 287–288.

"A Stroke of Good Fortune"
  McFarland, Dorothy T. *Flannery O'Connor,* 22–23.
  Zoller, Peter T. "The Irony of Preserving the Self: Flannery O'Connor's 'A
    Stroke of Good Fortune,' " *Kansas Q,* 9, ii (1977), 61–66.

"A Temple of the Holy Ghost"
McFarland, Dorothy T. *Flannery O'Connor*, 26–28.
Walden, Daniel, and Jane Salvia. "Flannery O'Connor's Dragon: Vision in 'A
Temple of the Holy Ghost,' " *Stud Am Fiction*, 4 (1976), 230–235.

"The Train"
May, John R. *The Pruning Word . . .*, 34–37.

"The Turkey"
May, John R. *The Pruning Word . . .*, 31–34.

"A View of the Woods"
Gross, Konrad. "Flannery O'Connor, 'A View of the Woods,' " in Freese,
Peter, Ed. . . . *Interpretationen*, 184–193.
McFarland, Dorothy T. *Flannery O'Connor*, 51–53.

"Why Do the Heathen Rage?"
May, John R. *The Pruning Word . . .*, 56–59.

"Wildcat"
May, John R. *The Pruning Word . . .*, 27–29.

"You Can't Be Any Poorer Than Dead" [expanded to become the first chapter of
The Violent Bear It Away]
May, John R. *The Pruning Word . . .*, 49–52.

FRANK O'CONNOR [MICHAEL O'DONOVAN]

"Achilles Heel"
Wohlgelernter, Maurice. *Frank O'Connor . . .*, 58–59.

"An Act of Charity"
Wohlgelernter, Maurice. *Frank O'Connor . . .*, 55.

"After Fourteen Years"
Wohlgelernter, Maurice. *Frank O'Connor . . .*, 78–79.

"Bones of Contention"
Matthews, James H. *Frank O'Connor*, 51–52.

"The Bridal Night"
Matthews, James H. "Frank O'Connor's Stories: The Contending Voice,"
Sewanee R, 84 (1976), 62–63; rpt. in his *Frank O'Connor*, 59–60.

"The Cheat"
Matthews, James H. *Frank O'Connor*, 78–79.

"The Corkerys"
Wohlgelernter, Maurice. *Frank O'Connor . . .*, 79–80.

"Counsel of Oedipus"
Wohlgelernter, Maurice. *Frank O'Connor . . .*, 105–106.

"Daydreams"
   Matthews, James H. "Frank O'Connor's Stories . . .," 69–70; rpt. in his *Frank
      O'Connor*, 73–74.

"Don Juan (Retired)"
   Wohlgelernter, Maurice. *Frank O'Connor* . . ., 106–107.

"The Drunkard"
   *Perrine, Laurence. *Instructor's Manual* . . . *"Story* . . .," 30–31; *Instructor's*
      Manual . . . *"Literature* . . .," 30–31.
   Wohlgelernter, Maurice. *Frank O'Connor* . . ., 88–89.

"The Eternal Triangle"
   Wohlgelernter, Maurice. *Frank O'Connor* . . ., 39–40.

"Expectations of Life"
   Wohlgelernter, Maurice. *Frank O'Connor* . . ., 107–108.

"Father and Son"
   Wohlgelernter, Maurice. *Frank O'Connor* . . ., 90–91.

"First Confession"
   Wohlgelernter, Maurice. *Frank O'Connor* . . ., 59.

"The Genius"
   Matthews, James H. "Frank O'Connor's Stories . . .," 68–69; rpt., with
      changes, in his *Frank O'Connor*, 70–71.

"The Grand Vizier's Daughter"
   Wohlgelernter, Maurice. *Frank O'Connor* . . ., 89–90.

"Guests of the Nation"
   Briden, Earl F. " 'Guests of the Nation': A Final Irony," *Stud Short Fiction*, 13
      (1976), 79–81.
   Cassill, R. V. *Instructor's Handbook* . . ., 163–166.

"The Holy Door"
   Wohlgelernter, Maurice. *Frank O'Connor* . . ., 80–81.

"The House That Johnny Built"
   Wohlgelernter, Maurice. *Frank O'Connor* . . ., 100–101.

"The Impossible Marriage"
   Matthews, James H. *Frank O'Connor*, 80–81.
   Wohlgelernter, Maurice. *Frank O'Connor* . . ., 70–71.

"In the Train"
   Matthews, James H. "Frank O'Connor's Stories . . .," 59; rpt. in his *Frank
      O'Connor*, 52–54.

"Judas"
   Matthews, James H. *Frank O'Connor*, 69–70.
   Wohlgelernter, Maurice. *Frank O'Connor* . . ., 93–94.

"A Life of Your Own"
Wohlgelernter, Maurice. *Frank O'Connor* . . ., 98–99.

"The Long Road to Ummera"
Matthews, James H. *Frank O'Connor*, 68–69.
Wohlgelernter, Maurice. *Frank O'Connor* . . ., 51–52.

"The Luceys"
Matthews, James H. *Frank O'Connor*, 63–65.

"The Mad Lomasneys"
Kane, Thomas S., and Leonard J. Peters. *Some Suggestions* . . ., 35–36.
Matthews, James H. "Frank O'Connor's Stories . . .," 64–66; rpt. in his *Frank O'Connor*, 65–68.

"The Majesty of the Law"
Matthews, James H. *Frank O'Connor*, 54–56.

"The Man of the World"
Matthews, James H. *Frank O'Connor*, 71–73.

"The Mass Island"
Matthews, James H. "Frank O'Connor's Stories . . .," 72–73; rpt., with changes, in his *Frank O'Connor*, 83–84.

"Michael's Wife"
Matthews, James H. "Frank O'Connor's Stories . . .," 60–62; rpt. in his *Frank O'Connor*, 57–59.

"Music When Soft Voices Die"
Wohlgelernter, Maurice. *Frank O'Connor* . . ., 99–100.

"My Oedipus Complex"
*Abcarian, Richard, and Marvin Klotz. *Instructor's Manual* . . ., 2nd ed., 18–19.
Wohlgelernter, Maurice. *Frank O'Connor* . . ., 69–70.

"Out-and-Out Free Gift"
Matthews, James H. *Frank O'Connor*, 76–77.

"The Paragon"
Wohlgelernter, Maurice. *Frank O'Connor* . . ., 96–98.

"The Party"
Wohlgelernter, Maurice. *Frank O'Connor* . . ., 91–92.

"Peasants"
Wohlgelernter, Maurice. *Frank O'Connor* . . ., 52–53.

"The Pretender"
Wohlgelernter, Maurice. *Frank O'Connor* . . ., 95–96.

"Requiem"
Wohlgelernter, Maurice. *Frank O'Connor* . . ., 53–54.

"The School for Wives"
Matthews, James H. *Frank O'Connor*, 79–80.

"The Sentry"
Wohlgelernter, Maurice. *Frank O'Connor* . . ., 55–56.

"September Dawn"
Wohlgelernter, Maurice. *Frank O'Connor* . . ., 36–37.

"A Set of Variations"
Matthews, James H. "Frank O'Connor's Stories . . .," 73–75; rpt. in his *Frank O'Connor*, 84–86.

"Song Without Words"
Matthews, James H. *Frank O'Connor*, 62–63.
Wohlgelernter, Maurice. *Frank O'Connor* . . ., 62–63.

"The Star That Bids the Shepherd Fold"
Matthews, James H. *Frank O'Connor*, 63.

"The Stepmother"
Wohlgelernter, Maurice. *Frank O'Connor* . . ., 94–95.

"The Teacher's Mass"
Matthews, James H. "Frank O'Connor's Stories . . .," 72; rpt., with changes, in his *Frank O'Connor*, 82–83.
Wohlgelernter, Maurice. *Frank O'Connor* . . ., 60–61.

"The Thief"
Wohlgelernter, Maurice. *Frank O'Connor* . . ., 87–88.

"Unapproved Route"
Wohlgelernter, Maurice. *Frank O'Connor* . . ., 103–104.

"Uprooted"
Matthews, James H. *Frank O'Connor*, 60–62.

"Vanity"
Wohlgelernter, Maurice. *Frank O'Connor* . . ., 57–58.

LAWRENCE O'DONNELL [CATHERINE L. MOORE]

"The Children's Hour"
Gunn, James. "Henry Kuttner, C.L. Moore, Lewis Padgett, *et al.*," in Clareson, Thomas D., Ed. *Voices for the Future* . . ., 201–202.

"Vintage Season"
Gunn, James. "Henry Kuttner . . . *et al.*," 206–208.

ŌE KENZABURŌ

"The Catch"
Yamanouchi, Hisaaki. *The Search for Authenticity* . . ., 163–164.

SEAN O'FAOLAIN

"Admiring the Scenery"
Rippier, Joseph. . . . *Descriptive Technique,* 59–64.
Sampson, Denis. " 'Admiring the Scenery': Sean O'Faolain's Fable of the
Artist," *Canadian J Irish Stud,* 3, i (1977), 72–79.

"A Broken World"
Duffy, Joseph. "A Broken World: The Finest Short Stories of Sean O'Faolain,"
Irish Univ R, 6 (1975), 33–35.
Dunn, Douglas. *Two Decades of Irish Writing* . . ., 234–235.

"Lovers of the Lake"
Rippier, Joseph. . . . *Descriptive Technique,* 141–144.

"Midsummer Night Madness"
Davenport, Gary T. "Sean O'Faolain's Troubles: Revolution and Provincialism
in Modern Ireland," *So Atlantic Q,* 75 (1976), 315–316.

"The Silence of the Valley"
Duffy, Joseph. "A Broken World . . .," 35–36.
Rippier, Joseph. . . . *Descriptive Technique,* 128–133, 137–141.

"The Small Lady"
Davenport, Gary T. "Sean O'Faolain's Troubles . . .," 316.

LIAM O'FLAHERTY

"The Bath"
Kelly, A. A. *Liam O'Flaherty* . . ., 101–102.

"The Blackbird's Mate"
Doyle, Paul A. *Liam O'Flaherty,* 57–58.

"The Caress"
Kelly, A. A. *Liam O'Flaherty* . . ., 44–46.

"The Ditch"
Kelly, A. A. *Liam O'Flaherty* . . ., 78–79.

"The Fairy Goose"
Doyle, Paul A. *Liam O'Flaherty,* 53–54.
Kelly, A. A. *Liam O'Flaherty* . . ., 43–44.

"Galway Bay"
Kelly, A. A. *Liam O'Flaherty* . . ., 49–50.

"Going into Exile"
Doyle, Paul A. *Liam O'Flaherty*, 47–48.

"The Hawk"
Kelly, A. A. *Liam O'Flaherty* . . ., 9–10.

"The Inquisition"
Kelly, A. A. *Liam O'Flaherty* . . ., 33–34.

"The Letter"
Kelly, A. A. *Liam O'Flaherty* . . ., 56–57.

"Milking Time"
Kelly, A. A. *Liam O'Flaherty* . . ., 15–16.

"The Mirror"
Kelly, A. A. *Liam O'Flaherty* . . ., 58–59.

"The Mountain Tavern"
Kelly, A. A. *Liam O'Flaherty* . . ., 60–61.

"The Outcast"
Kelly, A. A. *Liam O'Flaherty* . . ., 105–106.

"The Parting"
Kelly, A. A. *Liam O'Flaherty* . . ., 20–21.

"The Pedlar's Revenge"
Kelly, A. A. *Liam O'Flaherty* . . ., 102–103.

"The Post Office"
Doyle, Paul A. *Liam O'Flaherty*, 114–115.
Kelly, A. A. *Liam O'Flaherty* . . ., 103–104.

"Proclamation"
Kelly, A. A. *Liam O'Flaherty* . . ., 39–40.

"Red Barbara"
Doyle, Paul A. *Liam O'Flaherty*, 48–49.
Kane, Thomas S., and Leonard J. Peters. *Some Suggestions* . . ., 8–9.

"The Rockfish"
Doyle, Paul A. *Liam O'Flaherty*, 55–56.

"Sport: The Kill"
Kelly, A. A. *Liam O'Flaherty* . . ., 4–5.

"Spring Sowing"
Doyle, Paul A. *Liam O'Flaherty*, 46–47.

"A Strange Disease"
Kelly, A. A. *Liam O'Flaherty* . . ., 97–98.

"The Tent"
   Doyle, Paul A. *Liam O'Flaherty*, 51–52.

"The Terrorist"
   Kelly, A. A. *Liam O'Flaherty* . . ., 31–32.

"The Tramp"
   Doyle, Paul A. *Liam O'Flaherty*, 49–50.

"The Tyrant"
   Kelly, A. A. *Liam O'Flaherty* . . ., 30–31.

"Unclean"
   Kelly, A. A. *Liam O'Flaherty* . . ., 29–30.

"The Wounded Cormorant"
   Doyle, Paul A. *Liam O'Flaherty*, 56–57.

O. HENRY [WILLIAM SYDNEY PORTER]

"A Municipal Report"
   *Perrine, Laurence. *Instructor's Manual* . . . "*Story* . . .," 38–39; *Instructor's Manual* . . . "*Literature* . . .," 38–39.

TILLIE OLSEN

"Tell Me a Riddle"
   Cassill, R. V. *Instructor's Handbook* . . ., 166–168.

JUAN CARLOS ONETTI

"Avenida de mayo—Diagonal—Avenida de mayo"
   Kadir, Djelal. *Juan Carlos Onetti*, 130–131.

"The Face of Misfortune"
   Rodriguez Santibáñez, Marta. " 'La cara de la desgracia' o el sentido de la ambigüedad," *Cuadernos Hispanoamericanos*, 292–294 (1974), 320–333.

"El posible Baldi"
   Kadir, Djelal. *Juan Carlos Onetti*, 131–132.

JAMES OPPENHEIM

"Slag"
   Fine, David M. *The City* . . ., 92–93.

GEORGE ORWELL

"Animal Farm"
  Small, Christopher. *The Road to Miniluv* . . ., 104–116.

CYNTHIA OZICK

"Envy; or, Yiddish in America"
  Cohen, Sarah B. "The Jewish Literary Comediennes," in Cohen, Sarah B., Ed.
  Comic Relief . . ., 180–182.

"Usurpation (Other People's Stories)"
  Cohen, Sarah B. "The Jewish Literary Comediennes," 184–186.

"Virility"
  Cohen, Sarah B. "The Jewish Literary Comediennes," 182–184.

LEWIS PADGETT [CATHERINE L. MOORE and HENRY KUTTNER]

"Piggy Bank"
  Gunn, James. "Henry Kuttner, C. L. Moore, Lewis Padgett, *et al.,*" in Clareson,
  Thomas D., Ed. *Voices for the Future* . . ., 196–198.

"The Twonky"
  Gunn, James. "Henry Kuttner . . . *et al.,*" 196.

"When the Bough Breaks"
  Gunn, James. "Henry Kuttner . . . *et al.,*" 200–201.

THOMAS NELSON PAGE

"Marse Chan"
  MacKethan, Lucinde H. "Thomas Nelson Page: The Plantation as Arcady,"
  Virginia Q R, 54 (1978), 318–319.

"Meh Lady"
  MacKethan, Lucinde H. ". . . Plantation as Arcady," 328–329.

"No Haid Pawn"
  MacKethan, Lucinde H. ". . . Plantation as Arcady," 319–320.

"Ole 'Stracted"
  MacKethan, Lucinde H. ". . . Plantation as Arcady," 329–331.

ALBERT B. PAINE

"The Black Hands"
  Moskowitz, Sam. *Strange Horizons* . . ., 60–61.

GRACE PALEY

"The Used-Boy Raisers"
Cassill, R. V. *Instructor's Handbook* . . ., 169.

DOROTHY PARKER

"The Banquet of Crow"
Kinney, Arthur F. *Dorothy Parker*, 146–147.

"Big Blonde"
Cassill, R. V. *Instructor's Handbook* . . ., 170–171.
Kinney, Arthur F. *Dorothy Parker*, 136–137.

"Clothe the Naked"
Kinney, Arthur F. *Dorothy Parker*, 141–142.

"Soldier of the Republic"
Kinney, Arthur F. *Dorothy Parker*, 142–143.

"Such a Pretty Little Picture"
Kinney, Arthur F. *Dorothy Parker*, 128–129.

"Too Bad"
Kinney, Arthur F. *Dorothy Parker*, 139–140.

ELIZABETH PARSONS

"The Nightingales Sing"
Cassill, R. V. *Instructor's Handbook* . . ., 171–172.

BORIS PASTERNAK

"Tale"
Aucouturier, Michel. "The Metonymous Hero or the Beginnings of Pasternak
the Novelist," *Books Abroad,* 44 (1970), 225–226; rpt. Erlich, Victor, Ed.
Pasternak . . ., 48–50.

KENNETH PATCHEN

"Bury Them in God"
Smith, Larry R. *Kenneth Patchen*, 81–82.

WALTER PATER

"Sebastian Van Storck"
Inman, Billie A. " 'Sebastian Van Storck': Pater's Exploration into Nihilism,"
Nineteenth-Century Fiction, 30 (1976), 457–476.

S.J. PERELMAN

"Call Me Monty and Grovel Freely"
Cassill, R. V. *Instructor's Handbook* . . ., 173.

"Dial 'H' for Heartburn"
Kane, Thomas S., and Leonard J. Peters. *Some Suggestions* . . ., 29–30.

ITZHAK PERETZ

"Devotion Without End"
Gittleman, Sol. *From Shtetl to Suburbia* . . ., 139–141.

BENITO PÉREZ GALDÓS

"El pórtico de la gloria"
Hoar, Leo J. "Galdós' Counter-Attack on His Critics: The 'Lost' Short Story 'El pórtico de la gloria,' " *Symposium,* 30 (1976), 287–296.

JULIA PETERKIN

"Ashes"
Landess, Thomas H. *Julia Peterkin,* 41–42.

"Green Thursday"
Landess, Thomas H. *Julia Peterkin,* 42–46.

"Meeting"
Landess, Thomas H. *Julia Peterkin,* 46–49.

"The Red Rooster"
Landess, Thomas H. *Julia Peterkin,* 49–56.

"A Sunday"
Landess, Thomas H. *Julia Peterkin,* 56–59.

ANN PETRY

"The Witness"
Madden, David. "Ann Petry: 'The Witness,' " *Stud Black Lit,* 6, iii (1975), 24–26.

WILLIAM PICKENS

"The Vengeance of the Gods"
Berzon, Judith R. *Neither White Nor Black* . . ., 35–36.

PING HSIN [HSIEH WAN-YING]

"Since Her Departure"
Hsia, C. T. *A History* . . ., 74–76.

"The West Wind"
Hsia, C. T. *A History* . . ., 74–77.

LUIGI PIRANDELLO

"An Annuity for Life"
Radcliff-Umstead, Douglas. *The Mirror of Our Anguish* . . ., 60–61.

"A Breath"
Radcliff-Umstead, Douglas. *The Mirror of Our Anguish* . . ., 110–112.

"By Himself"
Radcliff-Umstead, Douglas. *The Mirror of Our Anguish* . . ., 70–71.

"Candelora"
Radcliff-Umstead, Douglas. *The Mirror of Our Anguish* . . ., 96–97.

"Captivity"
Radcliff-Umstead, Douglas. *The Mirror of Our Anguish* . . ., 196.

"The Choice"
Radcliff-Umstead, Douglas. *The Mirror of Our Anguish* . . ., 27–28.

"Ciaula scopre la Luna"
Radcliff-Umstead, Douglas. *The Mirror of Our Anguish* . . ., 88–90.

"A Day"
Radcliff-Umstead, Douglas. *The Mirror of Our Anguish* . . ., 119–120.

"The Destruction of Man"
Radcliff-Umstead, Douglas. *The Mirror of Our Anguish* . . ., 104–106.

"Double Tombs for Two"
Radcliff-Umstead, Douglas. *The Mirror of Our Anguish* . . ., 67–68.

"Flight"
Radcliff-Umstead, Douglas. *The Mirror of Our Anguish* . . ., 196.

"The Fly"
Radcliff-Umstead, Douglas. *The Mirror of Our Anguish* . . ., 61–62.

"The Gentle Touch of Death"
Radcliff-Umstead, Douglas. *The Mirror of Our Anguish* . . ., 73–74.

"Happiness"
Radcliff-Umstead, Douglas. *The Mirror of Our Anguish* . . ., 101–102.

"There's Someone Who Is Laughing"
Radcliff-Umstead, Douglas. *The Mirror of Our Anguish* . . ., 116–119.

"The Tragedy of a Character"
Radcliff-Umstead, Douglas. *The Mirror of Our Anguish* . . ., 297–299.

"The Trap"
Radcliff-Umstead, Douglas. *The Mirror of Our Anguish* . . ., 102–103.

"The Umbrella"
Radcliff-Umstead, Douglas. *The Mirror of Our Anguish* . . ., 79–80.

"Visit"
Radcliff-Umstead, Douglas. *The Mirror of Our Anguish* . . ., 113–116.

"Visiting the Sick"
Radcliff-Umstead, Douglas. *The Mirror of Our Anguish* . . ., 72–73.

"The Wave"
Radcliff-Umstead, Douglas. *The Mirror of Our Anguish* . . ., 95–96.

"The Wet Nurse"
Radcliff-Umstead, Douglas. *The Mirror of Our Anguish* . . ., 94.

"The Wheelbarrow"
Radcliff-Umstead, Douglas. *The Mirror of Our Anguish* . . ., 277–278.

"When I Was Mad"
Radcliff-Umstead, Douglas. *The Mirror of Our Anguish* . . ., 54–58.

"World News"
Radcliff-Umstead, Douglas. *The Mirror of Our Anguish* . . ., 74–75.

"The Wreath"
Radcliff-Umstead, Douglas. *The Mirror of Our Anguish* . . ., 66–67.

EDGAR ALLAN POE

"The Angel of the Odd"
Gargano, James W. "The Distorted Perception of Poe's Comic Narrators," *Topic*, 16, xxx (1976), 27–29.

"Berenice"
Billy, Ted. "The Teasing and Teething of 'Berenice,' " *Susquehanna Univ Stud*, 10 (1978), 255–259.
Staats, Armin. "Edgar Allan Poes symbolistiche Erzählkunst," *Beihefte zum Jahrbuch für Amerikastudien*, 20 (1967), 70–78.

"The Black Cat"
Anderson, Gayle D. "Demonology in 'The Black Cat,' " *Poe Stud*, 10 (1977), 43–44.

Rabkin, Eric S. *The Fantastic* . . ., 50–54.
Staats, Armin. ". . . Erzählkunst," 103–111.

"The Cask of Amontillado"
Clendenning, John. "Anything Goes: Comic Aspects in 'The Cask of Amontillado,' " in Brack, O.M., Ed. *American Humor* . . ., 13–25.
Pittman, Philip M. "Method and Motive in 'The Cask of Amontillado,' " *Malahat R,* 34 (1975), 87–100.
Stepp, Walter. "The Ironic Double in Poe's 'The Cask of Amontillado,' " *Stud Short Fiction,* 13 (1976), 447–453.
Sweet, Charles A. "Retapping Poe's 'Cask of Amontillado,' " *Poe Stud,* 8 (1975), 10–12.

"The Colloquy of Monos and Una"
Carter, Everett. *The American Idea* . . ., 159–161.

"A Descent into the Maelström"
Finholt, Richard. *American Visionary Fiction* . . ., 83–97.
Frank, Frederick S. "The Aqua-Gothic Voyage of 'A Descent into the Maelström,' " *Am Transcendental Q,* 29 (1975), 85–93.
Hennelly, Mark M. "Oedipus and Orpheus in the Maelström: The Traumatic Rebirth of the Artist," *Poe Stud,* 9 (June, 1976), 6–11.
Ljungquist, Kent. "Poe and the Sublime: His Two Short Sea Tales in the Context of an Aesthetic Tradition," *Criticism,* 17 (1975), 140–144.

"The Devil in the Belfry"
Gargano, James W. "The Distorted Perception . . .," 31–33.

"The Domain of Arnheim"
Staats, Armin. ". . . Erzählkunst," 158–170.

"The Duc de l'Omelette"
Hirsch, David H. " 'The Duc de l'Omelette' as Anti-Visionary Tale," *Poe Stud,* 10 (1977), 36–39.

"Eleonora"
Robinson, E. Arthur. "Cosmic Vision in Poe's 'Eleonora,' " *Poe Stud,* 9 (1976), 44–46.

"The Fall of the House of Usher"
Budick, E. Miller. "The Fall of the House: A Reappraisal of Poe's Attitude Toward Life and Death," *Southern Lit J,* 9 (Spring, 1977), 41–50.
Butler, David W. "Usher's Hypochondriasis: Mental Alienation and Romantic Idealism in Poe's Gothic Tales," *Am Lit,* 48 (1976), 1–12.
Cassill, R.V. *Instructor's Handbook* . . ., 174.
Flory, Wendy S. "Usher's Fear and the Flaw in Poe's Theories of the Metamorphosis of the Senses," *Poe Stud,* 7, i (1974), 17–19.
Girgus, Sam B. "Poe and R.D. Laing: The Transcendent Self," *Stud Short Fiction,* 13 (1976), 300–303.
St. Armand, Barton L. "Poe's Landscape of the Soul: Association Theory and 'The Fall of the House of Usher,' " *Mod Lang Stud,* 7, ii (1977), 32–41.
Staats, Armin. ". . . Erzählkunst," 118–130.

Wasserman, Renata R. M. "The Self, the Mirror, the Other: 'The Fall of the House of Usher,' " *Poe Stud,* 10 (1977), 33–37.

"Four Beasts in One"
Autrey, Max L. "Edgar Allan Poe's Satiric View of Evolution," *Extrapolation,* 5 (1977), 191–193.

"The Gold Bug"
Ricardou, Jean. "Gold in the Bug," trans. Frank Towne, *Poe Stud,* 9, ii (1976), 33–39.

"Hop-Frog"
Autrey, Max L. ". . . Evolution," 195–198.

"The Imp of the Perverse"
Finholt, Richard. *American Visionary Fiction . . .,* 91–93.

"The Island of the Fay"
Ljungquist, Kent. "Poe's 'The Island of the Fay': The Passing of Fairyland," *Stud Short Fiction,* 14 (1977), 265–271.

"Ligeia"
Deutsch, Leonard J. "The Satire of Transcendentalism in Poe's 'Ligeia,' " *Bull West Virginia Assoc Coll Engl Teachers,* 3, ii (1976), 19–22.
Staats, Armin. ". . . Erzählkunst," 78–93.
Sweet, Charles A. " 'Ligeia' and the Warlock," *Stud Short Fiction,* 13 (1976), 85–88.
Tritt, Michael. " 'Ligeia' and 'The Conqueror Worm,' " *Poe Stud,* 9 (June, 1976), 21–22.

"Loss of Breath"
Autrey, Max L. ". . . Evolution," 189–191.

"The Man That Was Used Up"
Curran, Ronald T. "The Fashionable Thirties: Poe's Satire in 'The Man That Was Used Up,' " *Markham R,* 8 (1978), 14–20.

"MS. Found in a Bottle"
Ljungquist, Kent. "Poe and the Sublime . . .," 136–139.
Staats, Armin. ". . . Erzählkunst," 131–134.

"The Masque of the Red Death"
Abcarian, Richard, and Marvin Klotz. *Instructor's Manual . . .,* 2nd ed., 19–20.
Pitcher, Edward W. "Horological and Chronological Time in 'Masque of the Red Death,' " *Am Transcendental Q,* 29 (1976), 71–75.

"Morella"
Bickman, Martin. "Animatopoeia: Morella as Siren of the Self," *Poe Stud,* 8, ii (1975), 29–32.
Gargano, James W. "Poe's 'Morella': A Note on Her Name," *Am Lit,* 47 (1975), 259–264.
Staats, Armin. ". . . Erzählkunst," 134–137.

"The Murders in the Rue Morgue"
Autrey, Max L. ". . . Evolution," 193–194.
Bronzwaer, W. "Deixis as a Structuring Device in Narrative Discourse: An Analysis of Poe's 'The Murders in the Rue Morgue,' " *Engl Stud,* 56 (1975), 345–359.
Keller, Mark. "Dupin in the 'Rue Morgue': Another Form of Madness?" *Arizona Q,* 33 (1977), 249–255.
Pollin, Burton R. "Poe's 'Murders in the Rue Morgue': The Ingenious Web Unravelled," *Stud Am Renaissance,* [n.v.] (1977), 235–259.

"The Narrative of Arthur Gordon Pym"
Chiesura, Fabrizio. "L'occhio di Poe," *Prospetti,* 46–47 (1977), 78–82.
DeFalco, Joseph M. "Metaphor and Meaning in Poe's 'The Narrative of Arthur Gordon Pym,' " *Topic,* 16, xxx (1976), 54–67.
Engel, Leonard W. "Edgar Allan Poe's Use of the Enclosure Device in 'The Narrative of Arthur Gordon Pym,' " *Am Transcendental Q,* 37 (1978), 35–44.
Forclaz, Roger. "A Voyage to the Frontiers of the Unconscious: Edgar Allan Poe's 'Narrative of A. Gordon Pym,' " trans. Gerald Bello, *Am Transcendental Q,* 38 (1978), 45–55.
Hinz, Evelyn J., and John J. Teunissen. "Poe, 'Pym,' and Primitivism," *Stud Short Fiction,* 14 (1977), 13–20.
Kennedy, J. Gerald. " 'The Infernal Twosome' in 'Arthur Gordon Pym,' " *Topic,* 16, xxx (1976), 41–53.
Ketterer, David. "Delicious Voyage: The Singular 'Narrative of A. Gordon Pym,' " *Am Transcendental Q,* 37 (1978), 21–33.
Ljungquist, Kent. "Descent of the Titans: The Sublime Riddle of 'Arthur Gordon Pym,' " *Southern Lit J,* 10, ii (1978), 75–92.
Ricardou, Jean. " 'The Singular Character of the Water,' " trans. Frank Towne, *Poe Stud,* 9, i (1976), 1–6.
Rose, Alan H. *Demonic Vision . . . ,* 53–56.
Rowe, John C. "Writing and Truth in Poe's 'The Narrative of Arthur Gordon Pym,' " *Glyph,* 2 (1977), 102–121.
St. Armand, Barton L. "The Dragon and the Uroboros: Themes of Metamorphosis in 'Arthur Gordon Pym,' " *Am Transcendental Q,* 37 (1978), 57–71.
Santraud, Jeanne-Marie. "Edgar Allan Poe 'en sa maison de superbe structure': Étude du Recit d'Arthur Gordon Pym,' " *Études Anglaises,* 29 (1976), 360–370.
Wells, Daniel A. "Engraved within the Hills: Further Perspectives on the Ending of 'Pym,' " *Poe Stud,* 10, i (1977), 13–15.

"The Oval Portrait"
Scheick, William J. "The Geometric Structure of Poe's 'The Oval Portrait,' " *Poe Stud,* 11, i (1978), 6–8.
Twitchell, James. "Poe's 'The Oval Portrait' and the Vampire Motif," *Stud Short Fiction,* 14 (1977), 387–393.

"The Pit and the Pendulum"
Staats, Armin. ". . . Erzählkunst," 137–142.

"A Predicament"
Lewis, Paul. "Laughing at Fear: Two Versions of the Mock Gothic," *Stud Short Fiction,* 15 (1978), 413–414.

"The Purloined Letter"
Bellei, Sergio L.P. " 'The Purloined Letter': A Theory of Perception," *Poe Stud*, 9 (1976), 40–44.
Rabkin, Eric S. *The Fantastic* . . ., 60–67.

"Silence—A Fable"
Fisher, Benjamin F. "The Power of Words in Poe's 'Silence,' " *Lib Chronicle*, 41 (1976), 56–72.

"The Spectacles"
Gargano, James W. "The Distorted Perception . . .," 23–27.

"The Sphinx"
Gargano, James W. "The Distorted Perception . . .," 29–30.

"The System of Dr. Tarr and Professor Fether"
Autrey, Max L. ". . . Evolution," 194–195.
Fisher, Benjamin F. "Poe's 'Tarr and Fether': Hoaxing in the Blackwood Mode," *Topic*, 31 (1977), 29–40.
Gargano, James W. "The Distorted Perception . . .," 30–31.

"The Tell-Tale Heart"
Fleurdorge, Claude. "Discours et contre-discours dans 'The Tell-Tale Heart,' " *Delta* (Montpellier), 1 (1975), 43–65.
Richard, Claude. "Le Double voix dans 'The Tell-Tale Heart,' " *Delta* (Montpellier), 1 (1975), 17–41.

"William Wilson"
Carlson, Eric W. " 'William Wilson': The Double as Primal Self," *Topic*, 16, xxx (1976), 35–40.
Casale, Ottavio M. "The Dematerialization of William Wilson: Poe's Use of Cumulative Allegory," *So Carolina R*, 11, i (1978), 70–79.
Kane, Thomas S., and Leonard J. Peters. *Some Suggestions* . . ., 9–10.
Rovner, Marc L. "What William Wilson Knew: Poe's Dramatization of an Errant Mind," *Lib Chronicle*, 41 (1976), 73–82; rpt. in Fisher, Benjamin F., Ed. *Poe at Work* . . ., 73–82.
Sullivan, Ruth. "William Wilson's Double," *Stud Romanticism*, 15 (1976), 253–263.

KATHERINE ANNE PORTER

"The Circus"
Hennessy, Rosemary. "Katherine Anne Porter's Model for Heroines," *Colorado Q*, 25 (1977), 309.

"The Fig Tree"
Hardy, John E. *Katherine Anne Porter*, 16–19.
Hennessy, Rosemary. ". . . Model for Heroines," 308–309.
Hughes, Linda K. "Katherine Anne Porter's 'The Fig Tree': The Tree of Knowing," *Pubs Arkansas Philol Assoc*, 3, iii (1977), 54–58.

"Flowering Judas"
   Hardy, John E. *Katherine Anne Porter*, 68–76.
   Kennedy, X. J. *Instructor's Manual* . . . , 20–21.
   Rohrberger, Mary. "Betrayer or Betrayed: Another View of 'Flowering Judas,' " *Notes Mod Am Lit*, 2, i (1977), Item 10.

"The Grave"
   Hardy, John E. *Katherine Anne Porter*, 20–24.
   Hennessy, Rosemary. ". . . Model for Heroines," 309–311.
   Rooke, Constance, and Bruce Wallis. "Myth and Epiphany in Porter's 'The Grave,' " *Stud Short Fiction*, 15 (1978), 269–275.

"Hacienda"
   Hardy, John E. *Katherine Anne Porter*, 113–115.

"He"
   Hardy, John E. *Katherine Anne Porter*, 35–38.

"Holiday"
   Hardy, John E. "Katherine Anne Porter's 'Holiday,' " *Southern Lit Messenger*, 1, i (1975), 1–5.

"The Jilting of Granny Weatherall"
   *Abcarian, Richard, and Marvin Klotz. *Instructor's Manual* . . . , 2nd ed., 20–21.
   Hardy, John E. *Katherine Anne Porter*, 89–96.

"The Journey"
   Hennessy, Rosemary. ". . . Model for Heroines," 303–304.

"Magic"
   Hardy, John E. *Katherine Anne Porter*, 41–44.

"Noon Wine"
   Groff, Edward. " 'Noon Wine': A Texas Tragedy," *Descant*, 22 (Fall, 1977), 39–47.
   Hardy, John E. *Katherine Anne Porter*, 97–108.
   Walsh, Thomas F. "Deep Similarities in 'Noon Wine,' " *Mosaic*, 9, i (1975), 83–91.

"Old Mortality"
   Cassill, R. V. *Instructor's Handbook* . . . , 176–179.
   Flanders, Jane. "Katherine Anne Porter and the Ordeal of Southern Womanhood," *Southern Lit J*, 9, i (1976), 55–60.
   Gray, Richard. *The Literature of Memory* . . . , 189–196.
   Hardy, John E. *Katherine Anne Porter*, 24–33.
   Hennessy, Rosemary. ". . . Model for Heroines," 305–308.
   Sullivan, Walter. *A Requiem* . . . , 3–8.

"The Old Order"
   Flanders, Jane. ". . . Southern Womanhood," 52–55.
   Gray, Richard. *The Literature of Memory* . . . , 186–196.

"Pale Horse, Pale Rider"

Flanders, Jane. "'The Other Side of Self-Reliance: The Dream-Vision of 'Pale
Horse, Pale Rider,' " *Regionalism & Female Imagination,* 4, ii (1978), 8–13.
Hardy, John E. *Katherine Anne Porter,* 76–89.
Hennessy, Rosemary. ". . . Model for Heroines," 311–314.

"Rope"

Hardy, John E. *Katherine Anne Porter,* 46–47.

"The Source"

Hennessy, Rosemary. ". . . Model for Heroines," 303.

"Theft"

Hardy, John E. *Katherine Anne Porter,* 63–68.
Smith, Charles W. "A Flaw in Katherine Anne Porter's 'Theft': The Teacher
Taught," *Coll Engl Assoc Critic,* 38, ii (1976), 19–21.
Stern, Carol S. "A Flaw in Katherine Anne Porter's 'Theft': The Teacher
Taught—A Reply," *Coll Engl Assoc Critic,* 39 (May, 1977), 4–8.

J. F. POWERS

"Prince of Darkness"

Hoenisch, Michael. "James F. Powers, 'Prince of Darkness,' " in Freese,
Peter, Ed. . . . *Interpretationen,* 84–89.

"The Valiant Woman"

Cassill, R. V. *Instructor's Handbook* . . . , 180–181.
Kane, Thomas S., and Leonard J. Peters. *Some Suggestions* . . . , 26–27.

PEDRO PRADO

"The Laugh in the Desert"
Kelly, John R. *Pedro Prado,* 111–114.

"Moonlight"
Kelly, John R. *Pedro Prado,* 108–109.

"Summer Picture: The Cripple"
Kelly, John R. *Pedro Prado,* 105–107.

"When You Are Poor"
Kelly, John R. *Pedro Prado,* 107.

"The Wise Woman"
Kelly, John R. *Pedro Prado,* 107–108.

PRAMOEDYA ANANTA TOER

"Things Vanished"
Siegel, James. " 'Thing(s) Vanished' Rediscovered," *Glyph,* 1 (1977), 87–99.

FLETCHER PRATT and LAURENCE MANNING

"City of the Living Dead"
Carter, Paul A. *The Creation* . . . , 208–209.

MUNSHI PREM CHAND [MUNSHI DHANPAT RAI]

"The Chess Player"
Sharma, Govind Narain. *Munshi Prem Chand,* 149–157.

"The Old Aunt"
Sharma, Govind Narain. *Munshi Prem Chand,* 148–149.

JAMES PURDY

"Color of Darkness"
Adams, Stephen D. *James Purdy,* 12–14.

"Cutting Edge"
Adams, Stephen D. *James Purdy,* 45–47.

"Daddy Wolf"
Adams, Stephen D. *James Purdy,* 17–19.

"Don't Call Me by My Right Name"
Meindel, Dieter. "James Purdy, 'Don't Call Me by My Right Name,' " in Freese, Peter, Ed. . . . *Interpretationen,* 175–183.

"Eventide"
Adams, Stephen D. *James Purdy,* 43–44.

"Home by Dark"
Adams, Stephen D. *James Purdy,* 16–17.

"63: Dream Palace"
Adams, Stephen D. *James Purdy,* 19–26.
Kennard, Jean E. *Number and Nightmare* . . . , 84–87.

"Why Can't They Tell You Why?"
Adams, Stephen D. *James Purdy,* 14–15.

ALEXANDER PUSHKIN

"The Queen of Spades"
Kodjak, Andrej. " 'The Queen of Spades' in the Context of the Faust Legend," in Kodjak, Andrej, and Kiril Taranovksy, Eds. and Trans. *Alexander Puškin* . . . , 87–118.
Leighton, Lauren G. "Numbers and Numerology in 'The Queen of Spades,' " *Canadian Slavonic Papers,* 19 (1977), 417–443.

Rosen, Nathan. "The Magic Cards in 'The Queen of Spades,' " *Slavic & East European J,* 19 (1975), 255–275.

"The Stationmaster"
  Debreczeny, Paul. "Puškin's Use of His Narrator in 'The Stationmaster,' " *Russian Lit,* N.S., 4, ii (1976), 149–166.
  Shaw, J. Thomas. "Pushkin's 'The Stationmaster' and the New Testament Parable," *Slavic & East European J,* 21 (1977), 3–29.

THOMAS PYNCHON

"Entropy"
  Bischoff, Peter. "Thomas Pynchon, 'Entropy,' " in Freese, Peter, Ed. . . . *Interpretationen,* 226–236.
  Redfield, Robert, and Peter L. Hays. "Fugue as a Structure in Pynchon's 'Entropy,' " *Pacific Coast Philol,* 12 (1977), 50–55.
  Simmons, John. "Third Story Man: Biblical Irony in Thomas Pynchon's 'Entropy,' " *Stud Short Fiction,* 14 (1977), 88–93.
  Slade, Joseph W. *Thomas Pynchon,* 32–40; rpt., with changes, Mendelson, Edward, Ed. *Pynchon . . . ,* 77–81.

"A Journey into the Mind of Watts"
  Slade, Joseph W. *Thomas Pynchon,* 45–47; rpt., with changes, Mendelson, Edward, Ed. *Pynchon . . . ,* 83–85.

"Low-lands"
  Slade, Joseph W. *Thomas Pynchon,* 25–32; rpt., with changes, Mendelson, Edward, Ed. *Pynchon . . . ,* 73–77.

"Mortality and Mercy in Vienna"
  Slade, Joseph W. *Thomas Pynchon,* 20–25; rpt., with changes, Mendelson, Edward, Ed. *Pynchon . . . ,* 71–73.

"The Secret Integration"
  Slade, Joseph W. *Thomas Pynchon,* 40–45; rpt., with changes, Mendelson, Edward, Ed. *Pynchon . . . ,* 81–83.

HORACIO QUIROGA

"A la deriva"
  Shoemaker, Roy H. "El tema de la muerte en los cuentos de Horacio Quiroga," *Cuadernos Americanos,* No. 220 (1978), 249–257.

"El hombre muerte"
  Shoemaker, Roy H. "El tema de la muerte . . . ," 257–261.

"Las moscas"
  Shoemaker, Roy H. "El tema de la muerte . . . ," 261–264.

WILHELM RAABE

"Zum wilden Mann"
  Thürmer, Wilfried. "Entfremdetes Behagen: Wilhelm Raabes Erzählung 'Zum wilden Mann' als Konkretion gründerzeitlichen Bewusstseins," *Jahrbuch der Raabe-Gesellschaft*, [n. v.] (1976), 151–161.

MOHAN RAKESH

"Savorless Sin"
  Williams, Richard A. "Jivan and Zindagi: An Analysis of Mohan Rakesh's Short Story 'Savorless Sin,' " *J So Asian Lit*, 13, i–iv (1977–1978), 39–43.

RAJA RAO

"The Cow of the Barricades"
  Gemmill, Janet P. "Raja Rao: Three Tales of Independence," *World Lit Written Engl*, 15 (1976), 143–146.

"In Khandesh"
  Gemmill, Janet P. "Raja Rao . . .," 139–143.

"Narsiga"
  Gemmill, Janet P. "Raja Rao . . .," 135–139.

CHARLES READE

"Art: A Dramatic Tale"
  Smith, Elton E. *Charles Reade*, 63–65.

"Clouds and Sunshine"
  Smith, Elton E. *Charles Reade*, 65–66.

PETER REDGROVE

"Mr. Waterman"
  Favier, Jacques. "Space and Settor in Short Science Fiction," in Johnson, Ira and Christiane, Eds. *Les Américanistes . . .*, 196–197.

F. ANTON REEDS

"Forever Is Not So Long"
  Carter, Paul A. *The Creation . . .*, 99–100.

JOSÉ REVUELTAS

"La frontera increíble"
  Brodman, Barbara L. C. *The Mexican Cult . . .*, 60–61.

"Los hombres en el pantano"
Brodman, Barbara L. C. *The Mexican Cult* . . ., 62–63.

"Lo que solo uno escucha"
Brodman, Barbara L. C. *The Mexican Cult* . . ., 61–62.

DOROTHY RICHARDSON

"Excursion"
Fromm, Gloria G. *Dorothy Richardson* . . ., 344–346.

"Nook on Parnassus"
Fromm, Gloria G. *Dorothy Richardson* . . ., 293–295.

"Ordeal"
Fromm, Gloria G. *Dorothy Richardson* . . ., 242–245.

"Tryst"
Fromm, Gloria G. *Dorothy Richardson* . . ., 338–339.

"Visit"
Fromm, Gloria G. *Dorothy Richardson* . . ., 346–347.

"Visitor"
Fromm, Gloria G. *Dorothy Richardson* . . ., 346.

HENRY HANDEL RICHARDSON
[ETHEL FLORENCE LINDESAY RICHARDSON]

"Succedaneum"
Palmer, Nettie. *Henry Handel Richardson,* 131–133.

RAINER MARIA RILKE

"Die Turnstunde"
Wonderley, Wayne. "An Analysis of Rilke's Novella 'Die Turnstunde,' " *Perspectives Contemp Lit,* 2 (May, 1976), 34–39.

AUGUSTO ROA BASTOS

"The Carpincho Hunters"
Foster, David W. *Augusto Roa Bastos,* 28–31.

"The Excavation"
Foster, David W. *Augusto Roa Bastos,* 34–36.

"Lying in State"
Foster, David W. *Augusto Roa Bastos,* 76–78.

"Nocturnal Games"
   Foster, David W. *Augusto Roa Bastos*, 79–84.

"Private Audience"
   Foster, David W. *Augusto Roa Bastos*, 32–33.

"Slaughter"
   Foster, David W. *Augusto Roa Bastos*, 69–73.

"To Tell a Story"
   Foster, David W. *Augusto Roa Bastos*, 83–84.

ALAIN ROBBE-GRILLET

"Behind the Automatic Door"
   Deneau, Daniel P. "A Glance at Robbe-Grillet's *Snapshots*," *So Dakota R,* 13
      (1976), 109.

"A Corridor"
   Deneau, Daniel P. ". . . Robbe-Grillet's *Snapshots*," 107–108.

"The Dressmaker's Dummy"
   Deneau, Daniel P. ". . . Robbe-Grillet's *Snapshots*," 84–86.

"The Escalator"
   Deneau, Daniel P. ". . . Robbe-Grillet's *Snapshots*," 107.

"The Replacement"
   Deneau, Daniel P. ". . . Robbe-Grillet's *Snapshots*," 86–90.

"Scene"
   Deneau, Daniel P. ". . . Robbe-Grillet's *Snapshots*," 99–102.

"The Secret Room"
   Deneau, Daniel P. ". . . Robbe-Grillet's *Snapshots*," 109–116.

"The Shore"
   Deneau, Daniel P. ". . . Robbe-Grillet's *Snapshots*," 103–107.

"The Way Back"
   Deneau, Daniel P. ". . . Robbe-Grillet's *Snapshots*," 92–99.

"The Wrong Direction"
   Deneau, Daniel P. ". . . Robbe-Grillet's *Snapshots*," 90–92.

CHARLES G. D. ROBERTS

"When Twilight Falls on the Stump Lots"
   Morley, Patricia. " 'We and the Beasts Are Kin': Attitudes Toward Nature in
      Nineteenth- and Early Twentieth-Century Canadian Literature," *World Lit
      Written Engl,* 16 (1977), 349–350.

FRANK M. ROBINSON

"The Wreck of the Ship *John B*"
  Favier, Jacques. "Space and Settor in Short Science Fiction," in Johnson, Ira
  and Christiane, Eds. *Les Américanistes* . . ., 188–189.

PHILIP ROTH

"The Conversion of the Jews"
  Cassill, R. V. *Instructor's Handbook* . . ., 182–183.
  Rodgers, Bernard F. *Philip Roth*, 21–23.
  Shaheen, Naseeb. "Binder Unbound, or, How Not to Convert the Jews," *Stud
  Short Fiction*, 13 (1976), 376–378.

"Courting Disaster, or Serious in the Fifties"
  Rodgers, Bernard F. *Philip Roth*, 143–146.

"Defender of the Faith"
  *Perrine, Laurence. *Instructor's Manual* . . . *"Story* . . .," 14–16; *Instructor's
  Manual* . . . *"Literature* . . .," 14–16.
  Rodgers, Bernard F. *Philip Roth*, 24–27.

"Eli, the Fanatic"
  Gittleman, Sol. *From Shtetl to Suburbia* . . ., 92–94.
  Hellweg, Martin. "Philip Roth, 'Eli, the Fanatic,' " in Freese, Peter, Ed. . . .
  Interpretationen, 215–225.
  Rodgers, Bernard F. *Philip Roth*, 27–31.

"Epstein"
  Gittleman, Sol. *From Shtetl to Suburbia* . . ., 169–170.
  Rodgers, Bernard F. *Philip Roth*, 23–24.

"Goodbye, Columbus"
  Bankston, Dorothy H. "Roth's 'Goodbye, Columbus,' " *Explicator*, 36, ii
  (1978), 21–22.
  Gittleman, Sol. *From Shtetl to Suburbia* . . ., 167–169.
  Rodgers, Bernard F. *Philip Roth*, 34–46.

" 'I Always Want You to Admire My Fasting'; or Looking at Kafka"
  Rodgers, Bernard F. *Philip Roth*, 155–156.

"In Trouble"
  Kimmey, John L., Ed. *Experience and Expression* . . ., 55.

"Salad Days"
  Rodgers, Bernard F. *Philip Roth*, 142–143.

JUAN RULFO

"La Cuesta de las Comadres"
  Brodman, Barbara L. C. *The Mexican Cult* . . ., 52–54.

"El llano an llamas"
Brodman, Barbara L. C. *The Mexican Cult* . . ., 56–57.

"Luvina"
Brodman, Barbara L. C. *The Mexican Cult* . . ., 50–52.
Cannon, Carlota B. " 'Luvina' o el ideal que pudo ser: En torno a un cuento de Juan Rulfo," *Papeles de Son Armadans,* 80 (1976), 203–216.
Leal, Luis. "El cuento de ambiente: 'Luvina,' de Juan Rulfo," in Giacoman, Helmy F., Ed. *Homenaje a Juan Rulfo* . . ., 91–98.

"The Man"
Coddou, Marcelo. "Fundamentos para la valoracion de la obra de Juan Rulfo (proposiciones para la interpretacion y analisis del cuento 'El hombre'),'' in Giacoman, Helmy F., Ed. *Homenaje a Juan Rulfo* . . ., 61–89.

"No oyes ladrar los perros"
Forgues, Roland. "La tecnica del suspenso dramatico en un cuento de Juan Rulfo: 'No oyes ladrar los perros,' " *Letras de Deusto,* 6, xi (1976), 175–185.

"Talpa"
Clinton, Stephen T. "Form and Meaning in Juan Rulfo's 'Talpa,' " *Romance Notes,* 16 (1975), 520–525.

FRED SABERHAGEN

"Goodlife"
Stewart, A.D. "Fred Saberhagen, Cybernetic Psychologist: A Study of the Berserker Stories," *Extrapolation,* 18 (1976), 45–46.

"In the Temple of Mars"
Stewart, A.D. ". . . Berserker Stories," 45.

"Patron of the Arts"
Stewart, A.D. ". . . Berserker Stories," 47–48.

"The Peacemaker"
Stewart, A.D. ". . . Berserker Stories," 46–47.

J.D. SALINGER

"De Daumier-Smith's Blue Period"
Kirschner, Paul. "Salinger and His Society: The Pattern of *Nine Stories* [Part II]," *Lit Half-Yearly,* 14, ii (1973), 71–74.
Ortseifen, Karl. "J.D. Salinger: 'De Daumier-Smith's Blue Period,' " in Busch, Frieder, and Renate S. Bardeleben, Eds. *Amerikanische Erzählliteratur 1950–1970,* 186–196.

"Down at the Dinghy"
Kirschner, Paul. "Salinger and His Society . . . [Part II]," 63–66.

"For Esmé—With Love and Squalor"
Kirschner, Paul. "Salinger and His Society . . . [Part II]," 66–70.

"Franny"
Cotter, James F. "Religious Symbols in Salinger's Short Fiction," *Stud Short Fiction*, 15 (1978), 121–132.

"Just Before the War with the Eskimos"
Kirschner, Paul. "Salinger and His Society: The Pattern of *Nine Stories* [Part I]," *Lit Half-Yearly*, 12, ii (1971), 56–58.

"The Laughing Man"
Kirschner, Paul. "Salinger and His Society . . . [Part I]," 58–60.

"A Perfect Day for Bananafish"
Kirschner, Paul. "Salinger and His Society . . . [Part I]," 52–54.
Simms, L. Moody. "Seymour Glass: The Salingerian Hero as Vulgarian," *Notes Contemp Lit*, 5, v (1975), 6–8.

"Pretty Mouth and Green My Eyes"
Kirschner, Paul. "Salinger and His Society . . . [Part II]," 70–71.

"Teddy"
Kirschner, Paul. "Salinger and His Society . . . [Part II]," 74–75.

"Uncle Wiggily in Connecticut"
Groene, Horst. "Jerome David Salinger, 'Uncle Wiggily in Connecticut,' " in Freese, Peter, Ed. . . . *Interpretationen*, 110–118.
Kirschner, Paul. "Salinger and His Society . . . [Part I]," 54–56.

"Zooey"
Cotter, James F. "Religious Symbols . . . ," 121–132.

WILLIAM SAROYAN

"Love, Here Is My Hat"
Cassill, R.V. *Instructor's Handbook* . . . , 183–184.

RUNAR SCHILDT

"Aapo"
Zuck, Virpi. "The Finno-Swedish Short Story: Runar Schildt," *Scandinavian Stud*, 49 (1977), 183–187.

ZALMAN SCHNEOUR

"The Girl"
Gittleman, Sol. *From Shtetl to Suburbia* . . . , 103–105.

ARTHUR SCHNITZLER

"Blumen"
Russell, Peter. "Schnitzler's 'Blumen': The Treatment of a Neurosis," *Forum Mod Lang Stud,* 13 (1977), 289–302.

"Fraulein Else"
Baharriell, Frederick J. "Schnitzler's 'Fraulein Else': 'Reality' and Invention," *Mod Austrian Lit,* 10, iii–iv (1977), 247–264.

"The Last Letters of a Litterateur"
Mahlendorf, Ursula. "Arthur Schnitzler's 'The Last Letters of a Litterateur': The Artist as Destroyer," *Am Imago,* 34 (1977), 238–256.

DELMORE SCHWARTZ

"The World Is a Wedding"
Lyons, Bonnie. "Delmore Schwartz and the Whole Truth," *Stud Short Fiction,* 14 (1977), 259–264.

WALTER SCOTT

"The Two Drovers"
Cooney, Seamus. "Scott and Cultural Relativism: 'The Two Drovers,' " *Stud Short Fiction,* 15 (1978), 1–9.

WILLIAM CHARLES SCULLY

"Afar in the Desert"
Doyle, John R. *William Charles Scully,* 119–120.

"The Battle of Ezinyoseni"
Doyle, John R. *William Charles Scully,* 191–193.

"By the Waters of Marah"
Doyle, John R. *William Charles Scully,* 120–121.

"Chicken Wings"
Doyle, John R. *William Charles Scully,* 115–116.

"Ghamba"
Doyle, John R. *William Charles Scully,* 70–71.

"The Gratitude of a Savage"
Doyle, John R. *William Charles Scully,* 121–122.

"The Imishologu"
Doyle, John R. *William Charles Scully,* 76–77.

"Noquala's Cattle"
Doyle, John R. *William Charles Scully,* 92–96.

"On Picket, An Episode of the South African War"
Doyle, John R. *William Charles Scully,* 190–191.

"The Quest of the Copper"
Doyle, John R. *William Charles Scully,* 63–69.

"Rainmaking"
Doyle, John R. *William Charles Scully,* 114–115.

"Ukushwama"
Doyle, John R. *William Charles Scully,* 72–74.

"The Vengeance of Dogolwana"
Doyle, John R. *William Charles Scully,* 77–79.

"The White Hecatomb"
Doyle, John R. *William Charles Scully,* 79–80.

"The Wisdom of the Serpent"
Doyle, John R. *William Charles Scully,* 112–114.

"The Writing on the Rock"
Doyle, John R. *William Charles Scully,* 118–119.

MENDELE MOCHER SEFORIM [SHALOM YA'AKOV ABRAMOVITSH]

"In the Days of Tumult"
Steinberg, Theodore L. *Mendele Mocher Seforim,* 148–149.

"In the Heavenly and Earthly Assemblies"
Steinberg, Theodore L. *Mendele Mocher Seforim,* 149–151.

"The Old Story" [same as "There Is No God in Jacob"]
Steinberg, Theodore L. *Mendele Mocher Seforim,* 145–148.

ANNA SEGHERS

"The End"
Kessler, P. "Der verwandelte Teufel Ivan Karamazovs in Anna Seghers' Erzählung 'Das Ende,' " *Zeitschrift für Slawistik,* 22 (1977), 325–337.

ERNEST THOMPSON SETON

"Lobo, the King of the Currumpaw"
Morley, Patricia. " 'We and the Beasts are Kin': Attitudes Toward Nature in Nineteenth- and Early Twentieth-Century Canadian Literature," *World Lit Written Engl,* 16 (1977), 351–352.

IRWIN SHAW

"The Girls in Their Summer Dresses"
    Cassill, R. V. *Instructor's Handbook* . . ., 185.
    Kane, Thomas S., and Leonard J. Peters. *Some Suggestions* . . ., 32–34.

SHEN TS'UNG-WEN

"Hsiao-hsiao"
    Hsia, C. T. *A History* . . ., 201–203.

"Hui Ming"
    Hsia, C. T. *A History* . . ., 200–201.

"Living"
    Hsia, C. T. *A History* . . ., 203–204.

"Quiet"
    , Hsia, C. T. *A History* . . ., 208–211.

SHIGA NAOYA

"The Diary of Claudius" [same as "Claudius' Journal"]
    Yamanouchi, Hisaaki. *The Search for Authenticity* . . ., 84–85.

HENRYK SIENKIEWICZ

"A Comedy of Errors"
    Krzyzanowski, Julian. "The Polish-Californian Background of H. Sienkiewicz's
    Burlesque 'A Comedy of Errors,' " in Erlich, Victor, *et al.*, Eds. *For Wictor ·
    Weintraub* . . ., 253–265.

LYDIA HUNTLEY SIGOURNEY

"The Father"
    Douglas, Ann. *The Feminization* . . ., 197–198.

"The Patriarch"
    Douglas, Ann. *The Feminization* . . ., 197–198.

ALAN SILLITOE

"The Loneliness of the Long-Distance Runner"
    Byars, John A. "The Initiation of Alan Sillitoe's Long-Distance Runner," *Mod
    Fiction Stud,* 22 (1977), 584–591.

IGNAZIO SILONE

"The Fox and the Camellias"
Leibowitz, Judith. *Narrative Purposes* . . ., 95–98.

JOSÉ ASUNCIÓN SILVA

"Pataguya"
Osiek, Betty T. *José Asunción Silva,* 143–144.

ROBERT SILVERBERG

"After the Myths Went Home"
Fredericks, S.C. "Revivals of Ancient Mythology in Current Science Fiction
and Fantasy," in Clareson, Thomas D., Ed. *Many Futures* . . ., 61–63.

"Woman's World"
Moskowitz, Sam. *Strange Horizons* . . ., 88–89.

CLIFFORD D. SIMAK

"The Big Front Yard"
Clareson, Thomas D. "Clifford D. Simak: The Inhabited Universe," in
Clareson, Thomas D., Ed. *Voices for the Future* . . ., 79–80.

"Hunger Death"
Clareson, Thomas D. ". . . The Inhabited Universe," 69–70.

"Shotgun Cure"
Clareson, Thomas D. ". . . The Inhabited Universe," 78–79.

CLIFFORD D. SIMAK and CARL JACOBI

"The Street That Wasn't There"
Carter, Paul A. *The Creation* . . ., 154–155.

WILLIAM GILMORE SIMMS

"The Two Camps"
Rose, Alan H. *Demonic Vision* . . ., 47–49.

MAY SINCLAIR

"Between the Lines"
Zegger, Hrisey D. *May Sinclair,* 63–65.

"The Finding of the Absolute"
Zegger, Hrisey D. *May Sinclair,* 139–140.

"The Gift"
Zegger, Hrisey D. *May Sinclair,* 61–62.

"The Intercessor"
Zegger, Hrisey D. *May Sinclair,* 62–63.

I. J. SINGER

"Sand"
Gittleman, Sol. *From Shtetl to Suburbia . . . ,* 101–103.

ISAAC BASHEVIS SINGER

"The Black Wedding"
Seed, David. "The Fiction of Isaac Bashevis Singer," *Critical Q,* 18 (1976), 74.

"The Captive"
Rice, Julian C. "I. B. Singer's 'The Captive': A False Messiah in the Promised Land," *Stud Am Fiction,* 5 (1977), 269–275.

"Gimpel the Fool"
Gittleman, Sol. *From Shtetl to Suburbia . . . ,* 103–107.

"The Little Shoemakers"
Gittleman, Sol. *From Shtetl to Suburbia . . . ,* 107–115.

"Powers"
Kimmey, John L. *Instructor's Manual . . . ,* 13–15.

"The Spinoza of Market Street"
Cassill, R. V. *Instructor's Handbook . . . ,* 186–187.

TESS SLESINGER

"A Life in the Day of a Writer"
Cassill, R. V. *Instructor's Handbook . . . ,* 187–188.

CORDWAINER SMITH

"The Game of Rat and Dragon"
Wolfe, Gary K. "Mythic Structure in Cordwainer Smith's 'The Game of Rat and Dragon,' " *Sci-Fiction Stud,* 4 (1977), 144–150.

"Scanners Live in Vain"
Scholes, Robert, and Eric S. Rabkin. *Science Fiction . . . ,* 172–173.

WILLIAM JOSEPH SNELLING

"The Bois Brulé"
Scheick, William J. "The Half-Breed in Snelling's *Tales of the Northwest*," *Old Northwest*, 2 (1976), 145–150.

ALEXANDER SOLZHENITSYN

"The Easter Procession"
Rothberg, Abraham. "Solzhenitsyn's Short Stories," *Kansas Q*, 9, ii (1977), 34.

"For the Good of the Cause"
Kodjak, Andrej. *Alexander Solzhenitsyn*, 114–119.
Rothberg, Abraham. "Solzhenitsyn's Short Stories," 38–40.

"An Incident at Krechetovka Station"
Kodjak, Andrej. *Alexander Solzhenitsyn*, 108–114.
Rothberg, Abraham. "Solzhenitsyn's Short Stories," 40–43.
Rzhevsky, Leonid. *Solzhenitsyn . . .*, 39–43.

"Matryona's House"
Kodjak, Andrej. *Alexander Solzhenitsyn*, 104–108.
Rothberg, Abraham. "Solzhenitsyn's Short Stories," 43–47.
Rzhevsky, Leonid. *Solzhenitsyn . . .*, 43–48.

"The Right Hand"
Kodjak, Andrej. *Alexander Solzhenitsyn*, 119–120.
Rothberg, Abraham. "Solzhenitsyn's Short Stories," 34–36.

"Zakhar the Pouch"
Kodjak, Andrej. *Alexander Solzhenitsyn*, 120–121.
Rothberg, Abraham. "Solzhenitsyn's Short Stories," 36–38.

MURIEL SPARK

"The Go-Ahead Bird"
Leibowitz, Judith. *Narrative Purposes . . .*, 73–75.

"Memento Mori"
Leibowitz, Judith. *Narrative Purposes . . .*, 72–73.

JEAN STAFFORD

"In the Zoo"
Cassill, R. V. *Instructor's Handbook . . .*, 188–191.

WILBUR DANIEL STEELE

"How Beautiful with Shoes"
 Sullivan, Ernest W. "Flowers, Verse, and Gems: Names in Wilbur Daniel
  Steele's 'How Beautiful with Shoes,' " *Pubs Arkansas Philol Assoc,* 4, ii
  (1978), 63–65.
 *Sundell, Roger H. and Julie P. " 'How Beautiful with Shoes,' " in Dietrich,
  R. F., and Roger H. Sundell. *Instructor's Manual . . . ,* 3rd ed., 113–122.

WALLACE STEGNER

"The Blue-Winged Teal"
 Robinson, Forrest G. and Margaret G. *Wallace Stegner,* 78–81.

"Carrion Spring"
 Ahearn, Kerry. "Heroes vs. Women: Conflict and Duplicity in Stegner,"
  Western Hum R, 31 (1977), 131–132.

"The Chink"
 Robinson, Forrest G. and Margaret G. *Wallace Stegner,* 73–75.

"Field Guide"
 Robinson, Forrest G. and Margaret G. *Wallace Stegner,* 87–92.

"Goin' to Town"
 Cassill, R. V. *Instructor's Handbook . . . ,* 191–192.

"Saw Gang"
 Robinson, Forrest G. and Margaret G. *Wallace Stegner,* 76–77.

"The Traveler"
 Robinson, Forrest G. and Margaret G. *Wallace Stegner,* 86–87.

"The Women on the Wall"
 Robinson, Forrest G. and Margaret G. *Wallace Stegner,* 82–86.

GERTRUDE STEIN

"The Gentle Lena"
 Hoffman, Michael J. *Gertrude Stein,* 29–31.

"The Good Anna"
 Hoffman, Michael J. *Gertrude Stein,* 29–31.
 Rose, Marilyn G. "Gertrude Stein and the Cubist Narrative," *Mod Fiction Stud,*
  22 (1977), 545–549.

"Melanctha"
 Hoffman, Michael J. *Gertrude Stein,* 32–37.

JOHN STEINBECK

"The Chrysanthemums"
  Cassill, R. V. *Instructor's Handbook* . . ., 193–194.
  *Miller, William V. "Sexual and Spiritual Ambiguity in 'The Chrysanthe-
    mums,' " in Hayashi, Tetsumaro, Ed. *A Study Guide* . . ., 1–10.
  Mitchell, Marilyn. "Steinbeck's Strong Women: Feminine Identity in the Short
    Stories," *Southwest R,* 61 (1976), 304–315.
  Osborne, William. "The Education of Elisa Allen: Another Reading of John
    Steinbeck's 'The Chrysanthemums,' " *Interpretations,* 8 (1976), 10–15.

"The Gift"
  *Benton, Robert M. "Realism, Growth, and Contrast in 'The Gift,' " in Hayashi,
    Tetsumaro, Ed. *A Study Guide* . . ., 81–88.

"The Great Mountain"
  *Peterson, Richard F. "The Grail Legend and Steinbeck's 'The Great Moun-
    tain,' " in Hayashi, Tetsumaro, Ed. *A Study Guide* . . ., 89–96.

"Johnny Bear"
  *French, Warren. " 'Johnny Bear': Steinbeck's 'Yellow Peril' Story," in
    Hayashi, Tetsumaro, Ed. *A Study Guide* . . ., 57–64.

"The Leader of the People"
  *Astro, Richard. "Something That Happened: A Non-Teleological Approach to
    'The Leader of the People,' " in Hayashi, Tetsumaro, Ed. *A Study Guide* . . .,
    105–111.

"The Murder"
  Davis, Robert M. "Steinbeck's 'The Murder,' " *Stud Short Fiction,* 14 (1977),
    63–68.
  Morseberger, Katharine M. and Robert M. " 'The Murder': Realism or Ritual?"
    in Hayashi, Tetsumaro, Ed. *A Study Guide* . . ., 65–71.

"The Promise"
  *Woodward, Robert H. "The Promise of Steinbeck's 'The Promise,' " in
    Hayashi, Tetsumaro, Ed. *A Study Guide* . . ., 97–103.

"Saint Katy the Virgin"
  *Marovitz, Sanford E. "The Cryptic Raillery of 'Saint Katy the Virgin,' " in
    Hayashi, Tetsumaro, Ed. *A Study Guide* . . ., 73–80.

"The Snake"
  *Garcia, Reloy. "Steinbeck's 'The Snake': An Explication," in Hayashi, Tet-
    sumaro, Ed. *A Study Guide* . . ., 25–31.

"The White Quail"
  Mitchell, Marilyn. "Steinbeck's Strong Women . . .," 304–315.
  *Simpson, Arthur L. " 'The White Quail': A Portrait of an Artist," in Hayashi,
    Tetsumaro, Ed. *A Study Guide* . . ., 11–16.

JAMES STEPHENS

"Desire"
Martin, Augustine. *James Stephens* . . . , 63–65.

"Etched in Moonlight"
Martin, Augustine. *James Stephens* . . . , 65–69.

"Hunger"
Martin, Augustine. *James Stephens* . . . , 70–72.

"Mongan's Frenzy"
Martin, Augustine. *James Stephens* . . . , 132–133.

ROBERT LOUIS STEVENSON

"Olalla"
Massey, Irving. *The Gaping Pig* . . . , 106–110.

"The Strange Case of Dr. Jekyll and Mr. Hyde"
Massey, Irving. *The Gaping Pig* . . . , 101–106.

ADALBERT STIFTER

"Abdias"
Pischel, Barbara. "Adalbert Stifters Novelle 'Abdias' ethnographisch interpretiert," *Adalbert Stifter Institut*, 27 (1978), 69–72.

"Brigitta"
Branscombe, Peter. "The Use of Leitmotifs in Stifter's 'Brigitta,' " *Forum Mod Lang Stud*, 13 (1977), 145–154.
Leibowitz, Judith. *Narrative Purposes* . . . , 27–30.

"Chips off the Old Block"
Aspetsberger, Friedbert. "Stifters Erzählung 'Nachkommenschaften,' " *Sprachkunst*, 6 (1975), 238–260.

"The *Condor*"
Mautz, Kurt. "Natur und Gesellschaft in Stifters 'Condor,' " in Arntzen, Helmut, *et al.*, Eds. *Literaturwissenschaft* . . . , 406–435.

"An Elderly Bachelor"
Adamy, Bernhard. "Beitrag zum Verständnis von Stifters Erzählung 'Der Hagestolz,' " *Adalbert Stifter Institut*, 25 (1976), 83–100.

"The Fountain in the Woods"
Hunter-Lougheed, Rosemarie. "Waldschlange Lerche im 'Waldbrunnen': Zu Tiervergleich und Tiersymbol bei Stifter," *Seminar*, 13 (1977), 99–110.

"Granite"
Swales, Martin. *The German "Novelle,"* 133–157.

"Limestone"
Reddick, John. "Tiger und Tugend in Stifters 'Kalkstein': Eine Polemik,"
   Zeitschrift für Deutsche Philologie, 95 (1976), 235–255.

"Turmaline"
Hertling, G. H. " 'Wer jetzt kein Haus hat, baut sich keines mehr': Zur Zentral-
   symbolik in Adalbert Stifters 'Turmalin,' " *Adalbert Stifter Institut,* 26
   (1977), 17–34.
Mason, Eve. "Stifter's 'Turmalin': A Reconsideration," *Mod Lang R,* 72
   (1977), 348–358.

"The Wanderer in the Forest"
Hunter, Rosemarie. "Wald, Haus und Wasser, Moos und Schmetterling: Zu den
   Zentralsymbolen in Stifters Erzählung 'Der Waldgänger,' " *Adalbert Stifter
   Institut,* 24 (1975), 23–36.

THEODOR STORM

"Aquis Submersus"
Coupe, W. A. "Zur Frage der Schuld in 'Aquis Submersus,' " *Schriften der
   Theodor-Storm-Gesellschaft,* 24 (1975), 57–72.
Cunningham, William L. "Zur Wassersymbolik in 'Aquis submersus,' "
   Schriften der Theodor-Storm-Gesellschaft, [n.v.] (1978), 40–49.

"Pole Poppenspäler"
Schroeder, Horst. " 'Pole Poppenspäler' und die Schule," *Schriften der
   Theodor-Storm-Gesellschaft,* 24 (1975), 36–56.

"The Rider of the White Horse"
Findlay, Ian. "Myth and Redemption in Theodor Storm's 'Der Schimmel-
   reiter,' " *Papers Lang & Lit,* 11 (1975), 397–403.
Köhnke, Klaus. "Storms 'Schimmelreiter': Zur Bedeutung des Rahmens,"
   Deutschunterricht in Südafrika, 9, i (1978), 4–20.
Langer, Ilse. "Volksaberglaube und paranormales Geschichten in einigen
   Szenen des 'Schimmelreiters,' " *Schriften der Theodor-Storm-Gesellschaft,*
   24 (1975), 90–97.
Leibowitz, Judith. *Narrative Purposes . . .,* 32–33.

AUGUST STRINDBERG

"The Boarders"
Johnson, Walter. *August Strindberg,* 98.

DAVID STRINGER

"High Eight"
Favier, Jacques. "Space and Settor in Short Science Fiction," in Johnson, Ira
   and Christiane, Eds. *Les Américanistes . . .,* 197–198.

JESSE STUART

"Another April"
  Leavell, Frank H. "The Boy Narrator in Jesse Stuart's 'Another April,' " *Jack London Newsletter*, 8 (1975), 83–91.

"Another Hanging"
  *Foster, Ruel E. "The Short Stories: Tales of Shan and Others," in LeMaster, J.R., Ed. . . . *Selected Criticism*, 154–159.

"Between Life and Death"
  *Foster, Ruel E. "The Short Stories . . .," 159–160.

"Clearing in the Sky"
  Miller, Jim W. "The Gift Outright: W-Hollow," in LeMaster, J.R., and Mary W. Clarke, Eds. *Jesse Stuart* . . ., 112–114.

"Frog Trouncin' Contest"
  *Sundell, Roger H. " 'Frog Trouncin' Contest,' " in Dietrich, R.F., and Roger H. Sundell. *Instructor's Manual* . . ., 3rd ed., 123–127.

"Rain on Tanyard Hollow"
  Clarke, Kenneth. "Jesse Stuart's Use of Folklore," in LeMaster, J.R., and Mary W. Clarke, Eds. *Jesse Stuart* . . ., 123–125.

"A Stall for Uncle Jeff"
  Foster, Ruel E. "The Short Stories of Jesse Stuart," in LeMaster, J.R., and Mary W. Clarke, Eds. *Jesse Stuart* . . ., 45.

"Sylvania Is Dead"
  *Foster, Ruel E. "The Short Stories . . .," 160–161.

"Testimony of Trees"
  Clarke, Kenneth. "Jesse Stuart's Use of Folklore," 126–127.

"This Farm for Sale"
  Miller, Jim W. "The Gift Outright . . .," 103–106.

"Word and Flesh"
  *Foster, Ruel E. "The Short Stories . . .," 161–162.

THEODORE STURGEON

"Bulkhead"
  Wolfe, Gary K. "The Known and the Unknown: Structure and Image in Science Fiction," in Clareson, Thomas D., Ed. *Many Futures* . . ., 97–98.

"Extrapolation"
  Sackmary, Regina. "An Ideal of Three: The Art of Theodore Sturgeon," in Riley, Dick, Ed. *Critical Encounters* . . ., 137–138.

"Rule of Three"
 Sackmary, Regina. "An Ideal of Three . . .," 135–137.

"The Touch of Your Hand"
 Sackmary, Regina. "An Ideal of Three . . .," 139–140.

"Twink"
 Sackmary, Regina. "An Ideal of Three . . .," 140–141.

RONALD SUKENICK

"The Birds"
 Pütz, Manfred. "Ronald Sukenick, 'The Birds,' " in Freese, Peter, Ed. . . .
 Interpretationen, 314–322.

JULES SUPERVIELLE

"L'Enfant de la haute mer"
 Cranston, Philip E. "Jules Supervielle: 'Le Village sur les flots' and 'L'Enfant de
 la haute mer': Sea Changes," *French Lit Series*, 2 (1975), 101–115.

ITALO SVEVO

"Generous Wine"
 Lebowitz, Naomi. *Italo Svevo*, 152–154.

"The Hoax"
 Lebowitz, Naomi. *Italo Svevo*, 143–152.

"The Mother"
 Lebowitz, Naomi. *Italo Svevo*, 217–218.

"The Nice Old Man and the Pretty Girl"
 Lebowitz, Naomi. *Italo Svevo*, 140–143.

"Short Sentimental Journey"
 Lebowitz, Naomi. *Italo Svevo*, 154–163.

RABINDRANATH TAGORE

"The Atonement"
 Lago, Mary M. *Rabindranath Tagore*, 89–90.

"Cloud and Sun"
 Lago, Mary M. *Rabindranath Tagore*, 95–97.

"The Devotee"
 Lago, Mary M. *Rabindranath Tagore*, 91–92.

"The Editor"
Lago, Mary M. *Rabindranath Tagore,* 94–95.

"The Girl Between"
Lago, Mary M. *Rabindranath Tagore,* 102–107.

"One Night"
Lago, Mary M. *Rabindranath Tagore,* 98–99.

"The Postmaster"
Lago, Mary M. *Rabindranath Tagore,* 83–85.

"Rashmoni's Son"
Lago, Mary M. *Rabindranath Tagore,* 90–91.

"The Return of Khokababu"
Lago, Mary M. *Rabindranath Tagore,* 85–86.

"The Troublemaker"
Lago, Mary M. *Rabindranath Tagore,* 86.

"We Crown Thee King"
Lago, Mary M. *Rabindranath Tagore,* 97–98.

"A Wife's Letter"
Lago, Mary M. *Rabindranath Tagore,* 108–111.

TANIZAKI JUN'ICHIRŌ

"Tattoo"
Yamanouchi, Hisaaki. *The Search for Authenticity . . .,* 109–110.

PETER TAYLOR

"Dean of Men"
Cassill, R. V. *Instructor's Handbook . . .,* 195–197.

"A Wife of Nashville"
Sims, Barbara B. "Symbol and Theme in Peter Taylor's 'A Wife of Nash-ville,' " *Notes Mod Am Lit,* 2, iii (1978), Item 22.

YVES THÉRIAULT

"La fleur qui faisait un son"
Francoeur, Marie and Louis. "Deux contes nord-américains considérés comme actes de langage narratifs," *Études Littéraires,* 8 (1975), 57–80.

DYLAN THOMAS

"The Peaches"
Cassill, R. V. *Instructor's Handbook* . . ., 198–199.

"A Story"
Kane, Thomas S., and Leonard J. Peters. *Some Suggestions* . . ., 44–46.

JAMES THURBER

"The Catbird Seat"
Kane, Thomas S., and Leonard J. Peters. *Some Suggestions* . . ., 25–26.
Perrine, Laurence. *Instructor's Manual* . . . *"Story* . . .," 29–30; *Instructor's Manual* . . . *"Literature* . . .," 29–30.

"The Greatest Man in the World"
Abcarian, Richard, and Marvin Klotz. *Instructor's Manual* . . ., 2nd ed., 21–22.

"You Could Look It Up"
Cassill, R. V. *Instructor's Handbook* . . ., 200.
May, Charles E. "Christian Parody in Thurber's 'You Could Look It Up,' " *Stud Short Fiction,* 15 (1978), 453–454.

LEO TOLSTOY

"The Death of Ivan Ilych"
*Abcarian, Richard, and Marvin Klotz. *Instructor's Manual* . . ., 2nd ed., 22–23.
Borker, David. "Sentential Structure in Tolstoy's 'Smert Ivana Il'iča,' " in Birnbaum, Henrik, Ed. *American Contributions* . . ., I, 180–194.
Calder, Angus. *Russia Discovered* . . ., 232–233.
Cate, Hollis L. "On Death and Dying in Tolstoy's 'The Death of Ivan Ilych,' " *Hartford Stud Lit,* 7 (1975), 195–205.
*Howe, Irving, Ed. *Classics of Modern Fiction* . . ., 2nd ed., 113–121.
Wasiolek, Edward. *Tolstoy's Major Fiction,* 167–179.
*Wellek, René. "Masterpieces of Nineteenth-Century Realism and Naturalism," in Mack, Maynard, *et al.,* Eds. . . . *World Masterpieces,* II, 4th ed., 726–727.

"Family Happiness"
Monter, Barbara H. "Tolstoj's Path Toward Feminism," in Terras, Victor, Ed. *American Contributions* . . ., II, 524–525.
Poggioli, Renato. *The Oaten Flute* . . ., 265–282.
Wasiolek, Edward. *Tolstoy's Major Fiction,* 39–50.

"God Sees the Truth, but Waits"
Cassill, R. V. *Instructor's Handbook* . . ., 201.

"Hadji Murad" [same as "Hadji Murat"]
Briggs, A. D. P. " 'Hadji Murat': The Power of Understatement," in Jones, Malcolm, Ed. *New Essays* . . ., 109–127.

Dworsky, Nancy. " 'Hadji Murad': A Summary and a Vision," *Novel,* 8 (1975), 138–146.

Fanger, Donald. "Nazarov's Mother: Notes Toward an Interpretation of 'Hadji Murat,' " in Baer, Joachim T., and Norman W. Ingham, Eds. *Mnemozina* . . ., 95–104.

"How Much Land Does a Man Need?"

Jahn, Gary R. "Tolstoj's Vision of the Power of Death and 'How Much Land Does a Man Need?' " *Slavic & East European J,* 22 (1978), 442–453.

"The Kreutzer Sonata"

Baehr, Stephen. "Art and 'The Kreutzer Sonata': A Tolstoian Approach," *Canadian-Am Slavic Stud,* 10 (1976), 39–46.

Calder, Angus. *Russia Discovered* . . ., 233–235.

Holthusen, Johannes. "Das Erzählerproblem in Tolstoj's 'Kreutzer-sonate,' " in Baer, Joachim T., and Norman W. Ingham, Eds. *Mnemozina* . . ., 193–201.

Jacks, Robert L. "Tolstoj's 'Kreutzer Sonata' and Dostoevskij's 'Notes from Underground,' " in Terras, Victor, Ed. *American Contributions* . . ., II, 280–284.

Monter, Barbara H. "Tolstoj's Path . . .," 525–527.

Wasiolek, Edward. *Tolstoy's Major Fiction,* 162–164.

"A Landowner's Morning"

Lee, Nicholas. "Ecological Ethics in the Fiction of L. N. Tolstoj," in Terras, Victor, Ed. *American Contributions* . . ., II, 423–426.

"Polikushka"

Debreczeny, Paul. "The Device of Conspicuous Silence in Tolstoj, Čexov, and Faulkner," in Terras, Victor, Ed. *American Contributions* . . ., II, 125–128.

Lee, Nicholas. "Ecological Ethics . . .," 426–430.

"Three Deaths"

Wasiolek, Edward. *Tolstoy's Major Fiction,* 29–33.

JEAN TOOMER

"Blood-Burning Moon"

Martin, Odette C. "*Cane*: Method and Myth," *Obsidian,* 2, i (1976), 10.

"Box Seat"

Bone, Robert A. *The Negro Novel* . . ., 85–87; rpt. Durham, Frank, Ed. *Studies in "Cane"* . . ., 62–63.

"Esther"

Berzon, Judith R. *Neither White Nor Black* . . ., 69.

Martin, Odette C. ". . . Method and Myth," 9–10.

"Fern"

Berzon, Judith R. *Neither White Nor Black* . . ., 68–69.

Jung, Udo O.H. "Jean Toomer: 'Fern,' " in Bruck, Peter, Ed. *The Black American Short Story . . .*, 55–65.

"Kabnis"
Bone, Robert A. *The Negro Novel . . .*, 87–88; rpt. Durham, Frank, Ed. *Studies in "Cane" . . .*, 64–65.
Durham, Frank. "Toomer's Vision of the Southern Negro," in Durham, Frank, Ed. *Studies in "Cane" . . .*, 111–113.
Gloster, Hugh M. *Negro Voices . . .*, 129–130; rpt. Durham, Frank, Ed. *Studies in "Cane" . . .*, 55–56.
MacKethan, Lucinda H. "Jean Toomer's *Cane*: A Pastoral Problem," *Mississippi Q,* 28 (1975), 433.
Martin, Odette C. ". . . Method and Myth," 13–18.
Solard, Alain. "The Impossible Unity: Jean Toomer's 'Kabnis,' " in Durand, Regis, Ed. *Myth and Ideology . . .*, 175–194.

"Karintha"
Martin, Odette C. ". . . Method and Myth," 7–8.

"Theater"
*Abcarian, Richard, and Marvin Klotz. *Instructor's Manual . . .*, 2nd ed., 23–24.

ESTELA PORTILLO TRAMBLEY

"Rain of Scorpions"
Lattin, Vernon E. "The City in Contemporary Chicano Fiction," *Stud Am Fiction,* 6 (1978), 97–98.

BRUNO TRAVEN

"The Night Visitor"
Baumann, Michael L. *B. Traven . . .*, 128–129.

LIONEL TRILLING

"Of This Time, Of That Place"
George, Diana L. "Thematic Structure in Lionel Trilling's 'Of This Time, Of That Place,' " *Stud Short Fiction,* 13 (1976), 1–8.

ANTHONY TROLLOPE

"Aaron Trow"
Stone, Donald D. "Trollope as Short Story Writer," *Nineteenth-Century Fiction,* 31 (1976), 35.

"Malachi's Cove"
Stone, Donald D. "Trollope . . .," 36–37.

"The Spitted Dog"
  Stone, Donald D. "Trollope . . .," 41–42.

FRANZ TUMLER

"The Coat"
  Himmel, Hellmuth. "Unsicherheit und Präzision: Zu Franz Tumlers Erzählung
  'Der Mantel,' " in Doppler, Alfred, and Friedbert Aspetsberger, Eds. *Erzähl-
  techniken . . .*, 46–63.

IVAN TURGENEV

"Bezhin Meadow" [same as "Byezhin Prairie"]
  Carden, Patricia. "Finding the Way to Bezhin Meadow: Turgenev's Intimations
  of Mortality," *Slavic R*, 36 (1977), 455–464.
  Pritchett, V. S. *The Gentle Barbarian . . .*, 60–63.

"The Brigadier"
  Pritchett, V. S. *The Gentle Barbarian . . .*, 191–193.

"First Love"
  Pritchett, V. S. *The Gentle Barbarian . . .*, 134–137.

"A Lear of the Steppes"
  Pritchett, V. S. *The Gentle Barbarian . . .*, 194–198.

"The Singers"
  Pritchett, V. S. *The Gentle Barbarian . . .*, 58–60.

"The Story of Lieutenant Erguynov"
  Pritchett, V. S. *The Gentle Barbarian . . .*, 193–194.

"Yermolia and the Miller's Wife"
  Pritchett, V. S. *The Gentle Barbarian . . .*, 56–58.

MARK TWAIN [SAMUEL L. CLEMENS]

"Baker's Blue-Jay Yarn"
  Gibson, William M. *The Art of Mark Twain*, 66–71.

"Captain Stormfield's Visit to Heaven"
  Gibson, William M. *The Art of Mark Twain*, 83–89.

"A Fable"
  Prince, Gilbert. "Mark Twain's 'A Fable': The Teacher as Jackass," *Mark
  Twain J*, 17, iii (1975), 7–8.

"The Man That Corrupted Hadleyburg"
  Gibson, William M. *The Art of Mark Twain*, 89–95.

Rucker, Mary E. "Moralism and Determinism in 'The Man That Corrupted Hadleyburg,' " *Stud Short Fiction,* 14 (1977), 49–54.

Werge, Thomas. "The Sin of Hypocrisy in 'The Man That Corrupted Hadleyburg' and *Inferno,* XVIII," *Mark Twain J,* 18 (Winter, 1976), 17–18.

"The Mysterious Stranger"

Delaney, Paul. "The Dissolving Self: The Narrators of Mark Twain's 'Mysterious Stranger' Fragments," *J Narrative Technique,* 6 (1976), 50–65.

Perkins, Vivienne E. "The Trouble with Satan: Structural and Semantic Problems in 'The Mysterious Stranger,' " *Gypsy Scholar,* 3 (1975), 37–43.

Scrivner, Buford. " 'The Mysterious Stranger': Mark Twain's New Myth of the Fall," *Mark Twain J,* 18 (Winter, 1976), 17–18.

Varisco, Raymond. "Divine Foolishness: A Critical Evaluation of Mark Twain's 'The Mysterious Stranger,' " *R Interamericana,* 5 (1975), 741–749.

"The Notorious Jumping Frog of Calaveras County"

Cassill, R. V. *Instructor's Handbook . . . ,* 40–42.

"A True Story, Repeated Word for Word as I Heard It"

Gibson, William M. *The Art of Mark Twain,* 76–79.

MIGUEL DE UNAMUNO

"Abel Sánchez"

Jiménez-Fajardo, Salvador. "Unamuno's 'Abel Sánchez': Envy as a Work of Art," *J Spanish Stud: Twentieth Century,* 4 (1976), 89–104.

"Aunt Tula"

Richards, Katharine C. "A Cultural Note on Unamuno's 'La tía Tula,' " *Hispania,* 58 (1975), 315–316.

"Saint Manuel the Good, Martyr"

Fernández-Turienzo, Francisco. " 'San Manuel Bueno, mártir,' un paisaje del alma," *Nueva Revista de Filología Hispánica,* 26 (1977), 113–130.

Molina, Ida. "Truth versus Myth in 'En la ardiente oscuridad' and in 'San Manuel Bueno, mártir,' " *Hispano,* 52 (1974), 45–49.

Predmore, Susan. " 'San Manuel Bueno, mártir': A Jungian Perspective," *Hispano,* 64 (1978), 15–29.

JOHN UPDIKE

"A & P"

Cassill, R. V. *Instructor's Handbook . . . ,* 202–203.

"The Astronomer"

Hunt, George W. "Kierkegaardian Sensations into Real Fiction: John Updike's 'The Astronomer,' " *Christianity & Lit,* 26, iii (1977), 3–17.

"The Doctor's Wife"

*Howard, Daniel F., and William Plummer. *Instructor's Manual . . . ,* 3rd ed., 81–82.

"Flight"
Allen, Mary. *The Necessary Blankness* . . ., 98–99.

"Four Sides of One Story"
Schmitt-von Mühlenfels, Franz. " 'Four Sides of One Story': Tristan und Isolde bei John Updike," *Germanisch-Romanische Monatsschrift,* 27 (1977), 98–113.

"Pigeon Feathers"
Shurr, William H. "The Lutheran Experience in John Updike's 'Pigeon Feathers,' " *Stud Short Fiction,* 14 (1977), 329–335.

"Tomorrow and Tomorrow and So Forth"
Herget, Winfried. "John Updike, 'Tomorrow and Tomorrow and So Forth,' " in Freese, Peter, Ed. . . . *Interpretationen,* 160–167.

EDWARD UPWARD

"The Railway Accident"
Bergonzi, Bernard. *Reading the Thirties* . . ., 17–20.

A. E. VAN VOGT

"Black Destroyer"
Carter, Paul A. *The Creation* . . ., 221–222.

GIOVANNI VERGA

"Black Bread"
Cecchetti, Giovanni. *Giovanni Verga,* 110–111.

"The Canary of No. 15"
Cecchetti, Giovanni. *Giovanni Verga,* 117–118.

"Cavalleria rusticana"
Cecchetti, Giovanni. *Giovanni Verga,* 56–58.

"Freedom" [same as "Liberty"]
Cecchetti, Giovanni. *Giovanni Verga,* 114–115.

"The Ghosts of Trazza Castle"
Cecchetti, Giovanni. *Giovanni Verga,* 38–39.

"Gramigna's Lover"
Cecchetti, Giovanni. *Giovanni Verga,* 51–53.

"The How, the When and the Wherefore"
Cecchetti, Giovanni. *Giovanni Verga,* 103–104.

"Ieli the Shepherd"
Cecchetti, Giovanni. *Giovanni Verga*, 59–63.

"Images"
Cecchetti, Giovanni. *Giovanni Verga*, 42–43.

"Malaria"
Cecchetti, Giovanni. *Giovanni Verga*, 105–107.

"Nanni Volpe"
Cecchetti, Giovanni. *Giovanni Verga*, 124–125.

"Nedda"
Cecchetti, Giovanni. *Giovanni Verga*, 31–37.

"Property"
Cecchetti, Giovanni. *Giovanni Verga*, 107–110.

"Rosso Malpelo"
Cecchetti, Giovanni. *Giovanni Verga*, 63–65.

"The She-Wolf"
Cecchetti, Giovanni. *Giovanni Verga*, 53–56.

"A Simple Tale"
Cecchetti, Giovanni. *Giovanni Verga*, 118–119.

"Stinkpot"
Cecchetti, Giovanni. *Giovanni Verga*, 66–67.

"Story of the Saint Joseph Donkey"
Cecchetti, Giovanni. *Giovanni Verga*, 111–113.

"The Wolf Hunt"
Cecchetti, Giovanni. *Giovanni Verga*, 153–154.

BORIS VIAN

"Les Fourmis"
*Cismaru, Alfred. "Two Representative Short Stories of Boris Vian," *French Lit Series*, 2 (1975), 117–120.

"Le Rappel"
*Cismaru, Alfred. "Two Representative Short Stories . . .," 120–124.

BJØRG VIK

"They Come in Small Groups"
Waal, Carla. "The Norwegian Short Story: Bjørg Vik," *Scandinavian Stud*, 49 (1977), 220–223.

KURT VONNEGUT

"All the King's Horses"
  Schatt, Stanley. *Kurt Vonnegut,* 133–134.

"The Ambitious Sophomore"
  Schatt, Stanley. *Kurt Vonnegut,* 127–128.

"EPICAC"
  Schatt, Stanley. *Kurt Vonnegut,* 121–123.

"The Foster Portfolio"
  Schatt, Stanley. *Kurt Vonnegut,* 129–130.

"The Manned Missiles"
  Cassill, R. V. *Instructor's Handbook . . .,* 204–205.

"Next Door"
  Kimmey, John L., Ed. *Experience and Expression . . .,* 12–13.

"The Powder Blue Dragon"
  Schatt, Stanley. *Kurt Vonnegut,* 130–131.

"Report on the Barnhouse Effect"
  Schatt, Stanley. *Kurt Vonnegut,* 120–121.

"Runaways"
  Schatt, Stanley. *Kurt Vonnegut,* 132–133.

"Tomorrow and Tomorrow and Tomorrow"
  Breinig, Helmbrecht. "Kurt Vonnegut, Jr., 'Tomorrow and Tomorrow and
    Tomorrow,' " in Freese, Peter, Ed. . . . *Interpretationen,* 151–159.
  Schatt, Stanley. *Kurt Vonnegut,* 124–126.

"Unready to Wear"
  Broer, Lawrence R. " 'Unready to Wear,' " in Dietrich, R. F., and Roger H.
    Sundell. *Instructor's Manual . . .,* 3rd ed., 38–41.

"Welcome to the Monkey House"
  Schatt, Stanley. *Kurt Vonnegut,* 123–124.

"Who Am I This Time?" [originally entitled "My Name Is Everyone"]
  Schatt, Stanley. *Kurt Vonnegut,* 131–132.

RICHARD WAGNER

"An End in Paris"
  Kestner, Joseph. "Richard Wagner's Paris Trilogy: 'A Pilgrimage to
    Beethoven,' 'A Happy Evening,' and 'An End in Paris,' " *Stud Short Fiction,*
    15 (1978), 259–261.

"A Happy Evening"
Kestner, Joseph. "Richard Wagner's Paris Trilogy . . .," 258–259.

"A Pilgrimage to Beethoven"
Kestner, Joseph. "Richard Wagner's Paris Trilogy . . .," 254–258.

ROBERT PENN WARREN

"Blackberry Winter"
Popp, Klaus-Jürgen. "Robert Penn Warren, 'Blackberry Winter,'" in Freese,
Peter, Ed. . . . *Interpretationen*, 77–83.
Rotella, Guy. "A Note on Warren's 'Blackberry Winter,'" *Notes Contemp Lit*,
8, iii (1978), 3–5.

"When the Light Gets Green"
Shaw, Patrick W. "A Key to Robert Penn Warren's 'When the Light Gets
Green,'" *Coll Engl Assoc Critic*, 38, ii (1976), 16–18.

PRICE WARUNG [WILLIAM ASTLEY]

"The Bullet of the Fated Ten"
Andrews, Barry. *Price Warung . . .*, 125–127.

"Captain Maconochie's 'Bounty for Crime'"
Andrews, Barry. *Price Warung . . .*, 130–133.

"The Consequences of Cunliffe's Crime"
Andrews, Barry. *Price Warung . . .*, 110–111.

"Dictionary Ned"
Andrews, Barry. *Price Warung . . .*, 66–68.

"Parson Ford's Confession"
Andrews, Barry. *Price Warung . . .*, 84–87.

"The Pure Merinoes' Ball"
Andrews, Barry. *Price Warung . . .*, 123–124.

EVELYN WAUGH

"Bella Fleace Gave a Party"
Blayac, Alain. " 'Bella Fleace Gave a Party' or, The Archetypal Image of
Waugh's Sense of Decay," *Stud Short Fiction*, 15 (1978), 69–73.

BEATRICE POTTER WEBB

"Pages from a Work-Girl's Diary"
Nadel, Ira B. "Beatrice Webb's Literary Success," *Stud Short Fiction*, 13
(1976), 441–446.

H.G. WELLS

"The Star"
  Ower, John. "Theme and Technique in H.G. Wells's 'The Star,' " *Extrapolation*, 5 (1977), 167–175.

"The Time Machine"
  Eisenstein, Alex. " 'The Time Machine' and the End of Man," *Sci-Fiction Stud*, 3 (1976), 165–174.
  Scholes, Robert, and Eric S. Rabkin. *Science Fiction . . .*, 200–204.

EUDORA WELTY

"Circe"
  Goudie, Andrea. "Eudora Welty's Circe: A Goddess Who Strove with Men," *Stud Short Fiction*, 13 (1976), 481–489.

"Clytie"
  Fialkowski, Barbara. "Psychic Distances in *A Curtain of Green*: Artistic Successes and Personal Failures," in Desmond, John F., Ed. *A Still Moment . . .*, 64–65.

"A Curtain of Green"
  Carson, Gary. "The Romantic Tradition in Eudora Welty's *A Curtain of Green*," *Notes Mississippi Writers*, 9 (1976), 97–100.

"Death of a Traveling Salesman"
  Fialkowski, Barbara. "Psychic Distances . . .," 65–66.

"First Love"
  Bonifas-Masserand, A.M. " 'First Love' ou la parole en creux," *Delta* (Montpellier), 5 (1977), 49–62.
  Warner, John M. "Eudora Welty: The Artist in 'First Love,' " *Notes Mississippi Writers*, 9 (1976), 77–87.

"June Recital"
  Corcoran, Neil. "The Face That Was in the Poem: Art and 'Human Truth' in 'June Recital,' " *Delta* (Montpellier), 5 (1977), 27–34.
  Messerli, Douglas. "Metronome and Music: The Encounter Between History and Myth in *The Golden Apples*," in Desmond, John F., Ed. *A Still Moment . . .*, 85–91.

"Keela, the Outcast Indian Maiden"
  Cochran, Robert W. "Lost and Found Identities in Welty's 'Keela, the Outcast Indian Maiden,' " *Notes Mod Am Lit*, 2, ii (1978), Item 14.
  Cooley, John R. "Blacks as Primitives in Eudora Welty's Fiction," *Ball State Univ Forum*, 14, iii (1973), 21–23.
  Fischer, John I. " 'Keela, the Outcast Indian Maiden': Studying It Out," *Stud Short Fiction*, 15 (1978), 165–171.

"The Key"
  Fialkowski, Barbara. "Psychic Distances . . .," 65–66.

"Livvie"

   Kloss, Robert J. "The Symbolic Structure of Eudora Welty's 'Livvie,' " *Notes Mississippi Writers,* 7, iii (1975), 70–82.

   Oppel, Horst. "Eudora Welty, 'Livvie,' " in Freese, Peter, Ed. . . . *Interpretationen,* 39–47.

"A Memory"

   Carson, Gary. "Versions of the Artist in *A Curtain of Green:* The Unifying Imagination in Eudora Welty's Early Fiction," *Stud Short Fiction,* 15 (1978), 422–427.

   Fialkowski, Barbara. "Psychic Distances . . .," 67–70.

"Moon Lake"

   Messerli, Douglas. "Metronome and Music . . .," 93–96.

"Music from Spain"

   Messerli, Douglas. "Metronome and Music . . .," 97–98.

"Old Mr. Marblehall"

   Coulthard, A.R. "Point of View in 'Old Mr. Marblehall,' " *Notes Mississippi Writers,* 8 (1976), 22–27.

"Petrified Man"

   Arnold, St. George T. "Mythic Patterns and Satiric Effect in Eudora Welty's 'Petrified Man,' " *Stud Contemp Satire,* 4 (1977), 21–27.

   Deer, Harriet. " 'Petrified Man,' " in Dietrich, R.F., and Roger H. Sundell. *Instructor's Manual* . . ., 3rd ed., 51–54.

   Kane, Thomas S., and Leonard J. Peters. *Some Suggestions* . . ., 30–32.

   Kennedy, X.J. *Instructor's Manual* . . ., 8–9.

"A Piece of News"

   Hollenbaugh, Carol. "Ruby Fisher and Her Demon Lover," *Notes Mississippi Writers,* 7 (1974), 63–68.

"Powerhouse"

   Adams, Timothy D. "A Curtain of Black: White and Black Jazz Styles in 'Powerhouse,' " *Notes Mississippi Writers,* 10 (1977), 57–61.

   Carson, Gary. "Versions of the Artist . . .," 427–428.

   Cassill, R.V. *Instructor's Handbook* . . ., 207–208.

   Cooley, John R. "Blacks as Primitives . . .," 25–27.

   Thomas, Leroy. "Welty's 'Powerhouse,' " *Explicator,* 36, iv (1978), 15–17.

"Shower of Gold"

   Pitavy, Danièll. " 'Shower of Gold' ou les ambiguïtés de la narration," *Delta* (Montpellier), 5 (1977), 63–81.

"Sir Rabbit"

   Messerli, Douglas. "Metronome and Music . . .," 91–93.

"The Wanderers"

   Messerli, Douglas. "Metronome and Music . . .," 98–100.

"The Whole World Knows"
   Messerli, Douglas. "Metronome and Music . . .," 96–97.

"Why I Live at the P.O."
   Herrscher, Walter. "Is Sister Really Insane? Another Look at 'Why I Live at the P.O.,' " *Notes Contemp Lit,* 5, i (1975), 5–7.

"The Wide Net"
   Bolsterli, Margaret. "A Fertility Rite in Mississippi," *Notes Mississippi Writers,* 8, ii (1975), 69–71.

"A Worn Path"
   Ardolino, Frank R. "Life out of Death: Ancient Myth and Ritual in Welty's 'A Worn Path,' " *Notes Mississippi Writers,* 9 (1976), 1–9.
   Bartel, Roland. "Life and Death in Eudora Welty's 'A Worn Path,' " *Stud Short Fiction,* 14 (1977), 288–290.
   Cassill, R. V. *Instructor's Handbook . . .,* 206.
   Cooley, John R. "Blacks as Primitives . . .," 23–25.
   Nostrandt, Jeanne R. "Welty's 'A Worn Path,' " *Explicator,* 34 (1976), Item 33.

NATHANAEL WEST

"A Cool Million"
   Rabkin, Eric S. *The Fantastic . . .,* 11–12.
   Ward, J. A. "The Hollywood Metaphor: The Marx Brothers, S.J. Perelman, and Nathanael West," *Southern R,* 12 (1976), 667–668.

"The Dream Life of Balso Snell"
   Ward, J. A. "The Hollywood Metaphor . . .," 666–667.

"Miss Lonelyhearts"
   Clarke, Bruce. " 'Miss Lonelyhearts' and the Detached Consciousness," *Paunch,* 42–43 (1975), 21–39.
   Donald, Miles. *The American Novel . . .,* 163–166.
   Hanlon, Robert M. "The Parody of the Sacred in Nathanael West's 'Miss Lonelyhearts,' " *Int'l Fiction R,* 4 (1977), 190–193.
   Leibowitz, Judith. *Narrative Purposes . . .,* 105–110.
   Nelson, Gerald B. *Ten Versions of America,* 75–90.
   Ward, J. A. "The Hollywood Metaphor . . .," 670–672.

WALLACE WEST

"The Last Man"
   Moskowitz, Sam. *Strange Horizons . . .,* 79–80.

"The Phantom Dictator"
   Carter, Paul A. *The Creation . . .,* 122–123.

EDITH WHARTON

"After Holbein"
  Lawson, Richard H. *Edith Wharton,* 86–87.
  McDowell, Margaret B. *Edith Wharton,* 90–91.

"Autres Temps . . ."
  Lawson, Richard H. *Edith Wharton,* 85–86.

"Beatrice Palmato"
  Wolff, Cynthia G. *A Feast of Words* . . ., 299–308.

"Bewitched"
  McDowell, Margaret B. *Edith Wharton,* 88–90.

"The Blond Beast"
  Lawson, Richard H. *Edith Wharton,* 83–85.

"Bunner Sisters"
  McDowell, Margaret B. *Edith Wharton,* 71–72.
  Saunders, Judith P. "Ironic Reversal in Edith Wharton's 'Bunner Sisters,' "
    Stud Short Fiction, 14 (1977), 241–245.
  Wolff, Cynthia G. *A Feast of Words* . . ., 67–72.

"The Choice"
  Wolff, Cynthia G. *A Feast of Words* . . ., 151–152.

"Cold Green-house"
  Wolff, Cynthia G. *A Feast of Words* . . ., 413–414.

"Ethan Frome"
  Eggenschwiler, David. "The Ordered Disorder of 'Ethan Frome,' " *Stud Novel,*
    9 (1977), 237–246.
  Hays, Peter L. "First and Last in 'Ethan Frome,' " *Notes Mod Am Lit,* 1, ii
    (1977), Item 15.
  Lawson, Richard H. *Edith Wharton,* 67–75.
  McDowell, Margaret B. *Edith Wharton,* 64–71.
  Shintri, Sarojini B. "In Defense of 'Ethan Frome,' " in Naik, M. K., *et al.,* Eds.
    Indian Stud . . ., 108–114.
  Wolff, Cynthia G. *A Feast of Words* . . ., 163–184.

"The Eyes"
  Lawson, Richard H. *Edith Wharton,* 87–88.
  McDowell, Margaret B. *Edith Wharton,* 87–88.
  Wolff, Cynthia G. *A Feast of Words* . . ., 156–159.

"The Fullness of Life"
  Wolff, Cynthia G. *A Feast of Words* . . ., 72–75.

"His Father's Son"
  Wolff, Cynthia G. *A Feast of Words* . . ., 153–155.

"The Last Asset"
Lawson, Richard H. *Edith Wharton*, 81–83.

"The Legend"
Wolff, Cynthia G. *A Feast of Words . . .*, 155.

"The Letters"
Wolff, Cynthia G. *A Feast of Words . . .*, 202–204.

"Madame de Treymes"
McDowell, Margaret B. *Edith Wharton*, 56–57.

"Mrs. Manstey's View"
Lawson, Richard H. *Edith Wharton*, 78–80.
Wolff, Cynthia G. *A Feast of Words . . .*, 65–67.

"The Muse's Tragedy"
Wolff, Cynthia G. *A Feast of Words . . .*, 101–103.

"The Other Two"
Lawson, Richard H. *Edith Wharton*, 80–81.
Wolff, Cynthia G. *A Feast of Words . . .*, 107–109.

"Summer"
McDowell, Margaret B. *Edith Wharton*, 69–71.

"The Valley of Childish Things, and Other Emblems"
Wolff, Cynthia G. *A Feast of Words . . .*, 82–84.

"Xingu"
Lawson, Richard H. *Edith Wharton*, 85.

E. B. WHITE

"The Second Tree from the Corner"
*Timko, Michael. "Kafka's 'A Country Doctor,' Williams' 'The Use of Force,'
and White's 'The Second Tree from the Corner,' " in Timko, Michael, Ed. *38
Short Stories*, 2nd ed., 692–706.

PATRICK WHITE

"Being Kind to Titina"
Argyle, Barry. *Patrick White*, 73–75.

"A Cheery Soul"
Argyle, Barry. *Patrick White*, 87–89.
Walsh, William. *Patrick White's Fiction*, 69–71.

"Clay"
Argyle, Barry. *Patrick White*, 77–79.

"Cocotte"
Argyle, Barry. *Patrick White*, 67.

"Dead Roses"
Argyle, Barry. *Patrick White*, 79–80.

"Down at the Dump"
Walsh, William. *Patrick White's Fiction*, 72–74.

"The Evening at Sissy Kamara's"
Argyle, Barry. *Patrick White*, 69–71.

"A Glass of Tea"
Argyle, Barry. *Patrick White*, 75–77.

"The Letters"
Argyle, Barry. *Patrick White*, 84–85.

"Miss Slattery and Her Demon Lover"
Argyle, Barry. *Patrick White*, 82–84.

"The Twitching Colonel"
Argyle, Barry. *Patrick White*, 66–67.

"Willy-Wagtail by Moonlight"
Argyle, Barry. *Patrick White*, 80–82.

"The Woman Who Wasn't Allowed to Keep Cats"
Argyle, Barry. *Patrick White*, 71–73.

WILLIAM ALLEN WHITE

"The Real Issue"
Elkins, William R. "William Allen White's Early Fiction," *Heritage of Kansas,*
8, iv (1975), 12–13.

"The Story of Aqua Pura"
Elkins, William R. ". . . White's Early Fiction," 9–11.

"The Story of the Highlands"
Elkins, William R. ". . . White's Early Fiction," 11–12.

RICHARD WILBUR

"A Game of Catch"
Kennedy, X. J. *Instructor's Manual . . .*, 26.

OSCAR WILDE

"The Birthday of the Infanta"
Ericksen, Donald H. *Oscar Wilde*, 70–71.

Shewan, Rodney. *Oscar Wilde* . . ., 56–62.
Walker, Mary. "Wilde's Fairy Tales," *Unisa Engl Stud,* 14, ii (1976), 37–39.

"The Canterville Ghost"
Cohen, Philip K. *The Moral Vision* . . ., 62–69.
Ericksen, Donald H. *Oscar Wilde,* 57–58.
Schroeder, Horst. "Oscar Wilde, 'The Canterville Ghost,' " *Literatur in Wissenschaft und Unterricht,* 10 (1977), 21–30.
Shewan, Rodney. *Oscar Wilde* . . ., 32–35.

"The Devoted Friend"
Ericksen, Donald H. *Oscar Wilde,* 65–66.
Shewan, Rodney. *Oscar Wilde* . . ., 47–49.
Walker, Mary. "Wilde's Fairy Tales," 34–35.

"The Fisherman and His Soul"
Cohen, Philip K. *The Moral Vision* . . ., 96–102.
Ericksen, Donald H. *Oscar Wilde,* 71–72.
Quintus, John A. "The Moral Prerogative in Oscar Wilde: A Look at the Fairy Tale," *Virginia Q R,* 53 (1977), 712–715.
Shewan, Rodney. *Oscar Wilde* . . ., 62–67.
Walker, Mary. "Wilde's Fairy Tales," 39–40.

"The Happy Prince"
Cohen, Philip K. *The Moral Vision* . . ., 86–88.
Ericksen, Donald H. *Oscar Wilde,* 60–62.
Walker, Mary. "Wilde's Fairy Tales," 30–32.

"A House of Pomegranates"
Walker, Mary. "Wilde's Fairy Tales," 40–41.

"Lord Arthur Savile's Crime"
Cohen, Philip K. *The Moral Vision* . . ., 53–62.
Ericksen, Donald H. *Oscar Wilde,* 55–56.
Shewan, Rodney. *Oscar Wilde* . . ., 27–32.

"The Model Millionaire"
Cohen, Philip K. *The Moral Vision* . . ., 79–80.
Ericksen, Donald H. *Oscar Wilde,* 58–59.

"The Nightingale and the Rose"
Cohen, Philip K. *The Moral Vision* . . ., 89–92.
Ericksen, Donald H. *Oscar Wilde,* 62–63.
Shewan, Rodney. *Oscar Wilde* . . ., 43–47.
Walker, Mary. "Wilde's Fairy Tales," 32–33.

"The Portrait of Mr. W. H."
Ericksen, Donald H. *Oscar Wilde,* 89–90.
Shewan, Rodney. *Oscar Wilde* . . ., 83–94.

"The Remarkable Rocket"
Cohen, Philip K. *The Moral Vision* . . ., 93–95.
Ericksen, Donald H. *Oscar Wilde,* 66–67.

Quintas, John A. "The Moral Prerogative . . .," 711.
Walker, Mary. "Wilde's Fairy Tales," 35.

"The Selfish Giant"
Ericksen, Donald H. *Oscar Wilde,* 63–65.
Shewan, Rodney. *Oscar Wilde* . . . , 42–43.
Walker, Mary. "Wilde's Fairy Tales," 33–34.

"The Sphinx Without a Secret" [originally "Lady Alroy"]
Ericksen, Donald H. *Oscar Wilde,* 56–57.
Shewan, Rodney. *Oscar Wilde* . . . , 25–26.

"The Star-Child"
Shewan, Rodney. *Oscar Wilde* . . . , 67–69.

"The Young King"
Ericksen, Donald H. *Oscar Wilde,* 68–70.
Quintas, John A. "The Moral Prerogative . . .," 711–712.
Shewan, Rodney. *Oscar Wilde* . . . , 51–56.
Walker, Mary. "Wilde's Fairy Tales," 35–37.

MICHAEL WILDING

"The Sybarites"
Harrison-Ford, Carl. "The Short Stories of Wilding and Moorhouse," *Southerly,* 33 (1973), 175–176.

HELEN MARIA WILLIAMS

"The History of Perourou; or, The Bellows-Maker"
Pitcher, E. W. "Changes in Short Fiction in Britain 1785–1810: Philosophic Tales, Gothic Tales, and Fragments and Visions," *Stud Short Fiction,* 13 (1976), 340–342.

JOHN A. WILLIAMS

"Son in the Afternoon"
Freese, Peter. "John A. Williams: 'Son in the Afternoon,' " in Bruck, Peter, Ed. *The Black American Short Story* . . . , 144–153.
Kennedy, X. J. *Instructor's Manual* . . . , 4–5.

JOY WILLIAMS

"Taking Care"
Cassill, R. V. *Instructor's Handbook* . . . , 209.

TENNESSEE WILLIAMS

"Desire and the Black Masseur"
 Schubert, Karl. "Tennessee Williams, 'Desire and the Black Masseur,' " in
 Freese, Peter, Ed. . . . *Interpretationen,* 119–128.

WILLIAM CARLOS WILLIAMS

"The Use of Force"
 Baker, William. "Williams' 'The Use of Force,' " *Explicator,* 37, i (1978),
 7–8.
 *Dietrich, R.F. " 'The Use of Force,' " in Dietrich, R.F., and Roger H.
 Sundell. *Instructor's Manual* . . ., 3rd ed., 17–23.
 *Timko, Michael. "Kafka's 'A Country Doctor,' Williams' 'The Use of Force,'
 and White's 'The Second Tree from the Corner,' " in Timko, Michael, Ed. *38
 Short Stories,* 2nd ed., 692–706.

JACK WILLIAMSON

"Breakdown"
 Carter, Paul A. *The Creation* . . ., 223–227.

"Non-Stop to Mars"
 Stewart, Alfred D. "Jack Williamson: The Comedy of Cosmic Evolution," in
 Clareson, Thomas D., Ed. *Voices for the Future* . . ., 18–19.

"Star Bright"
 Stewart, Alfred D. ". . . Cosmic Evolution," 19.

PUNYAKANTE WIZENAIKE

"My Daughter's Wedding"
 Nivens, Alastaire. "The Fiction of Punyakante Wizenaike," *J Commonwealth
 Lit,* 12 (August, 1977), 56–57.

GABRIELE WOHMANN

"The Boxing Match"
 Hughes, Kenneth. "The Short Fiction of Gabriele Wohmann," *Stud Short
 Fiction,* 13 (1976), 69.

"Hamster, Hamster!"
 Hughes, Kenneth. "The Short Fiction . . .," 62–63.

"Internal Excuse"
 Hughes, Kenneth. "The Short Fiction . . .," 64–65.

"The Sailing Regatta"
  Hughes, Kenneth. "The Short Fiction . . .," 65.

"A Scandal for the Park"
  Hughes, Kenneth. "The Short Fiction . . .," 63.

"Seaway"
  Hughes, Kenneth. "The Short Fiction . . .," 66–67.

"Sunday at the Kreisands' "
  Hughes, Kenneth. "The Short Fiction . . .," 63.

"The Truth About Us"
  Hughes, Kenneth. "The Short Fiction . . .," 62.

THOMAS WOLFE

"The Child by Tiger"
  *Perrine, Laurence. *Instructor's Manual . . . "Story . . .*," 2–4; *Instructor's Manual . . . "Literature . . .*," 2–4.

"The Web of Earth"
  Gray, Richard. *The Literature of Memory . . .*, 138–140.

LEONARD WOOLF

"Pearls and Swine"
  Heine, Elizabeth. "Leonard Woolf: 'Three Jews' and Other Fiction," *Bull N Y Pub Lib*, 79 (1976), 456–457.

"A Tale Told by Moonlight"
  Heine, Elizabeth. "Leonard Woolf . . .," 455–456.

"Three Jews"
  Heine, Elizabeth. "Leonard Woolf . . .," 448–450.

"The Two Brahmans"
  Heine, Elizabeth. "Leonard Woolf . . .," 454–455.

VIRGINIA WOOLF

"Kew Gardens"
  Cassill, R. V. *Instructor's Handbook . . .*, 211–212.

"Mrs. Dalloway in Bond Street"
  Saunders, Judith P. "Mortal Stain: Literary Allusion and Female Sexuality in 'Mrs. Dalloway in Bond Street,' " *Stud Short Fiction*, 15 (1978), 139–144.

"The New Dress"
  Kane, Thomas S., and Leonard J. Peters. *Some Suggestions . . .*, 40–42.

RICHARD WRIGHT

"Big Boy Leaves Home"
  Jackson, Blyden. *The Waiting Years* . . . , 130–145.
  *Kinnamon, Keneth. " 'Big Boy Leaves Home,' " in Timko, Michael, Ed. *38
    Short Stories,* 2nd ed., 671–676.

"Bright and Morning Star"
  Rubin, Steven J. "The Early Short Fiction of Richard Wright Reconsidered,"
    Stud Short Fiction, 15 (1978), 407–408.

"Down by the Riverside"
  Rubin, Steven J. "The Early Short Fiction . . . ," 406–407.

"Fire and Cloud"
  Karrer, Wolfgang. "Richard Wright: 'Fire and Cloud,' " in Bruck, Peter, Ed.
    The Black American Short Story . . . , 101–108.

"Long Black Song"
  Rubin, Steven J. "The Early Short Fiction . . . ," 407.

"The Man Who Lived Underground"
  *Abcarian, Richard, and Marvin Klotz. *Instructor's Manual* . . . , 2nd ed., 24–26.
  Gounard, J.F. "Richard Wright's 'The Man Who Lived Underground': A
    Literary Analysis," *J Black Stud,* 8, ii (1977), 381–386.
  Howard, Daniel F., and William Plummer. *Instructor's Manual* . . . , 3rd ed.,
    52–53.
  McNallie, Robin. "Richard Wright's Allegory of the Cave: 'The Man Who
    Lived Underground,' " *So Atlantic Bull,* 42 (May, 1977), 76–84.
  Real, Willi. "Richard Wright, 'The Man Who Lived Underground,' " in
    Freese, Peter, Ed. . . . *Interpretationen,* 54–63.

"The Man Who Was Almost a Man"
  Cassill, R.V. *Instructor's Handbook* . . . , 213–214.

WU TSU-HSIANG

"Fan Village"
  Hsia, C.T. *A History* . . . , 284–285.

JOHN WYNDHAM

"Consider Her Ways"
  Friend, Beverly. "Virgin Territory: The Bonds and Boundaries of Women in
    Science Fiction," in Clareson, Thomas D., Ed. *Many Futures* . . . , 149–150.

RICHARD YATES

"A Really Good Jazz Piano"
  Cassill, R.V. *Instructor's Handbook* . . . , 214–215.

YEH SHAO-CHÜN [YEH SHENG-T'AO]

"Autumn"
Hsia, C. T. *A History* . . ., 67–68.

"The English Professor"
Hsia, C. T. *A History* . . ., 65–66.

"Rice"
Hsia, C. T. *A History* . . ., 61–64.

YU DAFU [YÜ TA-FU]

"Late-Blooming Osmanthus"
Hsia, C. T. *A History* . . ., 106–107.

"The Past"
Hsia, C. T. *A History* . . ., 107–109.

"Sinking"
Egan, Michael. "Yu Dafu and the Transition to Modern Chinese Literature," in
Goldman, Merle, Ed. *Modern Chinese Literature* . . ., 312–317.
Hsia, C. T. *A History* . . ., 102–105.

"Ts'ia Shih Chi"
Hsia, C. T. *A History* . . ., 105–106.

EVGENIJ ZAMJATIN

"The Cave"
Layton, Susan. "The Symbolic Dimension of 'The Cave' by Zamjatin," *Stud
Short Fiction,* 13 (1976), 455–461.

ERACLIO ZEPEDA

"Benzulu"
Brodman, Barbara L. C. *The Mexican Cult* . . ., 77–78.

"El Caguamo"
Brodman, Barbara L. C. *The Mexican Cult* . . ., 79–80.

STEFAN ZWEIG

"Leporella"
Allday, Elizabeth. *Stefan Zweig* . . ., 43–44.

"Letter from an Unknown Woman" [same as "Brief einer Unbekannten"]
Allday, Elizabeth. *Stefan Zweig* . . ., 180–182.

"Schachnovelle" [same as "The Royal Game" and "The Chess Game"]
Allday, Elizabeth. *Stefan Zweig* . . ., 145–147.

A CHECKLIST OF BOOKS USED

Abcarian, Richard, and Marvin Klotz. *Instructor's Manual to Accompany "Literature: The Human Experience, Second Edition."* New York: St. Martin's Press, 1978.

————, Eds. *Literature: The Human Experience*, 2nd ed. New York: St. Martin's Press, 1978.

Adams, Stephen D. *James Purdy*. London: Vision Press, 1976; Am. ed. New York: Barnes & Noble, 1976.

Alazraki, Jaime, and Ivar Ivask, Eds. *The Final Island: The Fiction of Julio Cortázar*. Norman: Univ. of Oklahoma Press, 1978.

Albright, Daniel. *Personality and Impersonality: Lawrence, Woolf, and Mann*. Chicago: Univ. of Chicago Press, 1978.

Allday, Elizabeth. *Stefan Zweig: A Critical Biography*. Chicago: O'Hara, 1972.

Allen, Mary. *The Necessary Blankness: Women in Major American Fiction of the Sixties*. Urbana: Univ. of Illinois Press, 1976.

Andrews, Barry. *Price Warung (William Astley)*. Boston: Twayne, 1976.

Argyle, Barry. *Patrick White*. Edinburgh: Oliver & Boyd, 1967; Am. ed. New York: Barnes & Noble, 1967.

Arnzten, Helmut, Bernd Balzer, Karl Pestalozzi, and Rainer Wagner, Eds. *Literaturwissenschaft und Geschichtsphilosophie: Festschrift für Wilhelm Emrich*. Berlin: de Gruyter, 1975.

Astro, Richard, and Jackson J. Benson, Eds. *The Fiction of Bernard Malamud*. Corvallis: Oregon State Univ. Press, 1977.

Baer, Joachim T., and Norman W. Ingham, Eds. *Mnemozina: Studia Litteraria Russica in Honorem Vsevolod Setchkarev*. Munich: Fink, 1974.

Bair, Deirdre. *Samuel Beckett*. New York: Harcourt Brace Jovanovich, 1978.

Baldanza, Frank, Ed. *Itinerary 3: Criticism*. Bowling Green: Bowling Green Univ. Press, 1977.

Bangerter, Lowell A. *Hugo von Hofmannsthal*. New York: Ungar, 1977.

Banks, G. V. *Camus: "L'Étranger."* London: Edward Arnold, 1976.

Barnett, Louise K. *The Ignoble Savage: American Literary Racism, 1790–1890*. Westport: Greenwood Press, 1975.

Barnett, Ursula. *Ezekiel Mphahlele*. Boston: Twayne, 1976.

Bauer, Arnold. *Thomas Mann*, trans. Alexander and Elizabeth Henderson. New York: Ungar, 1971.

Baumann, Michael L. *B. Traven: An Introduction*. Albuquerque: Univ. of New Mexico Press, 1976.

Baym, Nina. *The Shape of Hawthorne's Career*. Ithaca: Cornell Univ. Press, 1976.

Beck, Warren. *Faulkner: Essays by Warren Beck*. Madison: Univ. of Wisconsin Press, 1976.

Benston, Kimberly W., Ed. *Imamu Amiri Baraka (Le Roi Jones): A Collection of Critical Essays*. Englewood Cliffs: Prentice-Hall, 1978.

Bergonzi, Bernard. *Reading the Thirties: Texts and Contexts*. London: Macmillan, 1978.

Bersani, Leo. *A Future for Astynax: Character and Desire in Literature*. Boston: Little, Brown, 1976.

Berzon, Judith R. *Neither White Nor Black: The Mulatto Character in American Fiction*. New York: New York Univ. Press, 1978.

Bettinson, Christopher. *Gide: A Study*. London: Heinemann, 1977; Am. ed. Totowa, N.J.: Rowman & Littlefield, 1977.

Birn, Randi. *Johan Borgen*. New York: Twayne, 1974.

Birnbaum, Henrik, Ed. *American Contributions to the Eighth International Congress of Slavists, Zagreb and Ljubljana, September 3–9, 1978*, Vol. I. Columbus: Slavica, 1978.

Bone, Robert A. *The Negro Novel in America*. New Haven: Yale Univ. Press, 1958; 2nd ed., 1965.

Bonham, Barbara. *Willa Cather*. Philadelphia: Chilton, 1970; Canadian ed. Toronto: Thomas Nelson, 1970.

Bowman, Frank P. *Prosper Mérimée: Heroism, Pessimism and Irony*. Berkeley: Univ. of California Press, 1962.

Brack, O. M., Ed. *American Humor: Essays Presented to John C. Gerber*. Scottsdale, Arizona: Areto Publications, 1977.

Brashers, Howard C. *Creative Writing: Fiction, Drama, Poetry and the Essay*. New York: American Book, 1968.

Brodman, Barbara L. C. *The Mexican Cult of Death in Myth and Literature*. Gainesville: Univ. of Florida Press, 1976.

Brooks, Peter. *The Melodramatic Imagination: Balzac, Henry James, Melodrama, and the Mode of Excess*. New Haven: Yale Univ. Press, 1976.

Bruck, Peter, Ed. *The Black American Short Story in the 20th Century: A Collection of Essays*. Amsterdam: Grüner, 1977.

Bryant, Paul T. *H. L. Davis*. Boston: Twayne, 1978.

Bufithis, Philip H. *Norman Mailer*. New York: Ungar, 1978.

Burgess, C. F. *The Fellowship of the Craft: Conrad on Ships and Seamen and the Sea*. Port Washington: Kennikat, 1976.

Burkhard, Marianne. *Conrad Ferdinand Meyer*. Boston: Twayne, 1978.

Busch, Frieder, and Renate Schmidt von Bardeleben, Eds. *Amerikanische Erzählliteratur 1950–1970*. Munich: Fink, 1975.

Butwin, Joseph. *Sholom Aleichem*. Boston: Twayne, 1977.

Calder, Angus. *Russia Discovered: Nineteenth-Century Fiction from Pushkin to Chekhov*. London: Heinemann, 1976; Am. ed. New York: Barnes & Noble, 1976.

Carter, A. E. *Charles Baudelaire*. Boston: Twayne, 1977.

Carter, Everett. *The American Idea: The Literary Response to American Optimism*. Chapel Hill: Univ. of North Carolina Press, 1977.

Carter, Paul A. *The Creation of Tomorrow: Fifty Years of Magazine Science Fiction*. New York: Columbia Univ. Press, 1977.

Cassill, R. V. *Instructor's Handbook [for] The Norton Anthology of Short Fiction*. New York: Norton, 1977.

Cecchetti, Giovanni. *Giovanni Verga*. Boston: Twayne, 1978.

Chametzky, Jules. *From the Ghetto: The Fiction of Abraham Cahan*. Amherst: Univ. of Massachusetts Press, 1977.

Chartier, Armand B. *Barbey D'Aurevilly*. Boston: Twayne, 1977.

Chesnutt, Margaret. *Studies in the Short Stories of William Carleton*. Gothenburg: Acta Univ. Gothoburgensis, 1976.

Clareson, Thomas D., Ed. *Voices for the Future: Essays on Major Science Fiction Writers*. Bowling Green: Bowling Green Univ. Popular Press, 1976.

————. *Many Futures, Many Worlds: Theme and Form in Science Fiction*. Kent: Kent State Univ. Press, 1977.

Clum, John M. *Paddy Chayefsky*. Boston: Twayne, 1976.

Coale, Samuel. *John Cheever*. New York: Ungar, 1977.

Cohen, Philip K. *The Moral Vision of Oscar Wilde*. Cranbury, N.J.: Associated Univ. Presses [for Fairleigh Dickinson Univ. Press], 1978.

Cohen, Sandy. *Bernard Malamud and the Trial by Love*. Amsterdam: Rodopi, 1974.

Cohen, Sarah B., Ed. *Comic Relief: Humor in Contemporary American Literature*. Urbana: Univ. of Illinois Press, 1978.

Cohn, Dorrit. *Transparent Minds: Narrative Modes for Presenting Consciousness in Fiction*. Princeton: Princeton Univ. Press, 1978.

Colmer, John. *E. M. Forster: The Personal Voice*. London: Routledge & Kegan Paul, 1975.

Cook, Sylvia J. *From Tobacco Road to Route 66: The Southern Poor White in Fiction*. Chapel Hill: Univ. of North Carolina Press, 1976.

Cox, Martha H., and Wayne Chatterton. *Nelson Algren*. Boston: Twayne, 1975.

Crackanthorpe, David. *Hubert Crackanthorpe and English Realism in the 1890s*. Columbia: Univ. of Missouri Press, 1977.

Creighton, Joanne V. *Joyce Carol Oates*. Boston: Twayne, 1979.

Cronin, John. *Gerald Griffin: A Critical Biography*. Cambridge: Cambridge Univ. Press, 1978.

Currie, Robert. *Genius: An Ideology in Literature*. New York: Schocken, 1974.

Daleski, H. M. *Joseph Conrad: The Way of Dispossession.* New York: Holmes & Meier, 1976.

Dauber, Kenneth. *Rediscovering Hawthorne.* Princeton: Princeton Univ. Press, 1977.

Day, A. Grove. *Eleanor Dark.* Boston: Twayne, 1976.

de Jonge, Alex. *Dostoevsky and the Age of Intensity.* London: Secker & Warburg, 1975.

Debreczeny, Paul, and Thomas Eekman, Eds. *Chekhov's Art of Writing: A Collection of Critical Essays.* Columbus: Slavica, 1977.

Desmond, John F. *A Still Moment: Essays on the Art of Eudora Welty.* Metuchen: Scarecrow Press, 1978.

Dietrich, R. F., and Roger H. Sundell. *Instructor's Manual for "The Art of Fiction, 3rd Ed."* New York: Holt, Rinehart & Winston, 1978.

Dillingham, William B. *Melville's Short Fiction, 1853–1856.* Athens: Univ. of Georgia Press, 1977.

Dolan, Paul J. *Of War and War's Alarms: Fiction and Politics in the Modern World.* New York: Free Press, 1976.

Donald, Miles. *The American Novel in the Twentieth Century.* Newton Abbot: David & Charles, 1978; Am. ed. New York: Barnes & Noble, 1978.

Donaldson, Scott. *By Force of Will: The Life and Art of Ernest Hemingway.* New York: Viking, 1977.

Doppler, Alfred, and Friedbert Aspetberger, Eds. *Erzähltechniken in der modernen österreichischen Literatur.* Vienna: Österreichischer Bundesverlag, 1976.

Douglas, Ann. *The Feminization of American Culture.* New York: Knopf, 1977.

Doyle, John R. *William Charles Scully.* Boston: Twayne, 1978.

Doyle, Paul A. *Liam O'Flaherty.* New York: Twayne, 1971.

Dunn, Douglas. *Two Decades of Irish Writing: A Critical Survey.* Cheshire: Carcanet Press, 1975.

Durand, Regis, Ed. *Myth and Ideology in American Culture.* Villeneuve d'Ascq: Univ. de Lille, 1976.

Durham, Frank, Ed. *Studies in "Cane."* Columbus: Merrill, 1971.

Dyer, Denys. *The Stories of Kleist: A Critical Study.* New York: Holmes & Meier, 1977.

Eakin, Paul J. *The New England Girl: Cultural Ideals in Hawthorne, Stowe, Howells, and James.* Athens: Univ. of Georgia Press, 1976.

Eibl, Karl. *Robert Musil: "Drei Frauen" — Text, Materialien, Kommentar.* Munich: Hanser, 1978.

Eisinger, Chester. *Fiction of the Forties.* Chicago: Univ. of Chicago Press, 1963.

Elder, Arlene A. *The "Hindered Hand": Cultural Implications of Early African-American Fiction.* Westport, Conn.: Greenwood, 1978.

Ericksen, Donald H. *Oscar Wilde.* Boston: Twayne, 1977.

Erlich, Victor, Ed. *Pasternak: A Collection of Critical Essays.* Englewood Cliffs: Prentice-Hall, 1978.

———, et al., Eds. *For Wictor Weintraub: Essays in Polish Literature, Language, and History Presented on the Occasion of His 65th Birthday.* The Hague: Mouton, 1975.

Evans, Patrick. *Janet Frame.* Boston: Twayne, 1977.

Ezergailis, Inta M. *Male and Female: An Approach to Thomas Mann's Dialectic.* The Hague: Nijhoff, 1975.

Farrow, Anthony. *George Moore.* Boston: Twayne, 1978.

Fine, David M. *The City, The Immigrant and American Fiction, 1880–1920.* Metuchen, N.J.: Scarecrow Press, 1977.

Finholt, Richard. *American Visionary Fiction: Mad Metaphysics as Salvation Psychology.* Port Washington: Kennikat, 1978.

Finke, Wayne H., Ed. *Estudios de historia, literatura y arte hispánicos ofrecidos a Rodrigo A. Molina.* Madrid: Insula, 1977.

Finney, Brian. *"Since How It Is": A Study of Samuel Beckett's Later Fiction.* London: Convent Garden Press, 1972.

Fisch, Harold. *S. Y. Agnon.* New York: Ungar, 1975.

Fisher, Benjamin F., Ed. *Poe at Work: Seven Textual Studies.* Baltimore: Poe Society, 1978.

Fisher, Marvin. *Going Under: Melville's Short Fiction and the American 1850s.* Baton Rouge: Louisiana State Univ. Press, 1977.

230 A CHECKLIST OF BOOKS USED

Fleming, Robert E. *Willard Motley.* Boston: Twayne, 1978.

Flores, Angel, Ed. *The Kafka Debate: New Perspectives for Our Time.* New York: Gordian, 1977.

_____. *The Problem of "The Judgment": Eleven Approaches to Kafka's Story.* New York: Gordian, 1977.

Ford, Arthur L. *Robert Creeley.* Boston: Twayne, 1978.

Foster, David W. *Augusto Roa Bastos.* Boston: Twayne, 1978.

Frank, Joseph. *Dostoevsky: The Seeds of Revolt, 1821–1849.* Princeton: Princeton Univ. Press, 1976.

Frank, Luanne, Ed. *Literature and the Occult: Essays in Comparative Literature.* Arlington: Univ. of Texas at Arlington, 1977.

Frank, William L. *Sherwood Bonner (Catherine [sic] McDowell).* New York: Twayne, 1976.

Franklin, H. Bruce. *Future Perfect: American Science Fiction of the Nineteenth Century,* 2nd ed. New York: Oxford Univ. Press, 1978.

_____. *The Victim as Criminal and Artist: Literature from the American Prison.* New York: Oxford Univ. Press, 1978.

Freese, Peter, Ed. *Die amerikanische Short Story der Gegenwart: Interpretationen.* Berlin: Schmidt, 1976.

Friedman, Alan W. *Multivalence: The Moral Quality of Form in the Modern Novel.* Baton Rouge: Louisiana State Univ. Press, 1978.

Friedman, Lenemaja. *Shirley Jackson.* Boston: Twayne, 1975.

Fromm, Gloria G. *Dorothy Richardson, A Biography.* Urbana: Univ. of Illinois Press, 1977.

Fryer, Judith. *The Faces of Eve: Women in the Nineteenth Century American Novel.* New York: Oxford Univ. Press, 1976.

Gale, Robert L. *John Hay.* Boston: Twayne, 1978.

Gallo, Rose A. *F. Scott Fitzgerald.* New York: Ungar, 1978.

Garfield, Evelyn P. *Julio Cortázar.* New York: Ungar, 1975.

Gekoski, R. A. *Conrad: The Moral World of the Novel.* London: Elek, 1978.

Gérin, Winifred. *Elizabeth Gaskell: A Biography.* London: Oxford Univ. Press, 1976.

Giacoman, Helmy F., Ed. *Homenaje a Fernando Alegría: Variaciones interpretativas en torno a su obra.* Long Island City: Las Américas, 1972.

_____. *Homenaje a Julio Cortázar: Variaciones interpretativas en torno a su obra.* Long Island City: Anaya-Las Américas, 1972.

_____. *Homenaje a Juan Rulfo: Variaciones interpretativas en torno a su obra.* Long Island City: Anaya-Las Américas, 1974.

Gibson, William M. *The Art of Mark Twain.* New York: Oxford Univ. Press, 1976.

Gifford, Douglas. *James Hogg.* Edinburgh: Ramsay Head Press, 1976.

Giles, James R. *Claude McKay.* Boston: Twayne, 1976.

Gillespie, Gerald, and Edgar Lohner, Eds. *Herkommen und Erneuerung: Essays für Oskar Seidlin.* Tübingen: Niemeyer, 1976.

Gilmore, Michael T. *The Middle Way: Puritanism and Ideology in American Romantic Fiction.* New Brunswick: Rutgers Univ. Press, 1977.

Gish, Robert. *Hamlin Garland: The Far West.* Boise: Boise State Univ., 1976.

Gittleman, Sol. *From Shtetl to Suburbia: The Family in Jewish Literary Imagination.* Boston: Beacon Press, 1978; Canadian ed. Toronto: Fitzhenry & Whiteside, 1978.

Glassman, Peter J. *Language and Being: Joseph Conrad and the Literature of Personality.* New York: Columbia Univ. Press, 1976.

Glendinning, Victoria. *Elizabeth Bowen: Portrait of a Writer.* London: Weidenfeld & Nicolson, 1977; Am. ed. New York: Knopf, 1978.

Glicksberg, Charles I. *The Sexual Revolution in Modern American Literature.* The Hague: Martinus Nijhoff, 1971.

Gloster, Hugh M. *Negro Voices in America.* Chapel Hill: Univ. of North Carolina Press, 1948.

Goldblatt, Howard. *Hsiao Hung.* Boston: Twayne, 1976.

Goldman, Merle, Ed. *Modern Chinese Literature in the May Fourth Era.* Cambridge: Harvard Univ. Press, 1977.

González Echevarría, Roberto. *Alejo Carpentier: The Pilgrim at Home*. Ithaca: Cornell Univ. Press, 1977.

Goonetilleke, D. C. R. A. *Developing Countries in British Fiction*. Totowa, N.J.: Rowman & Littlefield, 1977.

Gordon, David J. *Literary Art and the Unconscious*. Baton Rouge: Louisiana State Univ. Press, 1976.

Graham, Ilse. *Heinrich von Kleist—Word into Flesh: A Poet's Quest for the Symbol*. Berlin: de Gruyter, 1977.

Grant, Mary K. *The Tragic Vision of Joyce Carol Oates*. Durham: Duke Univ. Press, 1978.

Grant, Richard B. *Théophile Gautier*. Boston: Twayne, 1975.

Gray, Richard. *The Literature of Memory: Modern Writers of the American South*. Baltimore: Johns Hopkins Univ. Press, 1977.

Grubačic, Slobodan. *Heines Erzählprosa: Versuch einer Analyse*. Stuttgart: Kohlhammer, 1975.

Guerard, Albert J. *The Triumph of the Novel: Dickens, Dostoevsky, Faulkner*. New York: Oxford Univ. Press, 1976.

Hahn, Beverly. *Chekhov: A Study of the Major Short Stories and Plays*. Cambridge: Cambridge Univ. Press, 1977.

Hall, Robert A. *Antonio Fogazzaro*. Boston: Twayne, 1978.

Hall, Rodney. *J. S. Manifold: An Introduction to the Man and His Work*. St. Lucia: Univ. of Queensland Press, 1978.

Handy, William J. *Modern Fiction: A Formalist Approach*. Carbondale: Southern Illinois Univ. Press, 1971.

Hardy, John E. *Katherine Anne Porter*. New York: Ungar, 1973.

Hayashi, Tetsumaro, Ed. *A Study Guide to Steinbeck's "The Long Valley."* Ann Arbor: Pierian, 1976.

Hazell, Stephen, Ed. *The English Novel: Developments in Criticism Since Henry James*. London: Macmillan, 1978.

Hemenway, Robert E. *Zora Neale Hurston: A Literary Biography*. Urbana: Univ. of Illinois Press, 1977.

Hendrick, George. *Mazo de la Roche*. New York: Twayne, 1970.

Henning, Lawson, et al., Eds. *Studies by Members of the English Department, University of Illinois, in Memory of John Jay Parry*. Urbana: Univ. of Illinois Press, 1955; rpt. Freeport, N.Y.: Books for the Library Press, 1968.

Hingley, Ronald. *Dostoyevsky: His Life and Work*. New York: Scribner, 1978.

Hitchcock, Bert. *Richard Malcolm Johnston*. Boston: Twayne, 1978.

Hoffer, Peter T. *Klaus Mann*. Boston: Twayne, 1978.

Hoffman, Michael J. *Gertrude Stein*. Boston: Twayne, 1976.

Holquist, Michael. *Dostoevsky and the Novel*. Princeton: Princeton Univ. Press, 1977.

Holtz, William, Ed. *Two Tales by Charlotte Brontë: "The Secret" and "Lily Hart."* Columbia: Univ. of Missouri Press, 1978.

Howard, Daniel F., and William Plummer. *Instructor's Manual to Accompany "The Modern Tradition: Short Stories,"* 3rd ed. Boston: Little, Brown, 1976.

Howe, Irving, Ed. *Classics of Modern Fiction: Ten Short Novels*, 2nd ed. New York: Harcourt Brace Jovanovich, 1972.

Howe, Marguerite B. *The Art of the Self in D. H. Lawrence*. Athens: Ohio Univ. Press, 1977.

Hsia, C. T. *A History of Modern Chinese Fiction, 1917–1957*. New Haven: Yale Univ. Press, 1961; 2nd ed. 1971.

Huebener, Theodore. *The Literature of East Germany*. New York: Ungar, 1970.

Hulanicki, Leo, and David Savignac, Eds. and Trans. *Anton Čexov as a Master of Story-Writing*. The Hague: Mouton, 1976.

Ingwersen, Faith and Niels. *Martin A. Hansen*. Boston: Twayne, 1976.

Irwin, W. R. *The Game of the Impossible: A Rhetoric of Fantasy*. Urbana: Univ. of Illinois Press, 1976.

Jackson, Blyden. *The Waiting Years: Essays in American Negro Literature*. Baton Rouge: Louisiana State Univ. Press, 1976.

Jehlen, Myra. *Class and Character in Faulkner's South*. New York: Columbia Univ. Press, 1976.

Johnson, Ira and Christiane, Eds. *Les Américanistes: New French Criticism on Modern American Fiction*. Port Washington: Kennikat, 1978.

ʍ ʋ ᴄJohnson, Walter. *August Strindberg*. Boston: Twayne, 1976.

Jones, Edward T. *L. P. Hartley*. Boston: Twayne, 1978.

Jones, Granville H. *Henry James's Psychology of Experience: Innocence, Responsibility, and Renunciation in the Fiction of Henry James*. The Hague: Mouton, 1975.

Jones, Malcolm V. *Dostoevsky: The Novel of Discord*. London: Paul Elek, 1976.

_____ , Ed. *New Essays on Tolstoy*. Cambridge: Cambridge Univ. Press, 1978.

Kadir, Djelal. *Juan Carlos Onetti*. Boston: Twayne, 1977.

Kane, Thomas S., and Leonard J. Peters. *Some Suggestions for Using "The Short Story and the Reader: Discovering Narrative Techniques."* New York: Oxford Univ. Press, 1976.

Kannenstine, Louis F. *The Art of Djuna Barnes: Duality and Damnation*. New York: New York Univ. Press, 1977.

Karlinsky, Simon. *The Sexual Labyrinth of Nikolai Gogol*. Cambridge: Harvard Univ. Press, 1976.

Kellogg, Jean. *Dark Prophets of Hope: Dostoevsky, Sartre, Camus, Faulkner*. Chicago: Loyola Univ. Press, 1975.

Kelly, A. A. *Liam O'Flaherty the Storyteller*. London: Macmillan, 1976.

Kelly, John R. *Pedro Prado*. New York: Twayne, 1974.

ʍ ʋ ᴄKennard, Jean E. *Number and Nightmare: Forms of Fantasy in Contemporary Fiction*. Hamden: Shoe String Press, 1975.

Kennedy, X. J. *Instructor's Manual to Accompany "An Introduction to Fiction."* Boston: Little, Brown, 1976.

_____ , Ed. *An Introduction to Fiction*. Boston: Little, Brown, 1976.

Killam, G. D. *The Writings of Chinua Achebe*, 2nd ed. London: Heinemann, 1977.

Kimmey, John L. *Instructor's Manual for "Experience and Expression: Reading and Responding to Short Fiction."* Glenview: Scott, Foresman, 1976.

_____ , Ed. *Experience and Expression: Reading and Responding to Short Fiction*. Glenview: Scott, Foresman, 1976.

Kindt, Walther, and Siegfried J. Schmidt, Eds. *Interpretationsanalysen: Argumentationsstrukturen in literaturwissenschaftlichen Interpretationen*. Munich: Fink, 1976.

King, Bruce, and Kolawole Ogungbesan, Eds. *A Celebration of Black and African Writers*. Zaria: Ahmadu Bello Univ. Press, 1975; Oxford: Oxford Univ. Press, 1975.

Kinney, Arthur F. *Dorothy Parker*. Boston: Twayne, 1978.

Klibbe, Lawrence H. *Fernán Caballero*. New York: Twayne, 1973.

Kodjak, Andrej. *Alexander Solzhenitsyn*. Boston: Twayne, 1978.

_____ , and Kiril Taranovsky, Eds. and Trans. *Alexander Puškin: A Symposium on the 175th Anniversary of His Birth*. New York: New York Univ. Press, 1976.

Krag, Erik. *Dostoevsky: The Literary Artist*, trans. Sven Larr. Oslo: Universitetsforlag, 1976; Am. ed. New York: Humanities Press, 1976.

Kuna, Franz, Ed. *On Kafka: Semi-Centenary Perspectives*. London: Elek, 1976.

Lagmanovich, David, Ed. *Estudios sobre los cuentos de Julio Cortázar*. Barcelona: Hispam, 1975.

Lago, Mary M. *Rabindranath Tagore*. Boston: Twayne, 1976.

Landeira, Ricardo, and Carlos Mellizo, Eds. *Ignacio Aldecoa: A Collection of Critical Essays*. Laramie: Dept. of Modern & Classical Languages, Univ. of Wyoming, 1977.

ʍ ʋ ᴄLandess, Thomas H. *Julia Peterkin*. Boston: Twayne, 1976.

ᴍᴄ\ʍ ʋ ᴄLangbaum, Robert. *The Mysteries of Identity: A Theme in Modern Literature*. New York: Oxford Univ. Press, 1977.

Lawson, Richard H. *Edith Wharton*. New York: Ungar, 1977.

Lease, Benjamin. *That Wild Fellow John Neal*. Chicago: Univ. of Chicago Press, 1972.

Leavis, F. R. *Thought, Word and Creativity: Art and Thought in Lawrence*. London: Chatto & Windus, 1976.

Lebowitz, Naomi. *Italo Svevo*. New Brunswick: Rutgers Univ. Press, 1977.

Lee, L. L. *Vladimir Nabokov*. Boston: Twayne, 1976.

Leibowitz, Judith. *Narrative Purposes in the Novella*. The Hague: Mouton, 1974.

LeMaster, J. R., Ed. *Jesse Stuart: Selected Criticism*. St. Petersburg: Valkyrie Press, 1978.

LeMaster, J.R., and Mary W. Clarke, Eds. *Jesse Stuart: Essays on His Work*. Lexington: Univ. Press of Kentucky, 1977.
Levins, Lynn G. *Faulkner's Heroic Design: The Yoknapatawpha Novels*. Athens: Univ. of Georgia Press, 1976.
Light, Martin. *The Quixotic Vision of Sinclair Lewis*. West Lafayette: Purdue Univ. Press, 1975.
Linder, Erik H. *Hjalmar Bergman*, trans. Catherine Hjurklou. Boston: Twayne, 1975.
Lodge, David. *The Novel at the Crossroads*. Ithaca: Cornell Univ. Press, 1971.
Luker, Nicholas. *Alexander Kuprin*. Boston: Twayne, 1978.
Lundell, Torborg. *Lars Ahlin*. Boston: Twayne, 1977.
Lyell, William A. *Lu Hsün's Vision of Reality*. Berkeley: Univ. of California Press, 1976.
Lyngstad, Sverre. *Jonas Lie*. Boston: Twayne, 1977.
McDowell, Margaret B. *Edith Wharton*. Boston: Twayne, 1976.
McFarland, Dorothy T. *Flannery O'Connor*. New York: Ungar, 1976.
Mackenzie, Manfred. *Communities of Honor and Love in Henry James*. Cambridge: Harvard Univ. Press, 1976.
McLean, Hugh. *Nikolai Leskov: The Man and His Art*. Cambridge: Harvard Univ. Press, 1977.
McMurray, George R. *Gabriel García Márquez*. New York: Ungar, 1977.
Magill, C.P. *German Literature*. London: Oxford Univ. Press, 1974.
Martin, Augustine. *James Stephens: A Critical Study*. Dublin: Gill & Macmillan, 1977; Am. ed. Totowa, N.J.: Rowman & Littlefield, 1977.
Massey, Irving. *The Uncreating Word: Romanticism and the Object*. Bloomington: Indiana Univ. Press, 1970.
_____ . *The Gaping Pig: Literature and Metamorphosis*. Berkeley: Univ. of California Press, 1976.
Materer, Timothy. *Wyndham Lewis the Novelist*. Detroit: Wayne State Univ. Press, 1976.
Mathews, Richard. *Aldiss Unbound: The Science Fiction of Brian W. Aldiss*. San Bernardino: Borgo Press, 1977.
_____ . *Worlds Beyond the World: The Fantastic Vision of William Morris*. San Bernardino: Borgo Press, 1978.
Matthews, James H. *Frank O'Connor*. Cranbury, N.J.: Associated Univ. Presses [for Bucknell Univ. Press], 1976.
May, Charles E., Ed. *Short Story Theories*. Athens: Ohio Univ. Press, 1976.
May, John R. *The Pruning Word: The Parables of Flannery O'Connor*. Notre Dame: Univ. of Notre Dame Press, 1976.
Mendelson, Edward, Ed. *Pynchon: A Collection of Critical Essays*. Englewood Cliffs: Prentice-Hall, 1978.
Menton, Seymour. *Prose Fiction of the Cuban Revolution*. Austin: Univ. of Texas Press, 1975.
Mercier, Vivian. *Beckett/Beckett*. New York: Oxford Univ. Press, 1977.
Mercken-Spaas, Godelieve. *Alienation in Constant's "Adolphe": An Exercise in Structural Thematics*. Bern: Lang, 1977.
Meyers, Jeffrey. *Homosexuality in Literature 1890–1930*. Montreal: McGill-Queens Univ. Press, 1977.
Milliken, Stephen F. *Chester Himes: A Critical Appraisal*. Columbia: Univ. of Missouri Press, 1976.
Mochulsky, Konstantin. *Andrei Bely: His Life and Works*. Ann Arbor: Ardis, 1977.
Moreau, Geneviève. *The Restless Journey of James Agee*, trans. Miriam Kleiger and Morty Schiff. New York: Morrow, 1977.
Morrell, David. *John Barth: An Introduction*. University Park: Pennsylvania State Univ. Press, 1976.
Moskowitz, Sam. *Strange Horizons: The Spectrum of Science Fiction*. New York: Scribner, 1974.
Mulhern, Chieko I. *Kōda Rohan*. Boston: Twayne, 1977.
Myers, Andrew B., Ed. *1860–1974: A Century of Commentary on the Works of Washington Irving*. Tarrytown, N.Y.: Sleepy Hollow Restorations, 1976.

Naik, M. K., S. K. Desai, and S. M. Mokashi-Punekar, Eds. *Indian Studies in American Fiction.* Dharwar: Karnatak Univ., 1974; Delhi: Macmillan India, 1974.

Naumann, Marina T. *Blue Evenings in Berlin: Nabokov's Short Stories of the 1920s.* New York: New York Univ. Press, 1978.

Nelson, Charles, Ed. *Studies in Language and Literature.* Richmond: East Kentucky Univ., 1976.

Nelson, Gerald B. *Ten Versions of America.* New York: Knopf, 1972.

Ober, Kenneth H. *Meïr Goldschmidt.* Boston: Twayne, 1976.

O'Daniel, Therman B., Ed. *James Baldwin: A Critical Evaluation.* Washington: Howard Univ. Press, 1977.

Olander, Joseph D., and Martin H. Greenberg, Eds. *Isaac Asimov.* New York: Taplinger, 1977.

Orr, John. *Tragic Realism and Modern Society: Studies in the Sociology of the Modern Novel.* London: Macmillan, 1977; Am. ed. Pittsburgh: Univ. of Pittsburgh Press, 1978.

Osiek, Betty T. *José Asunción Silva.* Boston: Twayne, 1978.

Otten, Anna, Ed. *Hesse Companion.* Albuquerque: Univ. of New Mexico Press, 1977.

Page, Norman. *E. M. Forster's Posthumous Fiction.* Victoria: Univ. of Victoria Press, 1977.

Palmer, Nettie. *Henry Handel Richardson.* Sydney: Angus & Robertson, 1950.

Peake, C. H. *James Joyce, The Citizen and the Artist.* Stanford: Stanford Univ. Press, 1977.

Pearson, Lon. *Nicomedes Guzmán: Proletarian Author in Chile's Literary Generation of 1938.* Columbia: Univ. of Missouri Press, 1976.

Perrine, Laurence. *Instructor's Manual to Accompany "Literature: Structure, Sound, and Sense, Third Edition."* New York: Harcourt Brace Jovanovich, 1978.

———. *Instructor's Manual to Accompany "Story and Structure, Fifth Edition."* New York: Harcourt Brace Jovanovich, 1978.

———, Ed. *Story and Structure,* 5th ed. New York: Harcourt Brace Jovanovich, 1978.

Peters, Frederick G. *Robert Musil, Master of the Hovering Life: A Study of the Major Fiction.* New York: Columbia Univ. Press, 1978.

Peterson, Richard F. *Mary Lavin.* Boston: Twayne, 1978.

Piazza, Paul. *Christopher Isherwood: Myth and Anti-Myth.* New York: Columbia Univ. Press, 1978.

Pilling, John. *Samuel Beckett.* London: Routledge & Kegan Paul, 1976.

Pinion, F. B. *Thomas Hardy: Art and Thought.* London: Macmillan, 1977; Am. ed. Totowa, N.J.: Rowman & Littlefield, 1977.

———. *A D. H. Lawrence Companion: Life, Thought, and Works.* London: Macmillan, 1978; Am. ed. New York: Barnes & Noble, 1978.

Poggioli, Renato. *The Oaten Flute: Essays on Pastoral Poetry and the Pastoral Ideal.* Cambridge: Harvard Univ. Press, 1975.

Porter, Andrew, Ed. *The Book of Ellison.* New York: ALGOL Press, 1978.

Pratt, Louis H. *James Baldwin.* Boston: Twayne, 1978.

Pritchard, William H. *Seeing Through Everything: English Writers 1918–1940.* New York: Oxford Univ. Press, 1977.

Pritchett, V. S. *The Gentle Barbarian: The Life and Work of Turgenev.* New York: Random House, 1977.

Pullin, Faith, Ed. *New Perspectives on Melville.* Edinburgh: Edinburgh Univ. Press, 1978; Am. ed. Kent: Kent State Univ. Press, 1978.

Purdy, Strother B. *The Hole in the Fabric: Science, Contemporary Literature, and Henry James.* Pittsburgh: Univ. of Pittsburgh Press, 1977.

Rabkin, Eric S. *The Fantastic in Literature.* Princeton: Princeton Univ. Press, 1976.

Radcliff-Umstead, Douglas. *The Mirror of Our Anguish: A Study of Luigi Pirandello's Narrative Writing.* Cranbury, N.J.: Associated Univ. Presses [for Fairleigh Dickinson Univ. Press], 1978.

Radford, Jean. *Norman Mailer: A Critical Study.* London: Macmillan, 1975.

Rayfield, Donald. *Chekhov: The Evolution of His Art.* London: Paul Elek, 1975.

Rheinfelder, Hans, Pierre Christophorov, and Eberhard Müller-Bochat, Eds. *Literatur und Spiritualität: Hans Sckommodau zum siebzigten Geburtstag.* Munich: Fink, 1978.

Richardson, Robert D. *Myth and Literature in the American Renaissance.* Bloomington: Indiana Univ. Press, 1978.

ω υ ℮ Riley, Dick, Ed. *Critical Encounters: Writers and Themes in Science Fiction.* New York: Ungar, 1978.

| ωυ℮ Rimer, J. Thomas. *Modern Japanese Fiction and Tradition: An Introduction.* Princeton: Princeton Univ. Press, 1978.

Rimmon, Shlomith. *The Concept of Ambiguity—The Example of James.* Chicago: Univ. of Chicago Press, 1977.

Rippier, Joseph. *The Short Stories of Sean O'Faolain: A Study in Descriptive Technique.* Gerrards Cross, England: Colin Smythe, 1976.

Robinson, Forrest G. and Margaret G. *Wallace Stegner.* Boston: Twayne, 1977.

Rodgers, Bernard F. *Philip Roth.* Boston: Twayne, 1978.

Rohrberger, Mary H. *The Art of Katherine Mansfield.* Ann Arbor: Univ. Microfilms International, 1977.

Rolleston, James. *Kafka's Narrative Theater.* University Park: Pennsylvania State Univ. Press, 1974.

Romberg, Berthil. *Carl Jonas Love Almqvist.* Boston: Twayne, 1977.

M ℮ Roscoe, Adrian. *Uhuru's Fire: African Literature East and South.* London: Cambridge Univ. Press, 1977.

Rose, Alan H. *Demonic Vision: Racial Fantasy and Southern Fiction.* Hamden: Shoe String Press, 1976.

Rosen, Steven J. *Samuel Beckett and the Pessimistic Tradition.* New Brunswick: Rutgers Univ. Press, 1976.

ωυ℮ Roth, Martin. *Comedy and America: The Lost World of Washington Irving.* Port Washington: Kennikat, 1976.

Rowe, William W. *Through Gogol's Looking Glass: Reverse Vision, False Hope, and Precarious Logic.* New York: New York Univ. Press, 1976.

Rzhevsky, Leonid. *Solzhenitsyn: Creator and Heroic Dead.* University: Univ. of Alabama Press, 1978.

Salzman, Jack. *Albert Maltz.* Boston: Twayne, 1978.

ωυ℮ Schatt, Stanley. *Kurt Vonnegut.* Boston: Twayne, 1976.

Scheer, Steven C. *Kálmán Mikszáth.* Boston: Twayne, 1977.

Schneider, Daniel J. *The Crystal Cage: Adventures of the Imagination in the Fiction of Henry James.* Lawrence: Regents Press of Kansas, 1978.

Scholes, Robert, and Eric S. Rabkin. *Science Fiction: History, Science, Vision.* New York: Oxford Univ. Press, 1977.

Schweitzer, Darrell. *The Dream Quest of H.P. Lovecraft.* San Bernardino: Borgo Press, 1978.

Scott, James B. *Djuna Barnes.* Boston: Twayne, 1976.

Sears, Donald A. *John Neal.* Boston: Twayne, 1978.

Seinfelt, Frederick W. *George Moore: Ireland's Unconventional Realist.* Philadelphia: Dorrance, 1975.

Seyersted, Brita, Ed. *Norwegian Contributions to American Studies Dedicated to Sigmund Skard.* Americana Norvegica, IV. Oslo: Universitetsforlaget, 1973.

Sharma, Govind Narain. *Munshi Prem Chand.* Boston: Twayne, 1978.

Sherry, Norman, Ed. *Joseph Conrad: A Commemoration.* London: Macmillan, 1976: Am. ed. New York: Barnes & Noble, 1977.

Shewan, Rodney. *Oscar Wilde: Art and Egotism.* London: Macmillan, 1977.

Singleton, Mary A. *The City and the Veld: The Fiction of Doris Lessing.* Cranbury, N.J.: Associated Univ. Presses [for Bucknell Univ. Press], 1977.

Sjöberg, Leif. *Pär Lagerkvist.* New York: Columbia Univ. Press, 1976.

ωυ℮ Slade, Joseph W. *Thomas Pynchon.* New York: Warner Paperbacks Library, 1974.

M ℮ Slusser, George E. *The Bradbury Chronicle.* San Bernardino: Borgo Press, 1977.

MC _____ . *The Classic Years of Robert E. Heinlein.* San Bernardino: Borgo Press, 1977.

_____ . *Harlan Ellison: Unrepentant Harlequin.* San Bernardino: Borgo Press, 1977.

MC _____ . *The Space Odyssey of Arthur C. Clarke.* San Bernardino: Borgo Press, 1978.

Small, Christopher. *The Road to Miniluv: George Orwell, The State, and God.* London: Gollancz, 1975.

Smith, Elton E. *Charles Reade.* Boston: Twayne, 1976.

Smith, Larry R. *Kenneth Patchen.* Boston: Twayne, 1978.

Smith, Maxwell A. *Prosper Mérimée*. New York: Twayne, 1972.

Sokel, Walter H., Albert A. Kipa, and Hans Ternes, Eds. *Probleme der Komparatistik und Interpretation: Festschrift für André von Gronicka zum 65. Geburtstag am 25.5.1977*. Bonn: Bouvier, 1978.

Sola-Solé, Josep M., Alessandro S. Crisafulli, and Siegfried A. Schulz, Eds. *Studies in Honor of Tatiana Fotitch*. Washington: Catholic Univ. of America Press, 1978.

Sollors, Werner. Amiri Baraka/LeRoi Jones: The Quest for a "Populist Modernism." New York: Columbia Univ. Press, 1978.

Sorell, Walter. *Hermann Hesse: The Man Who Sought and Found Himself*. London: Oswald Wolff, 1974; Am. ed. Atlantic Highlands, N.J.: Humanities Press, 1975.

Spann, Meno. *Franz Kafka*. Boston: Twayne, 1976.

Spencer, Sharon. *Collage of Dreams: The Writings of Anaïs Nin*. Chicago: Swallow, 1977.

Spengemann, William C. *The Adventurous Muse: The Poetics of American Fiction, 1789–1900*. New Haven: Yale Univ. Press, 1977.

Sprich, Robert, and Richard W. Noland, Eds. *The Whispered Meaning: Selected Essays of Simon O. Lesser*. Amherst: Univ. of Massachusetts Press, 1977.

Springer, Mary D. *A Rhetoric of Literary Character*. Chicago: Univ. of Chicago Press, 1978.

Staal, Arie. *Hawthorne's Narrative Art*. New York: Revisionist Press, 1977.

Stade, George, Ed. *Six Contemporary British Novelists*. New York: Columbia Univ. Press, 1976.

Stavola, Thomas J. *Scott Fitzgerald: Crisis in an American Identity*. London: Vision Press, 1979.

Steinberg, Theodore L. *Mendele Mocher Seforim*. Boston: Twayne, 1977.

Sturrock, John. *Paper Tiger: The Ideal Fictions of Jorge Luis Borges*. Oxford: Clarendon Press, 1977.

Sullivan, Walter. *A Requiem for the Renascence: The State of Fiction in the Modern South*. Athens: Univ. of Georgia Press, 1976.

Swain, James O. *Juan Marin—Chilean: The Man and His Writings*. Cleveland, Tennessee: Pathway Press, 1971.

Swales, Martin. *The German "Novelle."* Princeton: Princeton Univ. Press, 1977.

Taylor, Welford D. *Sherwood Anderson*. New York: Ungar, 1977.

Terdiman, Richard. *The Dialectics of Isolation: Self and Society in the French Novel from the Realists to Proust*. New Haven: Yale Univ. Press, 1976.

Terras, Victor, Ed. *American Contributions to the Eighth International Congress of Slavists, Zagreb and Ljubljana, September 3–9, 1978*, Vol. II. Columbus: Slavica, 1978.

Tetel, Marcel, Ed. *Symbolism and Modern Literature: Studies in Honor of Wallace Fowlie*. Durham: Duke Univ. Press, 1978.

Tiusanen, Timo. *Dürrenmatt: A Study in Plays, Prose, Theory*. Princeton: Princeton Univ. Press, 1977.

Torrance, Robert. *The Comic Hero*. Cambridge: Harvard Univ. Press, 1978.

Tucker, Martin. *Joseph Conrad*. New York: Ungar, 1976.

Ueda, Makoto. *Modern Japanese Writers and the Nature of Literature*. Stanford: Stanford Univ. Press, 1976.

Wade, Michael. *Nadine Gordimer*. London: Evans, 1978.

Wagenknecht, Edward. *Eve and Henry James: Portraits of Women and Girls in His Fiction*. Norman: Univ. of Oklahoma Press, 1978.

Walsh, William. *Patrick White's Fiction*. Sydney: Allen & Unwin, 1977.

Wasiolek, Edward. *Tolstoy's Major Fiction*. Chicago: Univ. of Chicago Press, 1978.

Watts, Cedric. *Conrad's "Heart of Darkness": A Critical and Contextual Discussion*. Milan: Mursia International, 1977.

Weinstein, Arnold L. *Vision and Response in Modern Fiction*. Ithaca: Cornell Univ. Press, 1974.

White, Landeg. *V. S. Naipaul: A Critical Introduction*. London: Macmillan, 1975; Am. ed. New York: Barnes & Noble, 1975.

Williams, David L. *Faulkner's Women: Myth and the Muse*. Montreal: McGill-Queen's Univ. Press, 1977.

Wilson, Angus. *The Strange Ride of Rudyard Kipling: His Life and Works*. London: Secker & Warburg, 1977; Am. ed. New York: Viking, 1977.

Wohlgelernter, Maurice. *Frank O'Connor: An Introduction*. New York: Columbia Univ. Press, 1977.

Wolff, Cynthia G. *A Feast of Words: The Triumph of Edith Wharton*. New York: Oxford Univ. Press, 1977.

Worth, Katharine, Ed. *Beckett the Shape Changer*. London: Routledge & Kegan Paul, 1975.

Yamanouchi, Hisaaki. *The Search for Authenticity in Modern Japanese Literature*. Cambridge: Cambridge Univ. Press, 1978.

Yardley, Jonathan. *Ring: A Biography of Ring Lardner*. New York: Random House, 1977.

Yates, Donald A., Ed. *Otros mundos otros fuegos: Fantasía y realismo mágico en Iberoamérica*. East Lansing: Michigan State Univ. Latin-American Studies Center, 1975.

Zegger, Hrisey D. *May Sinclair*. Boston: Twayne, 1976.

Ziolkowski, Theodore. *The Novels of Hermann Hesse*. Princeton: Princeton Univ. Press, 1965.

A CHECKLIST OF JOURNALS USED

Acta Germanica   *Acta Germanica: Jahrbuch des Südafrikanischen Germanistenverbandes*

Adalbert Stifter Institut   *Adalbert Stifter Institut des Landes Oberöster-reich: Vierteljahresschrift*

Am Imago   *American Imago: A Psychoanalytic Journal for Culture, Science, and the Arts*

Am Lit   *American Literature: A Journal of Literary History, Criticism, and Bibliography*

Am Lit Realism   *American Literary Realism, 1870–1910*

Am Notes & Queries   *American Notes and Queries*

Am Transcendental Q   *American Transcendental Quarterly: A Journal of New England Writers*

      Analytische Psychologie

      Arbeiten aus Anglistik und Amerikanistik

Arcadia   *Arcadia: Zeitschrift für Vergleichende Literatur-wissenschaft*

Arizona Q   *Arizona Quarterly*

Asian Folklore Stud   *Asian Folklore Studies*

Aurora   *Aurora: Jahrbuch der Eichendorff Gesellschaft*

Australian Lit Stud   *Australian Literary Studies*

Ball State Univ Forum   *Ball State University Forum*

      Beihefte zum Jahrbuch für Amerikastudien

      Blätter der Thomas Mann Gesellschaft

Books Abroad   *Books Abroad* [retitled *World Literature Today: A Literary Quarterly of the University of Oklahoma*]

Boston Univ J   *Boston University Journal*

Bull Hispanic Stud   *Bulletin of Hispanic Studies*

Bull N Y Pub Lib	*Bulletin of the New York Public Library*
Bull Rocky Mt Mod Lang Assoc	*Bulletin of the Rocky Mountain Modern Language Association* [retitled *Rocky Mountain Review of Language and Literature*]
Bull West Virginia Assoc Coll Engl Teachers	*Bulletin of the West Virginia Association of College English Teachers*
Cahiers de la Compagnie	*Cahiers de la Compagnie Madeleine Renaud-Jean Louis Barrault*
	Cahiers de l'Association Internationale des Études Françaises
	Cahiers de Littérature et de Linguistique Appliquée
Cahiers Victoriens et Edouardiens	*Cahiers Victoriens et Edouardiens: Revue du Centre d'Études et de Recherches Victoriennes et Edouardiennes de l'Université Paul Valéry, Montpellier*
California Slavic Stud	*California Slavic Studies*
Canadian J Irish Stud	*Canadian Journal of Irish Studies*
Canadian R Am Stud	*Canadian Review of American Studies*
Canadian R Comp Lit	*Canadian Review of Comparative Literature/Revue Canadienne de Littérature Comparée*
Canadian Slavonic Papers	*Canadian Slavonic Papers: An Inter-Disciplinary Quarterly Devoted to the Soviet Union and Eastern Europe*
Canadian-Am Slavic Stud	*Canadian-American Slavic Studies*
Carleton Germ Papers	*Carleton Germanic Papers*
Centerpoint	*Centerpoint: A Journal of Interdisciplinary Studies*
Christianity & Lit	*Christianity and Literature*
Cithara	*Cithara: Essays in the Judaeo-Christian Tradition*
Claflin Coll R	*Claflin College Review*
Colby Lib Q	*Colby Library Quarterly*
Coll Engl Assoc Critic	*CEA Critic: An Official Journal of the College English Association*

Coll Engl Notes (N.J.)	*The Greater New York Regional CEA Newsletter*
Coll Lang Assoc J	*College Language Association Journal*
Coll Lit	*College Literature*
Colloquia Germanica	*Colloquia Germanica, Internationale Zeitschrift für Germanische Sprach- und Literaturwissenschaft*
Colorado Q	*Colorado Quarterly*
Commonwealth Q	*Commonwealth Quarterly*
Comp Lit	*Comparative Literature*
Conradiana	*Conradiana: A Journal of Joseph Conrad*
Contemp Lit	*Contemporary Literature*
Crit R	*The Critical Review*
Critical Q	*Critical Quarterly*
Criticism	*Criticism: A Quarterly for Literature and the Arts*
Critique	*Critique: Revue Générale des Publications Françaises et Étrangères*
Critique	*Critique: Studies in Modern Fiction*
	Cuadernos Americanos
Cuadernos Hispano-americanos	*Cuadernos Hispanoamericanos: Revista Mensual de Cultura Hispanica*
D.H. Lawrence R	*The D.H. Lawrence Review*
	Dada/Surrealism
Delta	*Delta: Revue du Centre d'Études et de Recherche sur les Écrivains du Sud aux États-Unis*
Descant	*Descant: The Texas Christian University Literary Journal*
Deutsche Vierteljahrs-schrift	*Deutsche Vierteljahrsschrift für Literaturwissenschaft und Geistesgeschichte*
Der Deutschunterricht	*Der Deutschunterricht: Beiträge zu seiner Praxis und wissenschaftlichen Grundlegung*
	Deutschunterricht in Südafrika

Diacritics	*Diacritics: A Review of Contemporary Criticism*
Discourse	*Discourse Processes: A Multidisciplinary Journal*
Durham Univ J	*Durham University Journal*
Dutch Q R	*Dutch Quarterly Review of Anglo-American Letters*
Edebiyat: J Middle Eastern Lit	*Edebiyat: A Journal of Middle Eastern Literatures*
	Encounter
Engl Lang Notes	*English Language Notes*
Engl Lit Hist	*Journal of English Literary History* [retitled *ELH*]
Engl Lit Transition	*English Literature in Transition*
Engl Stud	*English Studies: A Journal of English Language and Literature*
Engl Stud Canada	*English Studies in Canada*
Engl Stud Coll	*English Studies in College* (East Meadow, N.Y.)
ESQ: J Am Renaissance	*ESQ: Journal of the American Renaissance*
Essays French Lit	*Essays in French Literature*
Essays in Arts & Sciences	*Essays in Arts and Sciences*
Essays Lit	*Essays in Literature* (Western Illinois)
	Études Anglaises
	Études Germaniques
	Études Littéraires
Euphorion	*Euphorion: Zeitschrift für Literaturgeschichte*
	Explicación de Textos Literarios
	Explicator
Extracts	*Extracts: An Occasional Newsletter* [retitled *Melville Society Extracts*]
	Extrapolation
	Das Fenster Tiroler Kulturzeitschrift

Flannery O'Connor Bull	*Flannery O'Connor Bulletin*
	Forum (Houston)
Forum Mod Lang Stud	*Forum for Modern Language Studies*
	Le Français au Nigeria
French Lit Series	*French Literature Series*
French R	*French Review: Journal of the American Association of Teachers of French*
French Stud	*French Studies: A Quarterly Review*
Germ Life & Letters	*German Life and Letters*
Germ Notes	*Germanic Notes*
Germ Q	*German Quarterly*
Germ R	*Germanic Review*
	Germanica Wratislaviensia
Germanische-Romanische Monatsschrift	*Germanische-Romanische Monatsschrift, Neue Folge*
Glyph	*Glyph: Johns Hopkins Textual Studies*
Greyfriar	*Greyfriar: Siena Studies in Literature*
Gypsy Scholar	*Gypsy Scholar: A Graduate Forum for Literary Criticism*
Hartford Stud Lit	*University of Hartford Studies in Literature: A Journal of Interdisciplinary Criticism*
Harvard J Asiatic Stud	*Harvard Journal of Asiatic Studies*
	Hebbel-Jahrbuch
Hebrew Univ Stud Lit	*Hebrew University Studies in Literature*
Heritage of Kansas	*Heritage of Kansas: A Journal of the Great Plains*
Hispamerica	*Hispamerica: Revista la Literatura*
Hispania	*Hispania: A Journal Devoted to the Interests of the Teaching of Spanish and Portuguese*

Hispanic R	*Hispanic Review*
	Hispánica Moderna
Hispano	*Hispanófila*
	Ibero-Amerikanisches Archiv
Illinois Q	*Illinois Quarterly*
Indian J Am Stud	*Indian Journal of American Studies*
Indian Lit	*Indian Literature*
Interpretation: J Pol Phil	*Interpretation: Journal of Political Philosophy*
Interpretations	*Interpretations: Studies in Language and Literature*
Int' l Fiction R	*International Fiction Review*
Int' l J Symbology	*International Journal of Symbology*
Irish Univ R	*Irish University Review: A Journal of Irish Studies*
J Am Acad Psychoanalysis	*Journal of the American Academy of Psychoanalysis*
J Australasian Univs Lang & Lit Assoc	*Journal of the Australasian Universities Language and Literature Association: A Journal of Literary Criticism, Philology & Linguistics*
J Black Stud	*Journal of Black Studies* (Los Angeles)
J Commonwealth Lit	*The Journal of Commonwealth Literature*
J 1890's Soc	*Journal of the Eighteen Nineties Society*
J Engl & Germ Philol	*Journal of English and Germanic Philology*
J Folklore Institute	*Journal of the Folklore Institute*
J Libertarian Stud	*Journal of Libertarian Studies*
J Mod Lit	*Journal of Modern Literature*
J Narrative Technique	*Journal of Narrative Technique*
J Otto Rank Assoc	*Journal of the Otto Rank Association*
J So Asian Lit	*Journal of South Asian Literature*

J Spanish Stud: Twen- tieth Century	*Journal of Spanish Studies: Twentieth Century*
	Jack London Newsletter
	Jahrbuch der Grillparzer-Gesellschaft
	Jahrbuch der Raabe-Gesellschaft
Kansas Q	*Kansas Quarterly*
Kentucky Romance Q	*Kentucky Romance Quarterly*
Kipling J	*The Kipling Journal*
	Kwartalnik Neofilologiczny
Kyushu Am Lit	*Kyushu American Literature*
Lang Q	*The USF Language Quarterly*
Latin Am Lit R	*Latin American Literary Review*
	Letras de Deusto
Lib Chronicle	*Library Chronicle*
Linguistics in Lit	*Linguistics in Literature*
Lit & Psych	*Literature and Psychology*
Lit East & West	*Literature East and West*
Lit Half-Yearly	*Literary Half-Yearly*
Lit R	*Literary Review: An International Journal of Con- temporary Writing*
	Literatur in Wissenschaft und Unterricht
	Literatur und Kritik
Literature/Film Q	*Literature/Film Quarterly*
	Littérature
Lost Generation J	*Lost Generation Journal*
Malahat R	*Malahat Review: An International Quarterly of Life and Letters*

Mark Twain J	*Mark Twain Journal*
Markham R	*Markham Review*
Massachusetts R	*Massachusetts Review: A Quarterly of Literature, the Arts and Public Affairs*
	MELUS
Melville Soc Extracts	*Melville Society Extracts* [supersedes *Extracts: An Occasional Newsletter*]
Michigan Germ Stud	*Michigan Germanic Studies*
Midamerica	*Midamerica: The Yearbook of the Society for the Study of Midwestern Literature*
Midwest Q	*Midwest Quarterly: A Journal of Contemporary Thought*
	Minas Gerais, Suplemento Literário
Mississippi Q	*Mississippi Quarterly: The Journal of Southern Culture*
Mod Austrian Lit	*Modern Austrian Literature: Journal of the International Arthur Schnitzler Research Association*
Mod Brit Lit	*Modern British Literature*
Mod Fiction Stud	*Modern Fiction Studies*
Mod Lang Notes	*Modern Language Notes* [retitled *MLN*]
Mod Lang R	*Modern Language Review*
Mod Lang Stud	*Modern Language Studies*
Monatshefte	*Monatshefte: Für Deutschen Unterricht, Deutsche Sprache und Literatur*
Mosaic	*Mosaic: A Journal for the Comparative Study of Literature and Ideas*
Nantucket R	*Nantucket Review*
Nassau R	*The Nassau Review: The Journal of Nassau Community College Devoted to Arts, Letters, and Sciences*
Nathaniel Hawthorne J	*Nathaniel Hawthorne Journal*

Negro Am Lit Forum	*Negro American Literature Forum* [retitled *Black American Literature Forum*]
	Neophilologus
	Die Neueren Sprachen
Neuphilologische Mitteilungen	*Neuphilologische Mitteilungen: Bulletin de la Société Néophilologique/Bulletin of the Modern Language Society*
	Neusprachliche Mitteilungen aus Wissenschaft und Praxis
New England Q	*New England Quarterly: A Historical Review of New England Life and Letters*
New Germ Stud	*New German Studies*
New Laurel R	*New Laurel Review*
New Yorker	*The New Yorker*
	Nineteenth-Century Fiction
Nineteenth-Century French Stud	*Nineteenth-Century French Studies*
Notes & Queries	*Notes and Queries*
Notes Contemp Lit	*Notes on Contemporary Literature*
Notes Mississippi Writers	*Notes on Mississippi Writers*
Notes Mod Am Lit	*NMAL: Notes on Modern American Literature*
Nottingham French Stud	*Nottingham French Studies*
Novel	*Novel: A Forum on Fiction*
	Nueva Revista de Filología Hispánica
Obsidian	*Obsidian: Black Literature in Review*
Old Northwest	*The Old Northwest: A Journal of Regional Life and Letters*
Osmania J Engl Stud	*Osmania Journal of English Studies*
Österreich in Geschichte und Literatur	*Österreich in Geschichte und Literatur (mit Geographie)*

Pacific Coast Philol	*Pacific Coast Philology*
	Papeles de Son Armadans
Papers Lang & Lit	*Papers on Language and Literature: A Journal for Scholars and Critics of Language and Literature*
Paragone	*Paragone: Rivista Mensile de Arte Figurativa e Letteratura*
	Paunch
Perspectives Contemp Lit	*Perspectives on Contemporary Literature*
Philol Q	*Philological Quarterly*
Philosophy & Lit	*Philosophy and Literature*
Phylon	*Phylon: The Atlanta University Review of Race and Culture*
Poe Stud	*Poe Studies*
Poetica	*Poetica: Zeitschrift für Sprach- und Literatur-·wissenschaft*
	Prairie Schooner
Praxis	*Praxis: A Journal of Radical Perspectives on the Arts*
Proceedings Pacific Northwest Conference Foreign Langs	*Proceedings of the Pacific Northwest Conference on Foreign Languages*
Prospects	*Prospects: An Annual Journal of American Cultural Studies*
Prospetti	*Prospetti: Rivista Trimestrale*
Psychoanalytic R	*Psychoanalytic Review*
Pubs Arkansas Philol Assoc	*Publications of the Arkansas Philological Association*
R Interamericana	*Revista/Review Interamericana*
Rackham Lit Stud	*Rackham Literary Studies*
	RE: Artes Liberales
Reflection	*Reflection: Quarterly Journal of the Yale Divinity School*

Regionalism & Female Imagination	*Regionalism and the Female Imagination*
Renascence	*Renascence: Essays on Value in Literature*
Rendezvous	*Rendezvous: Journal of Arts and Letters*
Research Stud	*Research Studies*
	Review 73
	Review 72
	Revista de Estudios Hispánicos
	Revista de la Universidad de Costa Rica
Revista Hispánica Moderna	*Revista Hispánica Moderna: Columbia University Hispanic Studies*
	Revista Iberoamericana
	Revue des Langues Vivantes
	La Revue des Lettres Modernes
	Revue d'Histoire Lettéraire de la France
	Revue Romane
	Romance Notes
Romanic R	*Romanic Review*
Russian Lit	*Russian Literature*
Saggi	*Saggi e Ricerche di Letteratura Francese*
San José Stud	*San José Studies*
Scandinavian Stud	*Scandinavian Studies*
	Scando-Slavica
	Schriften der Theodor-Storm-Gesellschaft
Sci-Fiction Stud	*Science-Fiction Studies*
Seminar	*Seminar: A Journal of Germanic Studies*
Sewanee R	*Sewanee Review*
Slavic & East European J	*Slavic and East European Journal*

Slavic R	*Slavic Review: American Quarterly of Soviet and East European Studies*
So Atlantic Bull	*South Atlantic Bulletin: A Quarterly Journal Devoted to Research and Teaching in the Modern Languages and Literatures*
So Atlantic Q	*South Atlantic Quarterly*
So Carolina R	*South Carolina Review*
So Dakota R	*South Dakota Review*
Sophia Engl Stud	*Sophia English Studies*
Soundings	*Soundings: A Journal of Interdisciplinary Studies*
Southerly	*Southerly: A Review of Australian Literature*
Southern Hum R	*Southern Humanities Review*
Southern Lit J	*Southern Literary Journal*
Southern Lit Messenger	*Southern Literary Messenger: A Quarterly*
Southern R	*Southern Review* (Baton Rouge)
Southern R: Australian J Lit Stud	*Southern Review: An Australian Journal of Literary Studies*
Southern Stud	*Southern Studies: An Interdisciplinary Journal of the South*
Southwest R	*Southwest Review*
Sprachkunst	*Sprachkunst: Beiträge zur Literaturwissenschaft*
Stud Am Fiction	*Studies in American Fiction*
Stud Am Jewish Lit	*Studies in American Jewish Literature*
Stud Am Renaissance	*Studies in the American Renaissance*
Stud Black Lit	*Studies in Black Literature*
Stud Contemp Satire	*Studies in Contemporary Satire: A Creative and Critical Journal*
Stud Novel	*Studies in the Novel*
Stud Romanticism	*Studies in Romanticism*

Stud Short Fiction	*Studies in Short Fiction*
Stud Twentieth Century	*Studies in Twentieth Century Literature*
	Studi Germanici
	Style
	Symposium
Susquehanna Univ Stud	*Susquehanna University Studies*
Tennessee Stud Lit	*Tennessee Studies in Literature*
Texas Q	*The Texas Quarterly*
Texas Stud Lit & Lang	*Texas Studies in Literature and Language: A Journal of the Humanities*
Text und Kritik	*Text und Kritik: Zeitschrift für Literatur*
Thoth	*Thoth: Syracuse University Graduate Studies in English*
Topic	*Topic: A Journal of the Liberal Arts*
Travaux de Linguistique et de Littérature	*Travaux de Linguistique et de Littérature Publiés par le Centre de Philologie et de Littératures Romanes de l'Université de Strasbourg*
Twentieth Century Lit	*Twentieth Century Literature: A Scholarly and Critical Journal*
Unisa Engl Stud	*Unisa English Studies: Journal of the Department of English*
Univ Dayton R	*University of Dayton Review*
Univ Windsor R	*University of Windsor Review*
Virginia Q R	*Virginia Quarterly Review: A National Journal of Literature and Discussion*
Wascana R	*Wascana Review*
Weimarer Beiträge	*Weimarer Beiträge: Zeitschrift für Literaturwissenschaft, Ästhetik und Kulturtheorie*
Western Am Lit	*Western American Literature*
	Western Folklore

Western Hum R	*Western Humanities Review*
Western R	*Western Review*
Wirkendes Wort	*Wirkendes Wort: Deutsche Sprache in Forschung und Lehre*
World Lit Written Engl	*World Literature Written in English*
Yale French Stud	*Yale French Studies*
Yale R	*The Yale Review: A National Quarterly*
	Zeitschrift für Deutsche Philologie
	Zeitschrift für Slawistik

INDEX OF SHORT STORY WRITERS